Henry Hucks Gibbs, Henry Riversdale Grenfell

The Bimetallic Controversy

A Collection of Pamphlets, Papers, Speeches and Letters

Henry Hucks Gibbs, Henry Riversdale Grenfell

The Bimetallic Controversy
A Collection of Pamphlets, Papers, Speeches and Letters

ISBN/EAN: 9783744765862

Printed in Europe, USA, Canada, Australia, Japan

Cover: Foto ©Suzi / pixelio.de

THE

BIMETALLIC CONTROVERSY.

A COLLECTION OF

PAMPHLETS, PAPERS, SPEECHES AND LETTERS,

BY

HENRY H. GIBBS & HENRY R. GRENFELL,

FORMERLY GOVERNORS OF THE BANK OF ENGLAND;

Together with Contributions from

Earl Grey	Sir T. H. Farrer
Lord Sherbrooke	Mr. R. Giffen
Lord Bramwell	Mr. C. Daniell
Professor Bonamy Price	Mr. H. D. Macleod
Professor Jevons	M. Henri Cernuschi

Reprinted from the Originals.

LONDON:
EFFINGHAM WILSON, ROYAL EXCHANGE.

1886.

TABLE OF CONTENTS.

(*A detailed Index will be found at the end of the volume.*)

		PAGE
PREFACE.		
The Double Standard. (Gibbs.)	1881.	1
Letter on Mr. Daniell's Pamphlet "Gold in the East," by Mr. Grenfell.	*Economist*, August 2, 1879.	65
Reply by Mr. Daniell	" " 9, "	68
" Mr. Grenfell	" " 23, "	70
" Mr. Daniell	" " 30, "	72
The case against Bimetallism. (Giffen.) *Fortnightly Review*,	" "	75
Bimetallism. (Jevons.)	*Contemporary Review*, May, 1881.	99
What is a Pound? (Grenfell.)	*Nineteenth Century*, June, 1881.	111
Is the Value of Gold & Silver Money Artificial? "B." (Lord Bramwell.)	*The Times*, May 7, 1881.	131
" " "F." (Farrer.)	" " 21, "	138
" " Henri Cernuschi.	" " 26, "	142
" " "Chrysargyros." (Gibbs.)	" " 26, "	143
" " "F." (Farrer.)	" " 27, "	147
" " H. D. Macleod.	" " 28, "	148
" " Henri Cernuschi.	" June 1, "	149
" " "F." (Farrer.)	" " 2, "	150
The Double Standard. Correspondence between Earl Grey & Mr. Grenfell.	May—June, "	153
What is Money? (Lord Sherbrooke.)	*Nineteenth Century*, April, 1882.	183
What is a Standard? (Grenfell.)	" " May, "	197
Speech by Mr. Grenfell at a Meeting of the Association	March 8, "	219
" Mr. Gibbs "	" 8, "	225
The Scramble for Gold. (Gibbs.)	*Bullionist.* " 18, "	231
Concerning Faith in Treaties. (Gibbs.)	" April 15, "	237
The Value of Money. (Gibbs.)	" May 20, "	245
The Ratio of Value, &c. (Daniell.)	" " 20, "	251
Whither would the Dearer Metal go? (Grenfell.)	" June 24, "	259
Bimetallic England. (Gibbs.)	" " 24, "	267
Paper or Metallic Inflation. (Grenfell.)	" " 24, "	275
The Ratio between Gold & Silver. Two Letters by Mr. Gibbs.	*Economist*, October, "	281
Bimetallism Again. Correspondence between Mr. Grenfell & Professor Bonamy Price.	Sept. "	293
Correspondence: Sir T. H. Farrer, Mr. Gibbs & Lord Bramwell,	Mar. 1883.	335
The Gold Question & the Fall of Prices. (Gibbs.) *National Review.*	July, "	345
The Price of Silver. (Gibbs.) Letter to the *Economist*,	Sept. 19, 1885.	375
Concluding passages of Speech at Manchester. (Grenfell.)	Feb. 6, 1886.	381

LONDON,

September, 1886.

WE have been induced to make a collection of our writings and those of the most distinguished among our opponents on the subject of Bimetallism by the fact that so keen an interest in the question has been of late awakened in the public mind. The result of this has been that the Government have determined to act on the recommendation of the Royal Commission appointed to consider the causes of the Depression of Trade, and appoint a Special Commission to examine this and kindred questions.

This being so, it may be useful to recur to the arguments of two of the guardians of English currency who have given some time and labour to them, and who see no reason to doubt the accuracy of their information and the soundness of their conclusions in favour of the new doctrine.

Among the early contributions to the Bimetallic literature there were two, either of which would have served as an introduction to this collection, —namely, Mr. R. Gladstone's Catechism and Mr. Chapman's Memorandum,—but, in order to avoid all unnecessary repetition, we have preferred confining ourselves to the preliminary statement of the question in Mr. Gibbs' pamphlet, which is placed at the commencement of this collection. We have abstained, therefore, from asking permission to reprint these short and pithy papers.

The writers whose contributions have, with their permission, been inserted in this volume, are chiefly those with whom it is a subject of just pride to us that we have been privileged to contend. They are all celebrated for their powers of mind and for the part they have played in the practical solution of many difficult investigations. Many of these contributions are models of fair and serious treatment, affording a marked contrast to certain specious but hasty criticisms which have been published. There is only one omission which we regret, namely, that of the papers of the late Mr. Bagehot reprinted from the *Economist* and published after his death. Some of these we might, perhaps, have been permitted to include, but we found it impossible to do so, because we are not conscious of having made them specially the subject of our own replies: the fact being that when we took up the controversy the conditions of the question had somewhat altered since those papers were written.

H. H. G.

H. R. G.

THE DOUBLE STANDARD.

GOLD alone is the Standard Money of Great Britain. That is to say, the value of all commodities is measured by and expressed in the Pound sterling, consisting of 113·0016 grains of pure Gold, or 123·27447 grains of Standard Gold.

Silver coins are in this country merely tokens,—metallic notes representing portions of the Gold pound; thus, a crown is payable by law as the fourth of a Gold pound,* although the intrinsic or metallic value of the coin is much less.

In Germany, until the year 1872, Silver was the only Standard Money, and all commodities were in that country measured in Silver just as in this they are measured in Gold.

In France, as in the other countries belonging to the "Latin Union," Gold and Silver alike are the measure of value of all other commodities; 15½ ounces of pure Silver or one ounce of pure Gold being equally a discharge for a debt of 107·1342 francs, the Gold piece of 20 francs bearing that proportion to the Silver piece of 5 francs, and the debtor having in all cases by law the option of paying his debt in either metal.

I take, arbitrarily, these three countries, Great Britain, Germany (before 1872), and France, as representatives of their several systems; the last as an example (until 1874, when she suspended free mintage of standard Silver money) of the full use of the Double Standard, or what is now

* Subject to the 40*s*. limit.

called by the name of Bimetallism, and the two first as examples, severally, of the two varieties of a Single or Monometallic Standard.

It may be useful to give here a sketch of the position and progress of the Silver question since I first took it up in 1879.

The price of Silver towards the end of 1879 was higher than at present. Having been 60*d.* per ounce in 1872, it fell as low as 46¾*d.* in 1876, from which it rose by various fluctuations to 53½*d.* in November, 1879. It stood at the close of 1880 at about 51¾*d.*

The chief causes of the depreciation of Silver may be stated as follows :—

1. Increase of production of Silver, from 8½ millions in 1861 to about 16 millions in 1879.

2. Decrease in demand of Silver, owing to—

   (*a*) Demonetization of Silver in Germany, the Scandinavian States and Holland; and limitation of Silver coinage by the Latin Union.

   (*b*) Increase in amount of India Council Bills, coupled with less demand in India for coin, owing to bad harvests, &c.

3. Enhancement in the value of Gold, owing to—

   (*a*) Diminution in its supply, which fell from an estimated average annual production in 1852/6 of nearly 30 millions, to about 21 millions at present.

   (*b*) Increased demand for Gold—Germany and minor States absorbing about 86 millions, and the United States (since 1872) more than 40 millions, together about one-fifth of the total computed quantity in existence.

Mr. H. H. Gibbs.

Since 1878/9 the disturbing elements in Europe and India may be regarded as having ceased to be active. In general terms it may be said that the operations in Germany have not been extended; that the amount of India Council Bills has not increased; and that the improved condition of India and the East has maintained a due absorption of Silver.

Setting aside, therefore, for the moment, any further enquiry into these points, the subjects which appear to require examination, as having made some progress in the last two years, or as likely to hold a prominent place in influencing the immediate future, are—

1. The production of Silver and Gold, especially in America, as compared with previous years.
2. The operation of the American Silver coinage law, and the condition of things brought about under it.
3. The proposed arrangements in Italy for a new Gold Standard coinage.

Production of Silver and Gold.

During the past three years it would appear that so far as the United States is concerned, the production of Silver has remained nearly stationary.

Estimates, which are generally accepted, show that the production in 1879 amounted to £7,406,000 against £7,449,000 in 1878, and that last year (1880) it was about £7,500,000.

The following are the estimates of production in the United States for the last seven years:—

	£
1874	3,464,000
1875	6,521,000
1876	7,858,000
1877	9,169,000
1878	7,449,000
1879	7,406,000
1880	7,500,000

The production in other countries does not appear to have shown any considerable variation ; and as the estimates of supply in the year just ended are not in excess of the year 1879, it may be broadly stated that the greatly increased production prior to 1878 has, as was anticipated, not been maintained.

The production of Gold during the last three years appears to have diminished considerably.

In the United States, the production for the last four years, ending 30th June, is estimated by the mint authorities as follows :—

in 1877	9,380,000
1878	10,240,000
1879	7,780,000
1880	7,200,000

The production in Australia is stated also to have decreased though not so sensibly, while the prospect of any large supply of Gold from India is still uncertain.

The United States Coinage Law and its Results.

This law was passed in 1878. Its chief provisions are—

1. That the United States Treasury shall coin Silver monthly (whether it is required for trade or not) to an amount of not less than £400,000, or more than £800,000,—the necessary amount of Silver for this purpose being purchased by the Government at the market price.

2. Dollars so coined are to be of the weight of 412½ grains of standard Silver "as provided by the Act

Mr. H. H. Gibbs.

"of January, 1837," and are to be a legal tender, at their nominal value, for all debts and dues, public and private, "except where otherwise expressly "stipulated in the contract."

3. That any holder of this coin, in sums of not less than 10 dollars, may deposit it and obtain a certificate for it. These certificates are receivable for Customs, taxes, and all public dues, and may be re-issued.

It is of course difficult to ascertain with precision the working of a foreign law in a foreign country, but from the results it would appear, and, indeed, it seems to be admitted, that this Act has failed to fulfil the objects it aimed at.

It is stated that under the law about 80 millions of dollars (£16,000,000) had been coined before the close of last year, and that before the close of the present year the amount will, if the coinage continues, exceed 100 millions (£20,000,000). That, of the sum already coined, about three-fourths, say $60,000,000 (£12,000,000) remained in the Treasury vaults, belonging to the Treasury, or to Banks and others to whom the Treasury has issued certificates for them. That only about 20 million dollars (£4,000,000) remained out of the Treasury vaults, including all those actually held by the Banks; and that probably not more than 10 millions (£2,000,000) had gone into active circulation.

These dollars outside the limits of the United States are scarcely worth nine-tenths of a Gold dollar, though practically to a resident American they are equivalent to Gold. That they are, however, unacceptable is evident, and the question is exciting great attention. Prominent amongst the remedial measures has been the proposal to increase the weight of the dollar—but to make it equal to

Gold it must be raised from $412\frac{1}{2}$ grains to 455. At the late annual convention of bankers at Saratoga it was resolved to recommend that these dollars be melted back into bullion, a subsidiary coinage being issued only as required; and that certificates be issued for deposits of Silver bullion as nearly as possible at the market price. There is clearly a growing desire in some quarters to get rid of the Act altogether.

Whilst the Silver coined under this Act cannot be got into circulation, the absorption of the Gold coinage, especially in the West, is represented as being very great. According to an estimate by the United States Mint authorities, the Gold coinage circulation of the country was increased, by coinage and imports of coin, more than £20,000,000 between the 1st January, 1879, the date fixed for resumption, and the 1st November, 1880.

The Proposed Redemption of Forced Currency in Italy.

The Italian Government propose within the next two years to redeem so much of their paper circulation as will place the remainder in a satisfactory condition; and to this end, they purpose raising a loan of £25,760,000, of which £16,000,000 is to be in Gold. It would appear that the Government, so far as their views have been made known, entirely put aside, under present circumstances, the question of a Double Standard, and take the opportunity afforded by the substitution of a metallic for a forced paper currency of introducing a Gold standard.

On a review of the general position, so far as this has changed during the past eighteen months, the following appear to be some of the results:—

Mr. H. H. Gibbs.

1. The divergence between the value of Silver and Gold has widened.

That this is the case would appear from the following considerations :—

As regards Silver, the demand has not largely increased, if at all, whilst the production has remained nearly stationary. In the United States the coinage under the law of 1878 has been continued, but the country has not absorbed it. The coins lie idle, and do not even need the usual supply of Silver to maintain them in good condition. In Europe the limitation of Silver coinage by the Latin Union is still in force, and the former large Silver coinage of Germany and the Northern States needs no longer the supply formerly required to sustain it. Against this, however, must be placed an increased importation into India of more than four millions sterling last year over the previous year.

On the other hand the supply of Gold is not only less, but the demand for it has increased in every direction. Assuming the Australian yield to have been maintained at the diminished supply of the last few years, that of America is confessedly less. But as regards demand;—in the United States the absorption has been continuous. In Europe the increased amount of Gold coinage superseding Silver, and the extended area over which it prevails, needs for its maintenance a larger supply than formerly; whilst even India—probably owing to greater prosperity—has imported nearly £600,000 this year in excess of last. The diminution in the price of Silver from about 53½*d.* in November, 1879, to 51¾*d.* in December, 1880, probably represents the result of the operation of these causes.

2. Under the influence of circumstances within view, the probability is that the divergence of price will be greater rather than less.

The power of India and the East to absorb Silver is an unknown element. Although with prosperity it would increase, yet in such periods the importation of Gold (possibly for manufacturing purposes) increases also. But there does not appear to be any visible demand for Silver elsewhere; whilst any change in the present law of the United States, which is fast becoming intolerable, would lessen the demand there, and possibly release the accumulated useless stock.

Any action of the Italian Government, in the direction of introducing a Gold standard, would of course still further complicate the position; and any general revival of trade would stimulate all the causes now at work for a larger need of Gold in face of a diminishing supply.

Looking at the matter from the point of view of the advocates of a Double Standard, it would appear, that apart from all local considerations, and assuming no great Gold discoveries should alter the conditions, the natural causes which have been at work have been in the direction of strengthening the views of those who lean to that solution of the question; a view which of necessity is held most strongly by the United States as the chief Silver-producing country. The question may be asked whether any advance, and if so, to what extent, has been made in enabling them to enforce their will on Europe.

The working of the United States law of 1878 shows, if such a lesson were needed, the futility of a partial

Mr. H. H. Gibbs,

bimetallism. Had there been bimetallism, pure and simple, with free coinage of either metal to every one, America, as France in past time, would have brought up the value of Silver to its old point; though some have urged that she could not long maintain this service, unless a change arose in the relative value of the two metals, in the direction of making the less valuable the more valuable,—a view which I will discuss later on. But the United States did not establish bimetallism, and the question seems to be now before them, whether they shall establish it, or whether they will throw aside even the present semblance of a Silver legal tender, and revert to a single Gold standard, trusting that the constant absorption to meet the needs of an ever-extending area of population will tend to a settlement of the question in the direction they desire, and conscious of the power they possess as the great food-suppliers of the world.

The conditions would of course be modified by new discoveries of Gold; but, as it stands, it would appear that the question is being gradually narrowed to a monetary struggle between America and Europe. America is not likely by herself to introduce a Double Standard, as to do so would be to part with her present stock of Gold, and permit Europe to retain its single Gold standard; but she can follow, if Europe leads the way, and reap the benefits which would accrue from its establishment.

Before entering into the question whether the adoption by this country of the Double Standard would be, under any circumstances and in any degree, a remedy for the evils to which I have adverted in the Preface, I will set down what are supposed to be the comparative advantages of the two systems.

Shortly stated, the advantage of a single metallic standard is, that assuming the coins to be kept at their due weight and fineness, every one who buys, and every one who sells, knows precisely what it is that he gives and what it is that he receives for the commodity with which he is dealing, and that the calculations of commerce are more simple, for those who are engaged in it, whether they live in the same village or at opposite ends of the world, if they have but one medium for the exchange of their commodities.

The disadvantages which a Double Standard in one single country brings to that country itself are so notorious, and have been so constantly exposed in every treatise on the subject, from Locke to John Stuart Mill, that I need not enlarge on them.

The advantages which a Double Standard in one single country brings to other surrounding countries are obvious.

But the advantages which a Double Standard would bring to all countries simultaneously agreeing in adopting it is the point now under discussion; and it is that agreement, and the causes which seem to make it necessary, which alone present new features for our consideration.

These advantages are:

1. Uniformity, and therefore the removal of those variables which must be an encumbrance to commerce.

2. Increased steadiness of prices of commodities so far as they are affected by the quantity of the measure of value.

3. The providing a remedy, if not the only possible remedy, for the new state of things in Germany, Italy, and America, wherein these wealthy nations are entering into competition for the limited stock of Gold existing in the world.

1.—It is unnecessary to say more here on the obvious advantage to commerce of a uniform monetary system

Mr. H. H. Gibbs.

between nations. I will refer to it again when I speak of Lord Liverpool's Treatise.

2.—It is clear that the fluctuations of price under a Double Standard, though probably more frequent, are certainly less violent. The conclusion to which the Commission of 1868 unanimously came was confined to the assertion of greater frequency; and I cannot better illustrate my position than by referring to the work of Mr. Stanley Jevons—no partizan of the Double Standard—on *Money and the Mechanism of Exchange,* and particularly to pages 137-40, edition 1878, in which he discusses this point, and insists on what he calls the compensatory or equilibratory action of the Double Standard.

3.—I will now address myself to the question whether it is the only remedy, or whether a choice lies between a single standard of one metal only, and a compound standard of two metals, for adoption by the chief commercial nations.

I have no doubt myself that, as a matter of theory, a single standard would be the best for the whole world of commerce, and that Gold would be the most proper metal to serve as that standard. That is to say, that if we could suppose men to have set themselves at some time deliberately to choose a medium of exchange and measure of value, and Gold to have been ready to their hands in quantity sufficient for the convenience of commerce, nothing could have been more perfect than the selection of Gold for the purpose.

But this is, of course, mere imagination; for no nation or people ever did deliberately invent and choose a standard of value, and even had it been possible for them to do so, the same causes, or some of them, which led some to choose Gold, would have led others to choose Silver, brass, or iron, sheep and oxen, even salt, dried fish, shells, or other substances, as media of exchange.

No such deliberate choice could have taken place. The precious metals, I suppose, grew into being money by common consent and law united, and so grew because they were exceptionally suited to serve as money. They were imperishable, divisible, portable, beautiful, and rare, and thus possessed intrinsic metallic value.

I approach here an incidental portion of the argument in my former pamphlet, which drew down upon me the censure of almost all my critics. It was no important part of the argument, and might be conceded to the objectors without affecting in the least degree the correctness of my conclusions. It was only by way of illustration that I used the somewhat hyperbolical expression—"Gold and Silver "are a forced currency." The force I spoke of was *consent*, and no other; and it was no confutation of my statement to reply that nations would *not* consent to the use of a valueless currency. I nowhere said, or implied, that they would. My statement was but a truism, viz.: No commodity, however valuable, could become *money* without consent or tacit concurrence of those whose money it was to be. Even to a really forced currency imposed on a nation by the will of the Prince, consent, however unwilling, is a necessity.

I said, and I repeat, that it is from consent, and law which presupposes consent, that Gold and Silver derive their power *as money*. Their power as exchangeable commodities they derive, as wool and iron do, from their intrinsic worth and usefulness. To this phrase of mine objection was made, that I attributed their *value* to consent, meaning that consent and law could make that valuable which was not so without them, and that intrinsic worth was of no consequence. But I said nothing of the sort, but only that they derived their powers as money—their being money at all—from law and consent.

For if not, and if intrinsic worth alone suffice to cause a commodity to be money in proportion to its possession of

Mr. H. H. Gibbs.

it, then tin and platinum should also be money, which they are not; Gold should be money everywhere, which it is not; Silver should be money here, which it is not.

Again, in my former pamphlet, I said "the *metal* of "which the money is composed is indeed a commodity; "but when made into money it ceases to bear that character. "MONEY *is not a commodity, but a measure of commodities*," thus not undeservedly bringing upon myself a flood of criticism by using the term "commodity" in an ambiguous sense. I used the word as Locke used it, for "a thing that "can be valued in money"; and money, whether Gold or Silver, or both, cannot be valued in money. Money cannot buy money. Money considered as a measure of value, is not, in respect that it is money, a commodity as other commodities are. The substance of which it is made must be and must of course remain always a commodity, and no one I suppose thought that I so far believed in the transmutation of metals as to think otherwise. The sovereign which I hold in my hand is obviously as much a commodity as the purse in which I place it, and stamped or not it would be an exchangeable commodity like any other; but as money it has another function superadded, it is the medium of exchange between commodities, and so far differs from them all.

I have assumed that though Gold as a single metallic standard for all the world is theoretically the best, there is no practical possibility of its adoption.

In practice, the difficulties and even dangers of establishing it would be enormous. It would indeed be a mistake to allege as one of these difficulties that the stock of Gold would certainly be insufficient for the wants of commerce, for when once the adoption of a universal Gold Standard had been accomplished and the Gold distributed abroad, prices which would have been disturbed would after a time and by degrees adjust themselves, and fall into a normal condition. Besides which, the use by other civilised nations of the banking expedients employed by ourselves—of a system of convertible paper money (to speak only of sound expedients)—of cheques and clearings such as we have in England, would so economise the use of the metal, that there would, I imagine, be more than enough.

But setting aside the extreme improbability of such a change in the habits of other nations, the real danger in establishing a single Standard of Gold (or of Silver either) for all countries having commercial relations with each other would be the disturbance of prices to which I have referred above, by the contraction of the circulation, which would take place while the operation was proceeding, in every country of the world. Work is now done by both Gold and Silver, by Gold in some and by Silver in others, and the same work would then have to be done by one metal only. The adjustment of prices would then take a long time to perfect, and meanwhile the violent and continuous fall of prices would bring disaster, panic, and ruin in its train. Money would be harder to come by, and the debtor who owed and had to pay £100, would find that in order to raise it he must part with more commodities than could be bought with the money when he incurred the debt.

But though a single metal as money is only theoretically the best under present conditions, yet it is much more than mere theory which claims a single metal as absolutely the best money for any particular nation in its internal commerce; and it does not seem certain that the very arguments which prove this do not hold good for a uniform *system* of money for that greater nation which counts amongst its citizens the inhabitants of the whole commercial world. Every argument which Lord Liverpool uses for this country applies equally well to the whole family of nations; but he was not concerned for other states, he was not desirous of preaching a Gold standard, or even a uniform standard to other nations, and if he had desired to do so, it would have been at that time made all the more difficult by their several predilections either for Silver as a single standard, or for a double coinage of Gold and Silver; and also by the want of those facilities of communication which we now enjoy, and by the impossibility which then, at least, did exist of bringing about "international concert." But with respect to this country, for which alone Lord Liverpool intended his argument, it was capable of and received practical application, so that Gold became the single standard of these realms; of which result I will say that if nothing else had to be taken into consideration, and if we had dealings with no other country but the British Islands, our system would be perfect.

I will add that till of late years the inconveniences which have resulted have not made themselves manifest, and my only desire in writing these pages is to arouse the minds of the more experienced among us to the necessity of a careful examination of those inconveniences with a view to discover how far they are really dangerous to commerce, and to the well-being of England's dependencies, and how far they may overbalance the obvious benefits of a single Gold standard; and if it be found that they are of such a nature as to require a remedy, then to approach the question what that remedy shall be with an unprejudiced mind.

One of the remedies that has been suggested is the adoption of the second system of currency, spoken of in my first page; that is to say, of the Double Standard as it existed in full force in France till 1874.

Now, just as we shall find that many economists will declare that there are no inconveniences at all in the single Gold standard, or, if there are any, that they are not worth serious notice, so we shall find that there are enthusiastic defenders of the Double Standard who say that not only is its admitted action not disastrous even to a single country adopting it, but positively advantageous. Be that as it may, it is incontestable that what is called the Double Standard was, as applied at that time in France, really an alternative standard, or, more strictly speaking, produced an alternative currency. For some time before 1848, Gold, being the dearer of the two metals, had nearly left the country, and little but Silver was to be seen. Later on, when the construction of the Indian railways, and other causes, had greatly augmented the demand for Silver, that metal became the dearer of the two, and it became difficult to get change for a Gold napoleon.

Yet France was in neither case a monometallic country as has been sometimes assumed; for the bimetallic law was still in force, every one was at liberty to pay his debt in whichever metal he chose, and every one was entitled to receive 1000 pieces of 5 francs for 723·391 ounces of pure Silver, or 1000 pieces of 20 francs for 186·681 ounces of pure Gold, delivered at the mint.

But the dearer metal had in either case for the most part disappeared from common use, and France was so far left with the depreciated coinage only, of Gold or Silver as the case might be; a condition, according to some French economists, demanding congratulation as having brought gain to the country, but, according to most English economists, deserving commiseration as having brought loss, some going so far as to speak of "the misery endured by the "people of France under their changing system."

Mr. Cernuschi's contention is that if France has lost her Gold—to take that instance—it has not been taken from her against her will. She has freely offered it. If she has paid her debts to England in Gold, then for every 20-franc piece sent away she has had goods worth 20 Gold francs in exchange, or else she has received Silver for her Gold, and, by the hypothesis, more Silver than is contained in four

Mr. H. H. Gibbs.

5-franc pieces, for silver was cheaper than Gold in this market. So France, he thinks, as a nation, has gained all round.

Without either accepting the conclusion at which he arrives, or denying that there may be considerable inconvenience and disadvantage in a frequent shifting of currencies under a bimetallic law prevailing in a *single* nation, from which disadvantage a monometallic nation must be free, one may well doubt whether the prejudice is so great to the single bimetallic country as is commonly supposed.

That which seems to me to be urgently needed is a careful enquiry both into the reality of the alleged losses and inconveniences, and into the truth of the contention that they would be diminished under the operation of a bimetallic compact between all the principal nations of the earth.

I have seen no reason to alter the opinion expressed in my former pamphlet, that the alleged evils could not exist under the circumstances of such a compact, and that if England, the Latin Union, Germany and the United States were agreed, all other nations would find it to their advantage to follow their example; and that while the use of Silver as a medium of exchange would be legally extended over all the nations so agreeing, it would practically make very little or no difference in the metallic currency used by any particular nation in its internal commerce, inasmuch as all would still use that for which they have severally a preference. It may be, indeed, that the use of Gold of late years by the United States, and the present disinclination of the public in that country to use Silver, may add them to the list of the nations having a preference for Gold; but the effect of the prevalence of a bimetallic compact would be, in my opinion, that further change of habits in this respect would be not promoted but arrested.

Whether or not my belief is well founded that the disadvantages of the Double Standard as existing in any single country would be cured by a common accord amongst nations, the present question is whether the evils, whatever they may be, which now exist and are likely to increase, are such as to need a remedy which would, in anticipation at least, be so distasteful and so contrary to the traditions, and, which is of more importance, to the prejudices of a majority of Englishmen; and I propose to state the reasons which I will not say make such a change necessary, but which make a patient and thoughtful enquiry into the subject very desirable.

The question is a serious and important one, and scarcely deserves to be treated with the indifference and contempt with which some Political Economists are willing to treat it; for though the evils which now in my belief do result from the present state of things may or may not be found to need so radical a remedy, the evil which may hereafter result is a much wider one.

The inevitable end, if other nations are not in time awake to the danger, would seem to be that while we see the production of Gold decreasing, Gold may come to be adopted as a standard throughout the commercial world, with the evil consequences to which I have referred above; and this alone, without taking into account the present ill effects both of the fall in Silver, and of the uncertainty of its position from day to day, would afford a sufficient reason for grave enquiry.

It has been said that this fear of the appreciation of Gold is exaggerated, that the United States, a Silver-producing country, can never really desire the demonetization of Silver, and that if Italy intends to resume cash-payments in Gold, yet though she may be able to obtain it she will certainly not be able to keep it, and that Germany is too well aware of the loss she would sustain by selling the remainder of her stock of Silver, to persevere in her intention of substituting Gold for it.

Mr. H. H. Gibbs.

As to the United States, the fact remains that a large party loudly cry for the complete establishment of a Gold Standard, some because they have a theoretical preference for Gold, and some because they think that the threat of demonetization will be their best weapon wherewith to enforce on Europe their real desire, the adoption of the Double Standard.

As to Italy, if she has credit to obtain the loan which she desires, and if she cancels an amount of notes equal to the Gold remitted to her so that her circulation is not redundant, I do not see how having once got the Gold she can be with any certainty deprived of it. The only thing that can withdraw specie from a country is the indebtedness of that country, its imports exceeding its exports; that is to say, the state of the exchanges. The rate of interest is the weapon with which the battle of bullion will be fought. Some to obtain and others to retain that bullion will have to raise their rates one against the other, and the rise of the rate of interest implies the fall of prices.

If Italy then takes 16 millions; if the United States demonetize the 33 millions of Silver existing, according to computation, in the country, and supply the place of the half that is in circulation other than in the Treasury with Gold; if Germany absorbs an equal sum, and if France and other states should think themselves compelled to follow the example, the struggle for Gold would it seems be no light one, and the consequences of it could not fail to be prejudicial to England.

What is most to be dreaded in respect of Silver, and, if possible, provided against, is a further depreciation in its value.

I need not refer more particularly to the effect of the existing depreciation of Silver on the finances of India, and on all those who, whether in India or in other Silver-using countries, have fixed sums to receive in Silver, and fixed sums to remit in Gold.

It is the further depreciation, and, indeed, any abnormal fluctuation which affects for evil the interests of all those in Gold-using countries who have commercial dealings with Silver-using nations. Such fluctuation, acting on the exchanges, imparts an additionally speculative character to their business; they can make no just estimate of what they have to receive for their goods; the thing that they do receive is for them a commodity, just as wool is, or bark, or silk, or tea—neither more nor less.

I have been answered as to this point, that the merchant *does* know what he has to receive; for remittances being made in bills, it is all a matter of exchange, which must of necessity be subject to fluctuations.

I reply that it is precisely because it *is* a matter of exchange that my statement is correct.

What is it that regulates the rate of exchange between nations? Where their coins are the same in substance, and are equal (or by a fixed calculation are reduced to equality as the pound sterling and napoleon are) in weight or fineness, there are only two things which regulate the exchange. First, the cost of transmission of the coin; and second, the greater or less demand for bills in the market from whence the remittance takes place. But in such countries the rate cannot recede below the par of exchange less the cost of transmission. Thus the computed par of the sovereign, measured in French Gold, being frs. 25·21¾, and the cost of transmission being 8 or 9 cts., a rate of frs. 25·12½ causes the English debtor to send Gold rather than send or accept bills.

But if, on the other hand, the coins are not the same in substance, the exchange must also vary with the difference in value of the two substances each in the other market. The money of the country from which remittance is made is coined from a metal which is an article of merchandise in the State to which remittance is made, and thus an additional element of uncertainty comes into the calcula-

Mr. H. H. Gibbs.

tion. It matters not whether remittance is made in Silver, or tin, or bark; whether it is at so many pence per dollar, or so many pence per ounce of Silver or tin, or per pound of bark: it is a speculation in produce after all; and accordingly, in Silver-using countries, the exchange with England varies every day, not on the calculable value of a metal accepted as money, but on the variable value of an article of produce—on the ever-changing price of Silver in this market.

But it may be said that this also is one of the ordinary risks of trade, and involves merely an additional calculation to be made by the merchant here or by his correspondent in the Silver-using country; and even if the variation in the price of Silver occurs within the period of his transaction, and from day to day, there must be some means by which he can guard himself from loss.

I know of none; nor is it at all a question of having an extra calculation to make. The variations of price are *always* occurring during the period of a transaction, and the following example will show the evil which ensues.

Suppose a manufacturer to send two consignments of goods—one to Australia, and another to Calcutta, telling his correspondents that 30*s.* per piece is a covering price. The Australian has no difficulty at all; he knows the cost of transmission, and will not buy a bill for remittance on less favourable terms for the manufacturer than he could get by sending specie. His only calculation is as to the possible variation of the exchange between the date of his sale and the date of his recovering and remitting the proceeds; and a knowledge of the exports and imports will give him a reasonable clue to the probabilities of rise or fall in the exchange.

The Calcutta merchant can also estimate this; but there is another element on which he cannot calculate in the least when he makes his sale. What will be the price of Silver in England when he comes to buy his bill? Silver is to his English friend a mere commodity, and his remittance to him is in its essence a shipment of that commodity, and on the fluctuations of its price he cannot calculate at all. "But what then?" it may be answered; "These are only "the natural risks of Trade. Is our currency to be "revolutionised because a manufacturer has made a loss?" I answer that this is an extra risk which should and could be avoided; but the particular loss to the shipper is not the measure of the evil; for the risk forces him to suspend or curtail his shipments to the country, whereby both he and his correspondent in Calcutta suffer; he curtails his manufacture accordingly, whereby large classes in England suffer, and trade is injured all round.

As Gold is the only money current and recognised in this country, and as Silver is the only money recognised by certain other nations as current in their countries, and as therefore in these last Gold is but merchandise, just as in our country Silver is but merchandise, it must follow that the exchange of cotton goods—one kind of merchandise—for Silver—another kind of merchandise—is but a kind of barter. The exchange of English goods for so many ton weight of copper is confessedly barter, for copper is as much "produce" as wool is. The exchange for so many pounds weight of Silver, which is also as much "produce" as copper is, has only this difference, that we may send our Silver again to a place where it is money. To us it is, in a manner, barter; but barter with an alleviation.

But as to this I have been answered that "*Barter* is "where there is no medium or measure of exchange—where "a man who has more wheat than he wants, and wants "iron, must look out for a man who has more iron than he "wants, and who wants wheat. To call by the same name "the case where there are two media, and measures, Gold "and Silver, the relative value of which has to be deter-"mined, is surely to misuse terms,"—to which I reply that the phrase "two media" is an erroneous one. A *medium*

Mr. H. H. Gibbs.

of exchange must, I think, be something mutually accepted as such by two parties: *Two* "media," whereof one is a medium accepted by one party, and the other a medium accepted by another—one by England, and another by Mexico—have nothing to liken them to a medium accepted by both, nothing to take either one of them out of the category of merchandise in the country where it is not accepted as a medium.

Whether such dealings are properly called barter or not is wholly unimportant. My point is that it is an embarrassment to trade. So far as it *is* barter, it is disguised, as all barter is, in commercial countries by the use of bills of exchange.

I am told, and rightly, that the inconvenience of which I complain is only the same as is caused by paper-money issued in excess; and it is added that as we cannot remedy *that* mischief—for no agreement can prevent a nation in difficulties from issuing such paper—there is no reason why we should suffer ourselves to be disturbed by this, which is of the same kind.

But there is a great difference between the two cases, and it is clear that if the fluctuations in exchange in a country using inconvertible paper are due to the unforeseen and excessive emission of such paper-money, the case is worse than with Silver; but this is only because the difficulty of production is less; the printing press mine is more readily worked than the mountain mine; and the calculation of quantities is even more difficult. Mr. Goschen, in a speech on the Silver question, says that people do a very good business with countries where the fluctuations of exchange are enormous. But what *is* good business? Profitable business is done by some, but at the cost of much enhanced risk, a risk which makes business unprofitable to others. Such business can hardly be called *good.* Trade in the example quoted on p. 21, suffers all round—both with India, and generally—by the additional risk; first owing to the depreciation of the silver currency, which makes imports fall off, and secondly, and in a much greater degree, if the country with which we are dealing is forced, by stress of war or other emergency, to issue inconvertible paper. To send goods to such a country at any time may be risky: to send while the stress continues may be to give away, if notes are issued *ad libitum* and without warning.

True; nothing can prevent such a country from doing this: but nothing can prevent a Gold-using nation from taking the same evil course; and all the evils of a risky exchange would come upon us in our relations with it, and all the evils of the depreciation of Gold which its practical demonetization by a nation so acting would produce; and they would come on us, as I think can be shown, with two-fold force compared with what they would do if our money did not consist of Gold alone.

But that a rash issue of inconvertible paper will affect for evil the exchange of the issuing country, and do injury to trade, is no reason for sitting quietly under the more remediable evils of depreciated Silver, or appreciated Gold.

England, then, has suffered the inconvenience of exchanging her commodities, not for money, but for another commodity, exposed to a fluctuation in price, which cannot be sufficiently calculated—inconvenience which would certainly not occur if she, and the nations with which she dealt, used the same metal as money, nor, as I think, if they used the same metals as money.

How has she been able to bear such an uncivilised condition of commerce? It has only been possible because it has gone on, till of late, unperceived. There has been a safety-valve against the pressure, which has prevented the explosion —a salve for the sore, which has prevented the pain being felt. France has been there with her Double Standard of Gold and Silver, preserving the equilibrium of the two metals by receiving indifferently the Gold of England and the Silver of India, and acting as a clearing-house between the two countries. Mr. Giffen answered this reasoning of mine by saying, that through a long course of years before 1848, France had practically only a single standard, and having no Gold to give us could not therefore have done us this service. I reply, that the fact that one metal practically prevailed in France during a certain time is *nihil ad rem.* She had free mintage all the while for both. That her Gold (or Silver) was exported did not affect the question.

His contention is as follows:

"So long as anybody who has Gold will give it for 15½ "of Silver, Silver cannot fall below 15½."

"But if nobody, who is willing to give Gold for 15½ "of Silver, has any Gold to give, he has no power to "arrest the fall of Silver in relation to Gold."

"This was the case before 1848 in bimetallic countries. "They had no Gold to give for Silver. Therefore, they "could not prevent Silver falling to 16, 17, 18, 19, 20, or "any other price in relation to Gold."

"The bimetallic law was of no effect."

This is so far correct that if in a bimetallic country, which stands alone in its bimetallism, Gold becomes the dearer metal, it is theoretically true and practically possible that all the Gold bullion, and, perhaps, the greater portion of the Gold coin also, should leave the country; and then any one in it who may want Gold for any purpose, would have to give such an agio for it as might bring the nominal ratio in that country, between the Silver then become almost the sole current coin, and the desired Gold then become practically a commodity, to any point.

But that does not in the least invalidate my contention, which is not that the existence of a Gold and Silver currency in France affects the price of Silver in England, but that it is the law of Free Mintage, a necessary part of the law of the Double Standard, which of itself maintains a constant and comparatively even market for the metal;

and I maintain therefore that in England or any other monometallic Gold-using country, that law of free mintage must needs keep the price of the commodity Silver at a point dependent not at all on the power of getting Gold from France, or on the agio which may be paid for it there, but on the course of exchange between the two countries.

If, for example, France were to restore to-morrow the full operation of her bimetallic law, there can be no doubt that, on the same day, if exchange were about par, the price of Silver here would return to its old point. It would be wholly a question of exchange, and, supposing the exchange to vary only in its normal way under the influence of more or less abundant harvests in France, and more or less demand for foreign commodities of consumption, a chance remittance of $15\frac{1}{2}$ ounces of pure Silver to that country for sale would necessarily establish for the remitter a credit there for which he could draw. If exchange were at par he would sell his draft in this market for £4 4*s.* $11\frac{3}{4}$*d.*, which is the equivalent of one ounce of pure Gold, calculated at the rate of £3 17*s.* $10\frac{1}{2}$*d.* per ounce standard, or if it was above par, for somewhat more—in neither of these cases would he really remit the Silver—but if it was below par his power of remittance would inevitably fix the price below which Silver cannot go in this market. The presence or absence of Gold in Paris, the fact that France had or had not Gold to give us, would not in the least affect the question. It would be wholly a question of exchange—of the balance of trade between the two countries—on France being or not at the moment a debtor to England.

There would always exist the power of remitting the Silver to Paris for sale, and of drawing for the equivalent, so as to receive it in Gold in London.

This is exactly what happened in those years between 1827 and 1871, in which France was said to be denuded of Gold, yet the price of Silver in England only fluctuated between $58\frac{7}{8}$ and $60\frac{3}{8}$, the average of the lowest year (1845) being $59\frac{3}{8}$. Mr. Seyd gives the following list of prices from 1827:—

Year.	Lowest.	Highest.	Year.	Lowest.	Highest.
1827 ..	$59\frac{1}{2}$	$60\frac{1}{4}$	1854 ..	$60\frac{7}{8}$	$61\frac{7}{8}$
1828 ..	$59\frac{1}{4}$	$60\frac{1}{2}$	1855 ..	60	$61\frac{5}{8}$
1829 ..	$59\frac{1}{2}$	60	1856 ..	$60\frac{1}{2}$	$62\frac{1}{4}$
1830 ..	$59\frac{3}{4}$	60	1857 ..	61	$62\frac{3}{8}$
1831 ..	60	$60\frac{7}{8}$	1858 ..	$60\frac{3}{4}$	$61\frac{7}{8}$
1832 ..	$59\frac{3}{4}$	$60\frac{1}{4}$	1859 ..	$61\frac{3}{4}$	$62\frac{3}{4}$
1833 ..	$58\frac{3}{4}$	60	1860 ..	$61\frac{1}{4}$	$62\frac{3}{8}$
1834 ..	$59\frac{3}{4}$	$60\frac{3}{8}$	1861 ..	$60\frac{1}{8}$	$61\frac{1}{4}$
1835 ..	$59\frac{1}{4}$	60	1862 ..	61	$62\frac{1}{8}$
1836 ..	$59\frac{3}{8}$	$60\frac{3}{8}$	1863 ..	61	$61\frac{3}{4}$
1837 ..	59	$60\frac{3}{8}$	1864 ..	$60\frac{5}{8}$	$62\frac{1}{2}$
1838 ..	$59\frac{3}{8}$	$60\frac{1}{8}$	1865 ..	$60\frac{1}{2}$	$61\frac{7}{8}$
1839 ..	60	$60\frac{5}{8}$	1866 ..	$60\frac{3}{8}$	$62\frac{1}{4}$
1840 ..	$60\frac{1}{8}$	$60\frac{5}{8}$	1867 ..	$60\frac{5}{16}$	$61\frac{1}{4}$
1841 ..	$59\frac{3}{4}$	$60\frac{3}{8}$	1868 ..	$60\frac{1}{8}$	$61\frac{1}{8}$
1842 ..	$59\frac{1}{8}$	$59\frac{3}{4}$	1869 ..	60	61
1843 ..	59	$59\frac{5}{8}$	1870 ..	$60\frac{1}{4}$	62
1844 ..	$59\frac{1}{4}$	$59\frac{3}{4}$	1871 ..	$60\frac{3}{16}$	$60\frac{7}{8}$
1845 ..	$58\frac{7}{8}$	$59\frac{7}{8}$	1872 *	$59\frac{1}{4}$	$61\frac{1}{8}$
1846 ..	59	$60\frac{1}{8}$	1873 ..	$57\frac{7}{8}$	$59\frac{15}{16}$
1847 ..	$58\frac{7}{8}$	$60\frac{3}{8}$	1874 †	$57\frac{1}{4}$	$59\frac{1}{2}$
1848 ..	$58\frac{1}{2}$	60	1875 ..	$55\frac{1}{2}$	$57\frac{5}{8}$
1849 ..	$59\frac{1}{2}$	$60\frac{1}{8}$	1876 ..	$46\frac{3}{4}$	$58\frac{1}{2}$
1850 ..	$59\frac{1}{2}$	$61\frac{1}{2}$	1877 ..	$53\frac{1}{4}$	$58\frac{1}{4}$
1851 ..	60	$61\frac{5}{8}$	1878 ..	$49\frac{1}{2}$	$55\frac{1}{4}$
1852 ..	$59\frac{7}{8}$	$61\frac{7}{8}$	1879 ..	49	$53\frac{5}{16}$
1853 ..	$60\frac{5}{8}$	$62\frac{3}{8}$	1880 ..	$51\frac{5}{8}$	$52\frac{3}{4}$

* Demonetization of Silver by Germany.

† Suspension of free mintage of Silver by the Latin Union.

Though the difference between the profit of Gold and Silver produced at the mines was not abnormal, a difference existed, as is shown by the fact that France was denuded of Gold, the dearer metal; yet the price only fluctuated, as shown in the table.

The highest price in 1879 was $53\frac{3}{4}$, and the average price last year was $52\frac{3}{16}$. It is now $52\frac{1}{16}$.

It is quite possible that had the relative production of and demand for the two metals been maintained in due proportion the same steadiness of price would also have been maintained; but my contention is, that though that production and demand had varied, the power of claiming 107·1342 francs for my $15\frac{1}{2}$ ounces of pure Silver would have tended to steady the price, and that, without the necessity of actually making any such remittance, the other Silver-using countries would necessarily regulate the price they would give for Silver on the price obtainable by remittance to France.

It is indeed conceivable that an abnormal production of Silver in the mines, or a great diminution of the demand through falling off of trade, or cessation of the use of Silver as money in any country, would force merchants to realise their consignments of Silver by shipping them to France, and drawing against them. Then, possibly, unless the exports of France had kept pace with this change, either by absolute increase or by diminution of other imports, the exchange would go heavily against that country, and a proportionate fall in the price of Silver would be brought about; but it would then also be entirely a question of exchange, of the balance of exports and imports, including, of course, the import of Silver.

So long as there was plenty of Gold in France to remit, the fluctuation in the exchange, and consequently in the price of Silver in this market, would lie between very narrow limits, because the exchanges would be from time to time rectified by remittances of Gold, but when all that

Mr. H. H. Gibbs.

could go was gone, as in the time referred to before 1848, even then, if the exchanges remained at a point favourable to France, Silver could not fall.

It is true that a continued fall in the exchange, or even the expense of coining more Silver than was needed for internal commerce, would become intolerable to the bimetallic country, and cause it to do as France has done from fear of some such result, and suspend the full operation of the bimetallic law; but until that suspension took place, the free mintage guaranteed by that law must tie the price of Silver to the exchange between London and Paris.

Bimetallism, it is said, in one country only is an impossibility. That is only an equivocal use of the word "Bimetallism." A Bimetallic law, and the free mintage which is a necessary part of it, may perfectly well exist in one country alone, and has, in fact, existed in France about a hundred years; but if by bimetallism is meant the circulation of the two metals at the same time, it is quite true that Gold and Silver cannot long remain and perform the functions of a national currency in any single country while it has monometallic neighbours. For those neighbours the benefits of its bimetallic system will remain; for itself remain whatever inconveniences may attach to the system.

For the last sixty years those benefits have been ours; France acting as a clearing-house between England and India has been our safeguard against the inconveniences of the depreciation of the currency of the latter country, but now that the clearing-house has, for a time at least, suspended its operations, the last four or five years have shown us the existence of the evil, and the danger of its increase.

I do not think that anyone has endeavoured to show either that there is no evil at all, or, if there is, that it is bearable or incurable. Patience has been liberally prescribed to us, and other remedies proposed, which, it was thought, might be provided for us without any intervention or care of our own. Either (1) the over-production of Silver would cease, there would be at last an end to the abnormal flood of Silver poured on the market by the German sales of their demonetized coin, and trade would revive from its then existing depression, and when these things had happened, all would return to its normal condition, Silver and Gold would bear their accustomed ratio to one another, the losses of the Indian Government would cease, and stability return to our commerce with Silver-using countries.

Or, (2) if none of these things happened, then the pressure of the evil, if it was an evil, would force France into her old channel, and Germany, if not into her own old channel of Silver monometallism, at least into accord with bimetallic France, and all would be well.

Let us consider the first alternative.

The over-production in America has ceased, trade has in some measure improved, and for the present at least there is a cessation of German Silver sales, and these two circumstances, together with some demand for the Continent, did for a time cause a slight improvement in the price of the metal; but where is the return to the normal condition which prevailed from 1820 onwards? Where is the end of the losses of the Indian Government?

It is clear that even if the dead weight of the German Silver were removed from the market, in no case could Silver, while treated as a commodity, return to its former position with respect to Gold; for there would still remain one great cause of a lower price in the cessation of the demand for Germany (and some other countries) for coining. The Indian Government therefore would find its difficulties alleviated, but not removed; and we could expect no stability in whatever average price might be arrived at when the actual disturbing causes were removed,

Mr. H. H. Gibbs.

so long as the compensating balance afforded by the French Double Standard was not restored.

A new demonetization of Silver or Gold, a great discovery of either metal, great commercial disturbance in countries using one, while those using the other were in comparative prosperity—either of these causes might again bring about violent disturbance in the relations between Gold and Silver, and renew the evils of which we now complain.

A new influx of Silver and Gold from the mines is, of these disturbing causes, that one of which we need take least account. If such new discoveries are made, we cannot help it; we can neither predict them nor provide against them. If they come, they come; and nothing we can do can influence their coming or not coming. But demonetization by other countries is an evil which we may hasten or prevent. The example of Germany is already followed by some minor nations, and the more there are that adopt this course, the more do those who still use Silver feel their position to be a doubtful one, and the result may be that suggested in my Preface, namely, that others may be irresistibly driven to follow the example, and Silver may cease to be money in France and the Latin Union, in Germany and the United States.

As to the other alternative: No doubt all would be well if the other nations would agree in the use of the Double Standard, while we retain our present system unaltered, so far harmonizing with bimetallism that we have a Gold standard in one part of the empire, and Silver in another; but it may be doubted whether if the two nations most concerned in the Silver question, England for the sake of India, the United States for their own sakes, as producers of the metal, hold aloof, the others will step into the gap. Be this as it may, the United States have again opened the question, and a second Conference is to meet in a few days. It is much to be hoped that it will issue in some international accord, for if not, it is too likely that the affair will go from bad to worse, both in the appreciation of Gold and in the depreciation of Silver, and agreement, which is the only real remedy, will become every year more difficult.

It has, I think, been shown that agreement to adopt a single metal as the medium of exchange is practically impossible; but the adoption of the Double Standard by the chief nations of the world would provide them a common metallic basis which now does and still would amply suffice for the wants of commerce. Roughly speaking, one half the world uses Gold, and the other half uses Silver: the adoption of the Double Standard would make this change only, that all the world would use both Gold and Silver. There would be no more increase or diminution (consequent on such a measure) in the quantity of circulating medium among nations than if the whole quantity of both metals were fused into what the Romans called an *electrum*, that is to say, a compound metal of Gold and Silver. I have already said (and it is little more than a truism) that no metal has ever been the money of any country without national consent. Even an inconvertible paper currency, valueless though it is, may serve as the money of a nation, but it must have national consent to make it so serve, and that consent can make it serve notwithstanding that it is bad in principle and in use.

That any single metal should be universally money we need international consent; but neither for a Gold measure of value alone, nor for a Silver measure of value alone, have we that international consent, and I see nothing in the reason of the thing why all nations should not arrive at a common consent to use both together in a certain relative ratio, trusting to the establishment of free mintage to produce as its consequence continuous and unrestricted demand, and thus to preserve that ratio unaltered.

What that ratio should be, if such a thing be possible, I will discuss presently.

Mr. H. H. Gibbs.

That both metals are severally well fitted to be money all history shows, and the least costly of the two was "current money with the merchant" before the other was used except for ornament, probably because it was more abundant. A certain abundance is necessary; for there must be enough to serve as

"The . . . common drudge 'twixt man and man;"

but one principal necessity is that its natural cost, or rather difficulty, of production be considerable, so that there be not too much abundance, for that is a safeguard against the currency becoming redundant, and prices of commodities inconveniently rising. But as I have said above, there are other metals and other substances more difficult of access and more costly to produce than either Gold or Silver. Scarceness alone is not a sufficient qualification, nor imperishableness, nor portableness, necessary as these and other qualities are.

Nor, on the other hand, is inequality of cost, or cheapness of one portion of the metal used, a bar to its fitness to be a measure of value. That a great portion of the Gold discovered in Australia and California costs half or a quarter as much per ounce as the Gold discovered in some other countries, is no disparagement to the fitness of cheap and dear Gold alike to serve as a medium of exchange. Why should it be more prejudicial that a metal the production of which costs only a sixteenth of what Gold costs should be yoked with Gold in a certain proportion to do that service for the whole world, than that cheap Gold should be yoked with dear Gold. I can see little difference but one of degree in the two cases, and that the metal in question is white instead of yellow. We cannot distinguish between cheap Gold and dear Gold, and it seems needless to make any other distinction between cheap Silver and dear Gold than what nature has made at the time of their being yoked together.

But the objection usually raised to a Double Standard, to the concurrent use of Gold and Silver as money, is not that they ought not to be so yoked but that they could not; and I will now proceed to state the objections which are most commonly made, having first set down distinctly what it is that the advocates of the Double Standard desire.

Let the Governments of the chief commercial nations agree upon what is the present approximate ratio of Silver to Gold—we will assume, for the sake of having a basis to start from, that 15½ is to be that ratio. It is one on which, as we are informed, the Governments of France and the United States are already agreed, and which many of even our strongest opponents are willing to allow to be the only one possible, if the principle of the Double Standard itself could be accepted. Let our Government agree, then, that for the British Dominions 113·0016 grains of pure Gold (123·27447 Standard) or 1751·5247 grains of pure Silver (1893·5403 Standard) shall be indifferently a good discharge for a debt of one pound sterling, and that they will coin all Silver that any one brings to the Mint into pieces of 350·3049 grains pure, the debtor to have always the option of paying his debt either in Gold or Silver. For other countries the weight and denomination and currency of Silver and Gold coins would be specified in a corresponding manner. This is the whole Bill.

The answer to the question "What is a pound?" would be "either 113·0016 grains of pure Gold, or 1751·5247 pure "Silver, at the option of the payer."

Now the objections so far as I have been able to gather them are the following:—

I. It is impossible to regulate by legislative enactment the value of any commodity: Gold and Silver are commodities; therefore it is impossible to fix their relative values.

Mr. H. H. Gibbs.

II. If it be attempted, nature will revolt against it, and that which is in reality and in despite of law the cheaper of the two metals will prevail, and the other will leave the country, as has been the case in our own experience in France both with Gold and Silver.

III. But if it *were* possible, consent is admitted to be necessary; and consent is impossible.

IV. But if consent were possible, and if it sufficed to fix a reasonably approximate ratio between Gold and Silver, there would always be a preference for Gold, which will therefore bear a greater proportionate price; because, its bulk being smaller, it is (1) cheaper to transmit, and (2) easier to count.

V. Supposing a twofold standard established, the effects of a new flood of Silver from the mines would be disastrous. It would overwhelm commerce, give a sudden and dangerous impulse to prices, and disturb the relation between creditor and debtor.

VI. Supposing its establishment to be on the basis of a ratio of 15½ Silver to 1 Gold, while the existing proportion is perhaps 18, then the effect would be, first, that such a stimulus would be given to the working of Silver mines all over the world that this apprehended flood of Silver would really and inevitably come upon us; and secondly, that even if no increase of production took place, it would of itself increase the total circulation of the world by the addition to it of 2½ ounces for every 15½.

VII. There would also be the material inconvenience that all Silver token-coins would have to be called in and recoined.

VIII. We have gone on for sixty years in great prosperity with a single standard. Why change?

IX. It is impracticable; it may suit other nations, but it is impossible to present it in a form that can be acceptable to England.

I do not think I have misrepresented the objections, the first seven of which seem to me to be sufficiently cogent, and to deserve and require most careful answers. The two last are not, I think, of so much importance, but they have been seriously urged by good economists, and should be noticed.

I will now state what I have to urge against these objections.

I. "It is impossible to fix by law the value or rather "the price of any commodity, and the precious metals "being commodities, no price can be fixed for them."

There is no doubt of the truth of the proposition that it is impossible to fix by law the money value of any commodity; and were it possible, it would be as impolitic to enact that Silver should not be sold at less than 60*d.* an ounce, as it would be to ordain that wheat should never be sold at less than 60*s.* a quarter. But, by the hypothesis, Silver is to become part of the money of the country; Silver and Gold are to stand to one another in a different relation from that in which either of them stands to wheat. Under our present monetary law Gold stands to Silver in exactly the same relation as Gold stands to wheat, and it cannot be but that some change in those relations must result from Silver becoming equally with Gold the measure of value and means of payment for wheat—that is to say, that a debt of £3 17*s.* 10½*d.* incurred for wheat may be discharged either in an ounce of standard Gold, or in 15½ ounces of standard Silver. The words "price and value" seem to me to be misapplied in describing the mutual relation of the metals forming together what I venture to call one metallic standard of value, that is to say forming inseparable parts of one monetary system.

Mr. H. H. Gibbs.

Money cannot measure money, both metals being accepted as money. The question of price cannot arise between them, and their price cannot therefore be fixed by the State or otherwise. If their values measured in other commodities are by nature unequal, the State can by no law and no declaration make them equal; but in passing a law which makes 15½ ounces of Silver a good discharge for a debt of one ounce of Gold (we are supposing that to be the true proportion existing at the time of the making of the law) it does an act which, as I shall presently show, makes future inequality between the two metals unimportant, and their service as money unaccompanied by any injustice, inconvenience or irregularity.

It is true that in adopting a twofold standard, and fixing by law an arbitrary ratio of one of the constituent parts of that standard to the other, we *do* incidentally regulate the price of a commodity; but it is only incidentally, and as a consequence necessarily flowing from free mintage, and from what I have, I think, shown to be practicable and reasonable legislation. That is to say, we fix a price in Silver for that portion of Gold-yield which is used in the arts, and not for the purposes of coinage or currency, and a price in Gold of that portion of the Silver-yield which is used in the arts and not for circulation; but the quantities, whether of Silver or Gold, thus used are so small as compared with those doing duty as money, that the effect of thus fixing the price is certainly quite insignificant.

II. "The dearer metal would be exported and the " cheaper metal would take its place, thus causing a loss to " the country."

The cheapness of one metal in the market and the consequent export of the other are the two cardinal points on which the whole question turns, and I hope that in any answer to this which may appear some attempt will be made to show how, and by what steps, the supposed difference of market value could be brought about, and how, and by what steps, the "dearer" metal would disappear. Hitherto all that is alleged is that one metal *has* become dearer, and *has* disappeared under circumstances wholly different from those suggested.

The allegation is that there would be a difference between the mint price and market price of Silver, but it seems to me impossible. I wish to know how the market price could be quoted. In what would it be reckoned? Not in Gold, for it is not conceivable that a holder of Silver would sell his 15½ ounces standard for a less sum than £3 17*s.* 10½*d.* (or £3 17*s.* 9*d.* Bank price), when by taking them to the Mint he could by law have them coined for him into pieces of Silver (19 double florins and small change), which would be a legal discharge for a debt of that amount: not in commodities, for it is not conceivable that the seller of commodities would take less in Gold than he would in Silver, when he would have no reason to expect that his Gold would be worth more at home or abroad. Only if his Gold would buy him more Silver or more commodities elsewhere would he care in which metal his price was counted.

But by the hypothesis other commercial nations are to be in the same case with England, and he cannot, therefore, anywhere procure Silver at a cost of fewer commodities than he can Gold.

But the miner, it may be said, the cost of production of his Silver being less in proportion than that of Gold, will be able and willing to sell it for a lower price. Why should he do so? If he procures it at the cost of less labour and fewer commodities, so much the better for him. But he will not on that account part with it for a less number of dollars than he could get for it at the nearest mint, less cost of carriage and interest. The buyer would have to send it thither, and get the mint price: why should not the seller do the same? If not, and if he sells at a

Mr. H. H. Gibbs.

lower price than his buyer could thus obtain, he makes him a present of his profit. In discussing this question one of the most frequent mistakes is to confuse the profit of the miner with the supposed advantage of the debtor. It is commonly said that the debtor will be master of the situation, that he will be able to take advantage of the creditor and pay his debts in the cheaper metal. How is he to come by the "cheaper metal?" How will it be cheap to *him?* Were Englishmen able to pay their bills the easier because Gold was to be had in Australia for the picking up? The only effect of cheapness of production is to give profit to the miner and his men, and of course to enhance prices if cheapness of production increases the quantity produced; but they will be prices counted not in the miner's Silver only, but in his neighbour's Gold as well.

The cost of production will no doubt regulate the value of Gold or Silver reckoned in one another, or in other commodities, if *neither* metal is money; it will do so if *either* metal is money; *i.e.*, if one is a purchasable commodity, and the other money, the measure in which the value of that commodity is counted; but its effect will not be the same if *both* metals are money under an international compact. Their cost of production will then regulate their value not in one another, but in other commodities only.

Under such a compact Silver and Gold are as one metal—limbs of the same body, parts of the same whole—fused like an *electrum* into one mass; and when both are recognized as the measure of other commodities, whose value as a mass varies with the total quantity of that measure, the cost of production does not practically determine the mutual value of the two parts of it. I say "practically," because, though no law and no agreement can make the proportion between those two parts other than what nature and labour may have made it, my contention is that what law and agreement can do is to make the variations in that proportion wholly unimportant in the relation of the several metals to the commodities of which they are jointly the measure. Diminished cost of production, resulting in increased production of either part of the mass of metallic money cannot, I think, reduce the value of that part in respect of commodities, but the value of the whole mass.

But let us suppose for the sake of argument "one "metal or the other" to be the dearer of the two, and that therefore it "will leave the country," and the depreciated metal will remain. It is admitted on all hands that such was the case with France when she stood alone a bimetallic nation surrounded by monometallic neighbours; and that such must be the case with any single country so standing.

It must with equal unanimity be admitted that if *all* commercial nations without exception had but one mind in the matter and received Gold and Silver alike (in a fixed proportion) in payment of debt, no such exodus of one or other could take place. Whither would the dearer metal go? Surely the objectors will not say that it will leave all countries simultaneously!

But my contention is that the union for this purpose of two or more of the principal nations would be sufficient so to diminish whatever evil France may have suffered as to make it of very little consequence; and that if England were to lead the way not only would all Europe follow, but even if all did not, yet the fear of such an export, or, indeed, of any export at all of importance, when both metals were used by so large a combination, would be merely chimerical, and I think it certain that if such a compact were once made, there could be in effect no divergence between the nominal and real value of the precious metals measured in each other, and that therefore no debtor could gain in that way any advantage over his creditor. If the other nations, as is probable, did follow their example, assurance would be made doubly sure; but supposing some nations not to follow, could the dearest metal be attracted to them in any quantity? Could we

Mr. H. H. Gibbs.

send our Gold to Mexico, for instance, and fetch Silver from thence? Gold is for the Mexicans an article of merchandise. We might export Gold to that country, and it would probably be a bad speculation; but if we did so, why should the Mexican sell us or pay us 16 or 17 ounces of Silver for our ounce of Gold when he could himself send 15½ ounces to England, and buy not the ounce of Gold indeed, but the commodities that it would purchase?

It must, however, be admitted that Mexico, China, and any other country remaining outside the compact will stand in exactly the same relation towards the greater part of Europe, the United States, and all other nations within the compact, as the whole commercial world stood towards France when that country stood alone in her bimetallism.

It is scarcely necessary to point out how great would be the difference between the action of the whole commercial world upon France, and the action of a few nations upon a large number. The attracting force of those outside the compact would be infinitely less, and the diminution of the mass of the "dearer" metal held by those within it would be inappreciable.

I will take China as an instance. If China should absorb more Silver than she now does, more than the annual production would supply, it is possible, though highly improbable, that Silver might leave the bimetallic nations, or rise to a premium.

Or if China should indeed take to imitating the foreigner and adopt a Gold standard, she could, no doubt, remit her Silver to Europe, and establish credits there. Then, the debtor having the choice of metals, she would inevitably have to pay a premium for the Gold which would be remitted to her, and she would thus be deliberately making a loss without any compensatory gain; and if Europe did thus remain with the "cheaper" metal, it would be with a larger quantity of it that she would remain, and she would have lost nothing.

But in what respect would Europe be in a worse case under a bimetallic system than she would be *now* if China should choose to demonetize Silver? The bugbear is not of my raising, but of my opponents'. She would make her voluntary loss in a different way. She would take a leaf out of the German book, sell her Silver at a loss, and having thus established credits, would demand the Gold which in the other case she would have to buy.

III. "Consent between nations is impossible."

It is easier to allege than to prove the impossibility of agreement. Monetary concord between the various States of Germany would have seemed impossible a few years ago, and yet it has come to pass. There was no antecedent reason why it should have been possible to bring about the Latin Union, but it exists, and has been an important factor in the present condition of affairs. I believe that the only hindrance to international agreement lies in the attitude of this country, and in the opinions heretofore prevalent here; but if it can be shown that no real disadvantage to England in her internal commerce, and much advantage in her external relations, would attend the adoption of a twofold standard, that hindrance would, no doubt, disappear.

We already know that France and the United States are willing, provided only that others are willing also, that Germany was anxious for a Conference on the subject, and has, it is said, already nominated representatives. Austria would certainly make no demur, and Italy would lose, as the other nations would lose, the motives which are impelling her and them to resort to a single Gold standard; and the dangers which appear to me to threaten the commerce of England, and which lie in the increased and increasing appreciation of Gold, would be averted. Practically the decision rests with ourselves, and, if we were willing, that consent which is said to be impossible would at once exist.

But, it will be said, that even supposing all were to be willing to come to an agreement in principle, there is no probability of their being able to fix upon a ratio between the two metals that would commend itself to all the contracting powers, and at the same time be just to debtor and creditor alike.

The ratio was, indeed, theoretically, one of the great difficulties in the way of an agreement, but not practically. *Primâ facie* the just way would be to ascertain approximately the existing proportion between the two metals, and agree to fix that as the proportion at which the mints shall coin the Gold and Silver brought to them.

But how is that existing proportion to be ascertained? The market price will not show it, for the present position of Silver in the market is almost entirely the result of its demonetization, and the day Germany returned to a Silver currency Silver also would begin to return to its former level, even without any question of the Double Standard; and I believe that if Silver were as widely used as before it would be found that there would be very little difference between the true proportion and the ratio of 15½ which, by the necessity of the case, was always arbitrary, and more or less the result of a compromise.

I will discuss presently what would be the effect of fixing that ratio if it should really be much higher than the existing proportion, and what would be the effect of fixing it at 17 or 18 or any other ratio differing from 15½. This last has been the constant ratio for a much longer period than any other. Five-franc pieces bearing that relation to the Gold coinage of France are still legal tender in that country; thalers bearing that relation to the Gold coinage are still current in Germany at their full nominal value. In those two countries, therefore, the fixing the ratio at 17 or 18 would inflict some loss on the debtor, just as fixing it here at a higher rate than its existing market value would inflict some loss on the creditor, who might have to pay a debt in Silver to the foreigner. But as the present cheapness of the Silver which the creditor would in such a case have to buy arises from no action of his own country, and the renewed dearness would arise also without the necessity of any action of this country (for it would return by the action of the foreigner if Silver were remonetized and free mintage restored whether we retained our single standard or adopted the double one), he would have little reason to complain; and indeed the making his case worse by adopting too high a ratio under the Double Standard would not be so great an injustice as the making the debtor's worse by the depreciation of the lawful money of his country which would result from the adoption of too low a one.

It is quite true that the appreciation of Silver, whatever it may be, would involve a corresponding depreciation of Gold; and it has been asked whether, inasmuch as England is the greatest holder of Gold, it would not be England who more than any other would be injured by its depreciation, and whether, therefore, it is not unreasonable to expect that England should concur in the establishment of a Double Standard with such a fixed ratio between Gold and Silver as would ensure that depreciation.

Premising first that it is not alone the holders of the metal itself who would be affected by its depreciation, the answer is that the appreciation and depreciation of Silver and Gold respectively do not depend on our concurrence. The effect would be produced, either by a return on the part of Germany to the Single Silver Standard from which she departed in 1872, or by an agreement between France and the United States with or without other European States, to return to the Double Standard, with a fixed ratio of 15½ to 1.

But it may again be asked, "If it is certain that, in

"case no general agreement resulted from the Conference "one of the above-mentioned alternatives will happen, "why should England intervene, and why not rather main-"tain an expectant attitude and be in readiness to profit "by whatever may be the ultimate outcome of the delibe-"rations?"

If it *were* certain, and if the abstinence of England from co-operation did not involve a certain amount of instability in whatever action other nations may take, I could desire nothing better; but it is far from being certain, and the very knowledge that there is a strong and widely-spread opinion against bimetallism in this country will tend to make it even less probable than it would otherwise be.

But if the result is that neither is Silver reinstated in Germany, nor the Double Standard in France and the United States, that which does seem certain is that Gold will be inevitably adopted by those who are now in doubt, with the result upon prices to which I have before adverted.

Now it is worth while to inquire what practical effect for evil the supposed depreciation of Gold would have. Here is the sum of it. Suppose the Gold used for the purpose of money to be £500,000,000, and the Silver used for the same purpose to be £500,000,000 (the proportions are not correct, but near enough, probably, for an illustration). Then, if the present price of silver be 52*d.* an ounce (a ratio of about 18 to 1), these £500,000,000 are contained in 192,307,690 lbs. troy. Declare the ratio to be 15½ to 1, and each of those lbs. troy becomes the equivalent of about £3 sterling, and the £500,000,000 becomes £576,923,000—an apparent gain to the holders of Silver of some 15 per cent. But the whole £1,000,000,000 of circulation would have been inflated by an addition of £76,923,000, and depreciated, therefore, to the extent of about 7 per cent., which depreciation being shared by the Silver and Gold alike, the Gold-holders and Silver-holders alike would suffer a loss in the rise of prices, for their share of which loss the Silver-holders would be more than compensated. The loss would not be a very great one, even if this were the true state of the case; but if the measure is really advantageous for this country, even as the least of two evils, it may be desirable to sacrifice some exactness and to incur a small loss for the sake of bringing it about by common accord. I have shown that the mischief which could be done would be very small, even if the real difference were that between $15\frac{1}{2}$ and 18; but, as the difference would be only that between $15\frac{1}{2}$ and the true proportion under remonetization of Silver, the supposed prejudice would not be worth considering.

I have not desired to exaggerate the dangers which may follow upon the appreciation of Gold, but I think it well deserves careful examination whether they would not be more material than any which could be caused by a slight advance in the purchasing power of Silver.

Again, it may be objected, if the chief commercial nations had agreed on the principle of a Double Standard, and on the ratio between the two metals, what probability would there be of any such concert being maintained? Treaties are broken every day, and so, it may be thought, would this, if not by the reversion of one or more nations to one or other single standard, at least by a possible change in the ratio.

Other treaties may be broken, because by breaking them a nation seeks to bring advantage political or pecuniary to itself; but the Double Standard once established, I believe, the breaking of this treaty would touch home interests so widely spread, and so deeply rooted, that a change would not be lightly made.

In one particular indeed it must be admitted that there would be no guarantee for the maintenance of the treaty. Whatever the agreement, and however binding its terms, nothing can prevent any nation, party to it, from making short work of its metallic currency, by an issue, under

Mr. H. H. Gibbs.

stress of war, or for any other reason, of an inconvertible paper currency. The metallic money would in that case flow over into the currency of other nations.

But what happens *now* if a nation using a Gold Standard issues inconvertible paper? The Gold flows over into the Gold-using countries, affecting their prices more sharply than would the Gold and Silver which might leave a bimetallic country so acting, and would be spread over the whole world of commerce.

In any case the paper-issuing country would remain entirely without influence on the rest, when once her metallic money had left her. She would be outside the pale and would in no way affect the coherence of the others.

But some one may say, "If, after the ratio is once "ascertained and fixed, the relative market price of Silver "and Gold changes enormously, surely it must be not only "expedient but necessary to change the ratio. Suppose "Silver to become as rare as Gold—suppose it to become 50 "times commoner than Gold—is it conceivable that a ratio "of 15½ to 1 could be maintained?"

I have already shown, I think, that, when both were money, there could not be a market price as distinguished from a mint price of either metal—of Silver or Gold—their price would necessarily be measured in commodities, not in one another. Gold and Silver would be as one metal; and the only effect of such a change would be, that if the supposed rarity of Silver had produced a diminution of the common mass of money in the world the prices of other commodities would fall, or if its supposed abundance had produced an increase of that common mass, the prices of other commodities would rise; but such diminution or such enhancement must, in the nature of things, be gradual, and proportionate to the gradual diminution or increase of production; and to these the daily transactions of trade would adjust themselves without sudden or violent disturbance.

Secondly, the intrinsic danger and injustice of a change would be great.

Whatever ratio we now fix, no practical injury is done to the general interests of England. If we fix it a little too low or a little too high, the interest of a score of holders of Silver would be affected. That which they now hold as a commodity would be to a trifling extent raised or lowered in price, and there would be an end.

But a twofold standard once established, Silver becomes a money of the realm, and a change would affect the interest of every buyer and every seller, for the relation of money to all purchasable commodities would be violently altered. If, for example, we could suppose that the true proportion of Silver to Gold had come to be 20 to 1 instead of 15 to 1, and it should be decreed that the legal ratio should be changed accordingly, then the whole mass of Silver coin and bullion held in the country would be reduced in value by one-fourth, and the holder mulcted to that extent.

It needs but to mention the inconvenience which the mere apprehension of impending change would cause, if such change were supposed possible, to show that if England should once resolve on such a change as the adoption of Silver as a joint standard with Gold, she must surely adopt it once for all, and with no *arrière pensée* of future changes to and fro according as one or the other metal might seem to be relatively more abundant.

IV. The fourth objection depends on the statement that "there will always be a preference for Gold."

To this statement there is the short but decisive reply, that half the world has a preference for Silver.

Mr. H. H. Gibbs.

The reasons alleged for the statement—viz., cost of transmission, and labour of counting, can also, I think, be easily disposed of. In point of fact, it is *not* cheaper to transmit Gold than it is to transmit Silver, the freight and insurance being *ad valorem*, and the same for either. The bulk either of Silver or Gold is so small as to be of no moment in calculating the freight; and if there *be* any difference between them, Silver would have the advantage, inasmuch as Gold, by reason of its less bulk, value for value, is more exposed to the danger of robbery.

As to Gold being preferred because of its being easy to count, that point leads to the enquiry into what practical and material consequences would result from the adoption of a twofold standard by all nations, irrespective of any supposed effect on prices, to which latter point I will advert under Objection V.

Would currencies remain as they are, Gold in England, Silver in India, &c.?

I answer, certainly they would. Certainly no revolutionary change would be brought about by the admission of Silver into one country and Gold into the other as unlimited legal tender. Every one would be entitled to discharge any debt contracted after the passing of the law, in coins of standard Gold or in coins of standard Silver at his pleasure; but I see no reason to imagine that the latter would be more ready to his hand than the former, or indeed as ready. No one need fear that he will be in danger of receiving a sack of 5000 double florins for a debt of £1000, or of having to hire a porter to carry a bag of Silver when he has to pay his tailor. I apprehend that all large payments from hand to hand would be made as now by cheque; and all less ones of above £5 by notes; and all smaller ones by sovereigns and the Silver tokens representing parts of a sovereign. Payments in this country in Silver standard coins would be only exceptional. Silver is even now a legal tender up to 40*s*. Does anybody ever pay a debt of 40*s*. in Silver? I can imagine no reason why the Englishman should leave the "preference" which he now truly has for a Gold currency, nor the Indian his "preference" for a Silver currency. Those that use Gold for their daily transactions would use Gold still; and those that use Silver would use Silver still.

I presume, indeed, that the law would provide that debts or other payments falling due under contracts dated before the law came into operation might be demanded in Gold; but in reality there would be no reason why the debtor under such contracts should ordinarily prefer to pay in Silver rather than in Gold, nor why the creditor should prefer to receive in Gold rather than in Silver, any small sums not payable as usual by cheque or note.

Now suppose a bimetallic law passed to take effect on the 1st of January in any year, so soon as the Mint was made ready for the change; the actual thing which would happen is this: A shipment of Silver would arrive in course of time from Vera Cruz or some other port of shipment. It would be transhipped as now to India, or to any country in which there was a demand; just as a shipment of Gold is when the exchange is against the country, or when it has to be exported for any especial purpose. But if there should be no demand either to rectify the exchange or to supply (for example) a paper-using country with a required metal, the Silver would be taken to the Bank of England, and the directors, acting on the altered law, would issue notes against it. Those notes would fall into the Reserve of the Bank, and their sterling amount would be at the credit of the bringer, either in his own account in the books of the Bank or in that of his private banker; but as the law of the twofold standard could cause no increase in the quantities of the two metals, there could be no permanent increase in the Reserve; nor do I see any reason why Silver should flow to this country rather than Göld. Certainly, Gold alone would not come to the Bank, but

Mr. H. H. Gibbs.

I cannot see how caprice or interest will lead men to send Silver to it in preference. The debtor country, whose usual money is Silver, will pay its debts in Silver; and the debtor country, whose usual money is Gold, will send Gold. England is the monetary centre of the world, not because she uses Gold and not Silver, but because she is the centre of capital and trade. All the Gold and all the Silver of the world comes here now, except that which is retained for use in the country of its production. What more could happen if both Gold and Silver were accepted by us as money? Some imagine that all the Silver would come to the Bank of England, either instead of all the Gold or as well as all the Gold; and that in the latter case our issue of notes would rise to a point hitherto unknown. But I see no ground for supposing that we should issue one note more than we now do. The same balances would come, though sometimes in a different form; and whereas now shipment after shipment of Gold passes through England without entering into the Bank Reserve (when the state of the exchanges demands that it should go abroad), so it would be in the case of the Silver also.

But England, it is said, being a creditor country, would always be paid in the cheaper metal. This is to beg the question that there would or could be cheapness or dearness between the two parts of an accepted standard of value. Gold and Silver being jointly the measure of cheapness and dearness of other commodities could not have the same relation to one another that either one of them bears to any other commodity not so intimately connected with it.

The result would really be, I think, that the Bank would always hold both Silver and Gold bullion, as is already to a limited extent within its powers under the Act of 1844, and that the amounts of the two metals so held would be always varying, not by reason of any imaginary cheapness or dearness of either metal, but according to the varying condition of the balance of trade of the Silver-using or Gold-using countries respectively in relation to England.

The Silver received by the Bank would for the most part remain in the vaults, but some of it would be sent to the Mint to be coined into standard money, call them double florins or dollars, or what you will, in case it should be necessary to pay out any quantity of the new coin to the public; but, as I have said above, no great amount of it would be likely to go into active circulation.

The real difference that would result from a bimetallic law would be in international payments—in shipments of bullion to rectify the balance of trade between ourselves and other countries. The Bank of England would, as I have already said, hold Silver as well as Gold; and such shipments would be made in either metal at the option of the payer; but if made in coined metal, they would be made, as now, by weight and not by tale, so that the labour of counting will not enter into the question.

Some nations will have as they now have a preference for Gold for use in the daily transactions of life, but that they should therefore desire its employment in their international transactions is I think a chimera. No merchant will, as it has been suggested, stipulate that the Bills of Exchange which he may buy to be drawn on a bimetallic country shall be payable in Gold. Why should he do so? Are Bills on England now paid by transfer of metal from hand to hand? Is it really supposed that the effect of the establishment of the Double Standard in this country would be that a Bill for £1000 would be met by handing to the payee a sack of 1000 sovereigns, or five sacks of 1000 dollars each? When there really did exist an appreciable difference between the value of the two metals, and when it was therefore really of importance which of the two the payee received, is there any record of a bill being drawn on bimetallic Paris with such a stipulation on the face of it? Doubtless there is none.

Mr. H. H. Gibbs.

V. "A twofold standard once established, any great "influx of Silver from the mines would dangerously disturb "prices."

It is unquestionable that if England had a Silver as well as a Gold standard, the working of new mines of Silver and the production of an additional quantity of that metal, would have the result of enhancing prices; and if the quantity was very large and its production very sudden, the consequences might be severely felt.

But what if she adheres to her single standard, and the additional production be of Gold instead of Silver? That which has been (*e.g.* 1851 and onwards) may be again; and there can be no possible ground for saying that Silver *will* be found, and Gold will *not*. But if Gold be found again in extraordinary quantities, and the Double Standard be not adopted, then the flood would pour over half the world —the Gold-using half—and the immediate effect which the objector justly fears would be twice as great as if the flood were spread over the whole world, and affected equally the whole mass of currency; and this last would certainly be its operation if the Gold and Silver composing the mass were joined together in a bimetallic union.

What is the case at this moment? A flood of Silver was not long since let loose upon us, and that a double one, from the increased yield of the mines, and from the demonetization of Silver by Germany: Silver has been necessarily depreciated, and prices enhanced throughout all the Silver-using nations, and not only has the effect been twice as great because the area over which it extends is but half the commercial world, but it reacts also on the Gold-using nations.

I conclude, therefore, that this fifth objection is quite irrelevant to the question of a Double Standard; the particular danger which it suggests, and the consequent disturbance of the relations of creditor and debtor being at least as great under the present law as it could be under a bimetallic system of currency.

VI. "But supposing the bimetallic system to be "established on the basis of a ratio of 15½ while the real "existing proportion is perhaps 18, that difference will "give such a stimulus to the working of Silver mines, that "the dreaded flood of Silver would really come upon us; "and even if not, will of itself be an enlargement of the "Silver currency to the extent of about 15 per cent., and "consequently a depreciation of the whole mass of cur- "rency by about 7 per cent."

To the latter part of this objection I reply that I think I have already shown on p. 43 that the evil effect even on such a calculation would be more nominal than real, and that to take 18 or any such ratio as a basis for the calculation is untrue and misleading. As to the former part of the objection, I say that if there are indeed any mines which have been abandoned because of the fall of Silver from 5*s.* an ounce to 4*s.* 3*d.* or thereabouts, then a return to the price of 5*s.* might bring them again into bearing and so increase production; but I believe there is no evidence of any such abandonment, a much less price than 4*s.* 3*d.* being sufficient to make the working of all but perhaps a very insignificant number of workable mines remunerative.

VII. "It would be necessary to re-coin all our Silver "token-coinage."

This objection must arise from the supposition that standard florins, shillings, and sixpences would be coined, which would be undistinguishable from the token-coinage. But in fact no Silver standard money would be coined except double florins (dollars), and there is no more reason why they should not circulate concurrently with the Silver tokens, than there is why the existing French Silver tokens

Mr. H. H. Gibbs.

should not circulate in the same country with five-franc pieces. They would bear the same sort of relation to the subsidiary coinage as that shown in the following table to be borne by the five-franc piece to the French token-coinage:—

				Value in francs.
5-franc piece	900 millièmes ($\frac{9}{10}$) fine			5·
2 " "	835 "	Tokens		1·85½
1 " "	" "			·92½
½ " "	" "			·46

A shilling would still stand for the 20th part of a pound, whether that pound was 113·0016 grains of pure Gold, or 1751·5247 grains of pure Silver. If indeed Silver should be more widely demonetized it may possibly become necessary for Gold-using nations to call in and re-coin their silver tokens, because the nominal value of the shilling, &c., would be so far in excess of the real that an irresistible temptation would be held out to the maker of illicit silver coin. The rehabilitation of silver, by the adoption of the Double Standard or otherwise, would make such illicit coinage impossible.

VIII. "Our sixty years of prosperity."

This is the old fallacy of *Non causa pro causâ.* The objector sets before himself and us the varied facts of a prosperity which has developed itself in a hundred different ways since 1819, and passes *per saltum* to the conclusion that that prosperity has been caused by, or has had for one of its causes, the adoption of a single metal as our standard of value, but attempts no explanation of the mode in which so limited a cause has had so great an effect—an effect which, so far as it depends at all upon the character of the money of the realm, may be more justly attributed to our maintenance of an uncorrupted coinage of certain weight and fineness, and such, as I contend, we should have maintained, whether the metal of which it was composed were of Gold or Silver or of Gold and Silver.

An array of facts without cohesion—of premisses with no logical relation to the conclusion—is a frequent resource of the *soi-disant* practical man who would oppose what conflicts with his prejudices.

But the "practical" man is not unfrequently the ignorant man under another name, and is scarcely less dangerous than the theorist who, having no practical knowledge, constructs his facts for himself and deduces from them his own preconceived conclusions.

The true practical man is he who, resting on his own experience and knowledge, is able to arrange his facts in logical sequence and construct a theory on which such facts can be shown to lead inevitably to a certain conclusion.

Secondly, I must add that those who use this argument seem to take no account of change of circumstances. England has prospered for about sixty years, they say, *i.e.* since 1816. But what of the last four years or thereabouts? England suffered nothing from her single Gold standard, notwithstanding her relations with other countries where a single Silver standard prevailed, so long as France kept open a door of escape; but now that the aid of France is no longer afforded to us, our prosperity has not been so exemplary as to provide a very helpful argument to the advocates of the theory that our well-being has been owing to the fact that our standard money was of one metal alone.

I have already mentioned Lord Liverpool (p. 11). His *Treatise on the Coins of the Realm* is the foundation of our present system of money, and his great authority, and that of the eminent men whom he quotes, must, if the altered circumstances of the world be left out of the account, be a stumbling-block at the feet of those who dare to ask for an examination of the question, whether the

Mr. H. H. Gibbs.

system of the Double Standard is not more suitable to those altered circumstances.

No one at the present day would venture or desire to controvert the principles which he so lucidly states. Least of all would I do so. He proved to the satisfaction of the Government of his day—

I. That coins which were to be the measure of property should be, if possible, of one metal only.

II. That that metal should be Gold.

III. That the other coins should be as they now are, tokens; or, as we may call them, notes, representing parts of a sovereign, and made of metal instead of paper.

In support of the first proposition he adduces the authority of Sir William Petty, Mr. Locke, and Mr. Harris; but as he sets aside the opinion of Mr. Locke that Silver should be that one metal, on the ground that circumstances had so much altered that this opinion was no longer tenable, and thinks that Locke, had he lived then, would have been of that mind also, so I venture to think it not impossible that, if Lord Liverpool and the great men whom he quotes had lived in this age, they might have recognised that his first proposition, excellent in theory, might carry with it in practice, under the changed conditions of the mercantile world, inconveniences which would demand a remedy; and I think it can be shown that the main reasons which he adduced in support of it, and which were applicable to England as a single nation, are no less applicable, in the more developed condition of commerce, to the whole commercial world.

The evil which presented itself to his mind was one that does not and cannot now exist in England, viz.: that the currency was composed of English coins of uncertain weight and fineness, and included also some few coins, no less irregular in quality, of foreign coinage, and without any safeguard: so that men when they received this current coin in their daily transactions could not know for certain what it was they did receive.

There is, I say, no fear of this in England, but the uncertainty still exists in England's transactions with foreign nations, and even with her own dependencies, where a different kind of money is current. Lord Liverpool's care was to remedy the mischief as it then manifested itself, and to provide that the same monetary system should prevail through the length and breadth of this land; but the means of communication have been so much improved, that America is as near London as Scotland was in his time, and the several nations have been drawn more nearly together since those days. Then the policy of all nations was to look wholly to themselves for the promotion of their own exclusive interests, whereas now the promotion of the common good is better seen to be the promotion of individual good. If it was then desirable that the measure of value for England should be one, and one only, so that all men who traded with one another should know exactly what it was they were to receive for their wares, so is it also now desirable that the measure of value should be one for the nations forming the whole world of commerce, who, far more than in Lord Liverpool's time, may be said to be one community. But unity of money, in the sense of causing a single metal to suffice for all, has been shown to be an impossibility, both by reason of the preference of nations for one or other of the metals now used, and of the insufficiency of either one alone to provide all at once for the needs of all. Is it not, then, our best resource to approximate as nearly as possible to unity by causing the two metals, under prescribed regulations, to perform together the service of a metallic standard for the world? The world is already bimetallic; but it is an unregulated and haphazard bimetallism which prevails among us; and I must believe that a due regulation of it is both possible and desirable.

I have shown that the "traffic in coins," which is the chief inconvenience attaching, in Lord Liverpool's opinion, to a bimetallic measure of property, would be, under such regulation, impossible.

It is curious that the account which he gives of the bad condition of the currency in some other countries, and of the remedy which had been there applied, should afford one of the most striking instances of the great difference between our times and his.

His words are very remarkable. He says:—" There is " no circumstance that more clearly proves and illustrates " the truth of this principle, ' That coins which are to be " ' the principal measure of property can be made of one " ' metal only,' than the practice which (he says) has long " prevailed in several commercial states and countries on " the continent, of making foreign bills of exchange, and " sometimes other bills, exceeding a certain amount, payable " in what is usually called Bank-Money," that is to say, " *recepisses*, receipts, or notes, in return for the Gold or " Silver bullion . . . placed by individuals in their " custody," which receipts "are regulated by, and therefore " represent some one of the national coins current in each " of those states, exactly according to the standard of their " respective mints,"* so that they have and retain an undisputed value, and have come to be the fixed standard or measure according to which great payments are made.

He goes on to say that in Great Britain no such establishment has ever existed—that one such bank would not suffice, and that the establishment of many would be inconvenient—that Great Britain scarcely needs such a system, inasmuch as unauthorised foreign coins rarely enter

* *Treatise on the Coins of the Realm.* Reprint, 1880, pp. 136, 137.

it to serve as currency, and the coins of the realm are therefore necessarily the instruments of commerce, and the only legal tender whether to natives or foreigners; "and "from thence," he says, "results the necessity in this "country of having coins made of one metal only, which "should serve as an invariable measure, . ." &c.

He appends a note saying that it is unnecessary to advert to the Acts making Bank of England notes temporarily legal tender during suspension of cash payments, "as that "is not part of our recognised monetary system."

It is hardly necessary for me to point out how entirely all this has changed.

The exact system to which Lord Liverpool refers as non-existent, as insufficient for our needs, and unnecessary for the particular purpose, is, and has long been, established in England.

The notes of the Bank of England are issued practically as receipts for bullion; they are legal tender, like the *recepisses* to which he refers, and serve to make, as he says of the others, all "great mercantile payments," except where the use of the notes is again economised by the employment of cheques and other expedients of trade.

Lord Liverpool's argument seems to be that, in order to remedy the inconvenience of diversity of coins and uncertainty of weight and fineness, other nations had used a system of vouchers representing but one metal and one coin, which vouchers served for all transactions of moment, the debased coinage serving for small transactions of daily life; that, as in England we could not have such a system of vouchers, we could not safely permit a coinage of uncertain weight and fineness.

But we now have such a system, and may contend that the diversity of metal under a true bimetallic system is not at all open to the condemnation which he pronounces against the bimetallic coinage of his time. And, as in this one particular of a National Bank, I have shown that what he deemed impossible is actually existent, so also, I think I have shown cause for believing that the other considerations which I have mentioned might have been of sufficient weight to have led him to allow that circumstances might occur, and have now occurred, which should make it necessary for the well-being of English commerce, that, theoretically excellent as his system is, and practically irreproachable when applied to the internal commerce of a nation, we should not now treat the question of departing from it as one to be dismissed without careful consideration.

IX. In the foregoing paper I have endeavoured to answer the IXth objection. I have endeavoured to show that there is no impracticability in the adoption of a Double Standard, that whatever suits other nations must now of necessity suit the whole family of nations, and I would fain hope that I have presented it in a form which may prove not only acceptable to England, but a remedy for some grievous and pressing evils.

Again, in conclusion, I appeal to the wisdom and forethought of all men interested in the commerce of England; I urge every one who has at heart the prosperity of that commerce, not to close their eyes to the dangers of the immediate future, but to consider seriously what will be the result of the action which may in this very year be taken by foreign nations.

Two courses only are open to those nations: for it is impossible that they can remain as they are. They may adopt the Double Standard without the concurrence of England, or they may be driven to follow the example of Germany and adopt a Gold standard.

They may take the former course, though it will necessarily be very much against the grain that they should do what we tell them is bad for themselves and for our advantage. That it would be satisfactory to us and sufficient for us that they should do it is certain. But what are the chances of its being carried out? If they do take such a course they will be exposed, as all admit, to see their Gold leave them and flow into our coffers. Gold will not leave a bimetallic union in which England is included to flow into the coffers of a nation whose commerce is insignificant; but it will leave a bimetallic union of which England does not form a part, and, when circumstances lead it, flow into England, which is the commercial centre of the world.

It would not indeed do them any great harm, for no more Gold could come to and remain in England than what is needed for the full circulation of the country, and that we already have; but the apparent attraction of Gold hitherwards, and the feeling that England was not doing her part in the common work, might become intolerable to the bimetallic nations, and the present agitation might begin again, with the certain result of their recourse to the second alternative.

We have all seen what has been the consequence of the demonetization of Silver by Germany and the consequent absorption of Gold by that nation, and that prices as measured in Gold have fallen considerably wherever other circumstances have not concurred to maintain them. What will be the case if France and the Latin Union and the United States should be driven to do the same? The consequent and sudden fall in prices will be not fourfold but fortyfold, and the peril to our commerce will be incalculable.

The only real and permanent remedy would then be our adhesion to the principle of the Double Standard as set forth in these pages.

I know that my arguments rest on the hypothesis of general agreement, and the theory that such agreement would completely alter the conditions under which the Double Standard has not been found to work well.

Mr. H. H. Gibbs.

Before my readers deny the possibility of my hypothesis, and in haste reject my theory, let me ask them to read a quotation from the late Mr. Henry Drummond's *Elementary Propositions on the Currency.**

"The proportion of the magnitudes of the heavenly "bodies to each other rests purely upon hypothesis. The "annual and diurnal revolution of the earth, directly "opposed to the daily sensations and eyes of the *practical* "ploughboy, are founded on hypothesis. So absurd, in-"deed, did this revolution appear to all sober *practical* men "when it was first demonstrated, that Copernicus dared "not mention it for many years: the *practical* men in Italy "constrained the Pope reluctantly to put Galileo in prison, "and made him learn penitential psalms by heart to purge "away his philosophy; and when Jacquier and Le Seuri "published at Rome, so late as 1742, the theories of that "speculative heretic, Sir Isaac Newton, upon the same "subject, they wisely inserted in a preface, that they did "not presume to believe that which they had proved to be "true, unless that *practical* man, the Pope, should happen "to be of the same opinion."

* *Speeches in Parliament.* Vol. ii. p. 11.

GOLD IN THE EAST.*

From the *Economist*, August 2, 1879.

THE following letter is from a valued correspondent of considerable experience in the subject on which he writes, which we have pleasure in publishing:—

TO THE EDITOR.

SIR, I have read Mr. Daniell's pamphlet, and I think facts could be adduced to show that the thing which he proposes is impossible.

Colonel Smith proposes to make a gold standard, and to declare at once that the thing which is written as 10 rupees shall mean a golden sovereign.

By the method which he suggested for carrying out this operation, it is admitted that it could be done if the Government could succeed in keeping silver coinage from being smuggled into the country.

Colonel Smith, as a good official, thought of two things, and of two things only—the Government Budget and his

* *Gold in the East:* Being observations on a practical method of establishing a gold currency in India, and its influence on the trade and finance of that country. By Clarmont J. Daniell, Bengal Civil Service. Strahan & Co., Limited, 34, Paternoster Row, London. Price 1*s*.

F

own salary, or that of his fellow-workers and successors. Of the Indian cultivator and people he thought nothing.

His plan, as developed, is shortly disposed of by two answers—one by Baron Bramwell, at the Political Economy Club—

"If you can raise the rupee from 1*s.* 7*d.* to 2*s.* by a "stroke of the pen, why not raise it to 2*s.* 6*d.*?"

The other by Mr. Daniell himself, at the end of page 15, and beginning of page 16.

Mr. Daniell proposes that the customs and sums for revenue exceeding x should all be paid in gold.

Upon the suggestion arising that he is bound to state where the gold is to come from, he boldly faces it by saying that there is a very large stock of gold in India, and that, once make gold a legal tender, that hidden stock will come out, and be brought into general circulation.

If this large stock exists at all, or if it exists in the hands of any people ready to make use of it, it is very strange that use is not made of it now. If it could be melted into bars, and sold to the Government, who want it, why does it not now come into market? It cannot matter to a man who has got gold to dispose of whether its future destination is a legal tender sovereign or an unlegal tender gold mohur, if he can get his price for it in legal tender silver, which is all he wants.

I doubt the existence of any such disposable stock.

You might just as well have made a calculation of the gold in the green vaults at Dresden, or in the jewel boxes of the Sovereigns of Bavaria or Hanover, when you undertook to introduce a gold coinage in Germany.

In fact, Mr. Daniell sees that the real objection to his scheme is that the stock of gold for the use of the countries using a gold standard is already too small, and that to add India to those countries would inevitably tend to augment the gold famine, if I may use the expression. To meet that objection he has evolved from his

Mr. H. R. Grenfell.

inner consciousness the power of getting at this supposed stock in India.

Mr. Lowe, in his article in the *Fortnightly*, says: "If "I am asked where the gold is to come from, I frankly "state I do not know."

Mr. Daniell, however, does know, and propounds his undeveloped and unused stock existing in India.

This stock is wholly hypothetical. What we have got before us as an example is that Germany undertook to change its standard from silver to gold.

To enable it to perform that operation it took from France all the gold it could get. And yet, having this enormous sum to perform the operation, it has still lost enormously in carrying it out.

But that is not all.

The demand for gold for Germany has upset all the gold markets of the world, and all the silver markets.

The theory that the discoveries in America have had anything to do with the dislocation in the prices of the precious metals is now almost universally rejected.

If you were to add to those countries which have either changed their standard, or ceased to coin silver *ad libitum*, the Anglo-Indian Empire, gold would rise still higher, and silver fall still more.

The Indian producers would share in the fall of prices all over the world, from which they have been protected. They would have to buy the tool, money, for 2*s*. + X., which they now get for 1*s*. 7*d*.

Mr. Daniell says, and says rightly, that "Gold is the "measure of value of the Indian export trade." That is, it is the measure of value in the market of the world, *i.e.*, England.

The value of the lowest necessaries of life, such as wheat, &c., is ultimately determined by the cost of production; and in so far as the cost of production in India is affected by the value there of the lowest necessaries + wages + rent, which are reckoned in silver, the Indian producer is able to make a profit where a gold currency producer can not.

It matters not to a producer whether his profit comes by a high scale or a low purchase for one transaction, but the profit is more likely to continue from the latter than the former.

If wheat has fallen in the market of the world from 120 to 100, it has equally fallen to the Indian exporting cultivator; but then, with his 100, he procures 120 in that currency with which he pays his wages, his rent, and any debts written in anyone's books against him.

I remain, &c.

L.

(H. R. GRENFELL.)

From the *Economist*, August 9, 1879.

TO THE EDITOR.

SIR,—I do not wish to draw you into a discussion on the subject of "Gold in the East"; but as the letter you published on the 2nd inst. is calculated to warn readers off the book, and my object in publishing it is that its contents should be widely known and generally understood, will you allow me space in the *Economist* for the following remarks? The "impossibility" of introducing gold into the Indian currency appears to "L." to depend on the fact that there is no large stock of gold in India. This stock of gold in India he describes as "wholly hypothetical." So well is its existence ascertained, that "L." might with as much reason describe the stock of bullion and coins in the vaults of the Bank of England as "wholly hypothetical." The following extract from "L.'s" letter contains a very extraordinary statement, as coming from a "correspondent "of considerable experience" in currency matters:—"It "cannot matter to a man who has got gold to dispose of "whether its future destination is a legal tender sovereign "or an unlegal tender gold mohur." There is in the writer's opinion no difference, for purposes of trade, between legal tender coin and bullion. Were he to stand behind the counter of the Bank of England, and offer to merchants drawing large supplies of gold the gold bars which pass through the Bank on their way to the Mint, instead of sovereigns, and tell them at the same time that the coinage of gold had been stopped, and that no bank notes, or gold in the form of coin, would in future be procurable, he would soon, I think, have reason to alter his opinion. "L.'s" argument amounts to this; and he seems to think that gold bullion is as efficient in the East for purchases as gold coin in the West.

I am described as proposing that the Anglo-Indian Empire should cease to coin silver "*ad libitum.*" Had "L." examined my proposals with ordinary care, he would have found that I expressly insist on the necessity of keeping the Indian mints open for the coinage of any amount of silver brought to them; and that my plan for working a bimetallic currency on the principle of maintaining the intrinsic ratio of value between the gold and silver coins in the currency unaltered could not be carried on for a week, if the Government of India ceased to coin silver "*ad libitum.*" I forbear to notice other inaccuracies in "L.'s" letter, or to follow him into the discussion which the conclusion of his letter raises, or to comment on the singular confusion of terms in his last paragraph, as your space is limited. I hope that I have said enough to draw attention to the subject, the importance of which is sufficiently great to deserve more considerate treatment than it meets with from "L."

I remain, SIR, your obedient servant,

CLARMONT DANIELL.

From the *Economist*, August 23, 1879.

TO THE EDITOR.

SIR,—Mr. Daniell's letter in the *Economist* of the 9th, in answer to some portion of my letter of the 2nd, calls for a short rejoinder.

In order to compress what I have to say into the shortest space I use the baldest terms I can find. This must be my excuse for what is called "inconsiderate treat-"ment."

Mr. Daniell's first quotation is incomplete. Had he inserted the close of the sentence he would have seen that the meaning he gave it could not have been intended by me.

I expressed no "opinion" "as to the difference, for "purposes of trade, between legal tender coin and bullion."

Allow me to use "flour" instead of gold, and re-state the proposition.

"The miller who has flour to sell does not care whether "the baker makes cakes or puddings with it, provided he "gets his money for it."

What I wished to show was that Mr. Daniell's assertion that a stock of gold exists in India is only tantamount to an assertion that gold exists in the bowels of the earth.

At page 36 of his pamphlet he recognises this analogy.

If it does exist in India it is either for sale or it is not.

If it be for sale, the willingness to part with it must depend on the price, not on whether it is destined for coin or bars.

If he is right in supposing that making gold legal tender would bring this gold to market, it could only be because a higher price would be offered for it than can now be got.

Mr. H. R. Grenfell.

But it is the essence of my case that to make gold a legal tender in India would enhance the value of gold all over the world, and increase the dislocation in the relative price of the precious metals which has assisted in disarranging the commerce of the world.

His next point is, that I described him as proposing that the Indian mints should cease to coin silver *ad libitum.*

In this I have followed the best known currency authorities, whose doctrine it is that the amount of coin current cannot be increased *ad libitum*, and that if, for State purposes, you add to the existing currency of one metal another currency of another metal, the one will displace the other, not add to the total volume.

Persons bring silver to be coined because they want the coins. Under Mr. Daniell's proposition, gold, in certain cases, would be brought instead, and silver would thereby to that extent cease to be brought to be coined.

In substance, I adhere to what I stated. At page 19, in one sentence, he seems to recognise the truth of the statement himself. But in the following sentence he appears to dispute it.

My last paragraph appears to him confused. It refers to the large question of whether any one wins by the present state of exchange between England and India.

It was suggested by his own criticism on Colonel Smith's plan, which appears to me to be well founded.

I will endeavour to make my meaning clear.

The relative prices of the precious metals being in what Colonel Smith calls their normal state, a German exporter of wheat and an Indian exporter of wheat each pay 100 in its production, the one in gold, the other in silver, and each receives, as price for it, 120, or 20 per cent. profit.

The next year the price of wheat falls from 120 to 100 in gold, and the relative prices of gold and silver become abnormal, as at present.

The German, having to pay in gold, loses all his profit.

The Indian receives 100 in gold, but procures with it 120 in that currency, with which he paid his costs of production.

His 20 per cent. profit remains.

I called this, in my first letter, being protected from the fall in prices all over the world.

I remain, yours faithfully,

L.

(H. R. GRENFELL.)

From the *Economist*, August 30, 1879.

TO THE EDITOR.

SIR,—I will ask you for a little space in the *Economist* to reply finally to "L.'s" remarks of August 23rd on my scheme for introducing gold into the Indian currency, since, apart from my own opinions being criticised, which is a matter of little consequence, the importance of the subject requires that it should not be argued on wrong issues. "L." complains that on August 9th I quoted incompletely the words he used on August 2nd. This I did for the sake of brevity. "L.'s" contention was, that it is immaterial for a man who sought to turn his gold into coin whether he succeeded in doing so or not, provided he got silver coin in its place. The argument on "Gold in the East" is directed to prove that gold coin is required in India, and my answer of August 9th illustrated the position that the holders of gold are placed in, who, having gold, are unable to coin it, but can only use it in a crude form. "L.," on the 23rd, replies with the metaphor of the miller, as follows:—"The "miller who has flour to sell does not care whether the baker "makes cakes or puddings with it, provided he gets his

Mr. C. Daniell.

"money for it." True, but the miller would care very much if he found that his flour could be made into neither cakes nor puddings; and the Indian owner of gold is in much the same case who cannot turn it into coin. The question is one of the use of gold in currency, not of the use of gold in merchandise. It is, whether gold is of more use for currency in the form of legal tender coins, or non-legal tender bars; not whether gold as coin will or will not buy more silver than in the form of bars. "L.," on August 23rd, modifies his opinion that the stock of gold which I described as existing in India is "wholly hypothetical." It is probably more than 150 millions sterling in amount. "L." says, "if "it is there it is either for sale or it is not." Anyone who examines the price lists of the Presidency ports, will find that gold is offered for sale every day in the year in India. "L." says that, "to make gold legal tender would not "bring it into the market unless a higher price were offered "for it than now." This term, price, includes the advantage a trader would derive from trading on a gold rather than a silver basis. To be brief, it is the inability to obtain such an advantage which underlies the complaints that the Chambers of Commerce so justly make to the Indian Government of the effect which the state of the currency has on their trade. "L.'s" next point, that to make gold legal tender in India would enhance its value, and increase the confusion in trade now arising from the use of silver, I must, with much regret, pass over, as it is impossible to argue this part of the case within the limits to which I feel bound to confine this letter. "L." will, I hope, excuse my expressing an opinion that a careful consideration of the whole scheme I propose, in all its bearings, especially in relation to the ability of India to absorb silver and furnish gold, and of that part of it which provides for the invariable currency of silver and gold on equal terms, would, perhaps, convince him that the result he fears will be minimised, or not occur at all, and that a probability exists that in no long time it is gold which might be depreciated, and not silver, under its operation. "L.'s" next remark, that to add to the existing currency of one metal another currency of another metal will lead to the displacement of the former, makes no allowance for the power of expansion which the currency of every country, whose trade is in a healthy condition, possesses. It assumes that the quantity of silver required for coin in India is a fixed quantity, and that the silver which the gold displaces has no further use. The array of facts which prove that neither of these assumptions are true of India is too great, and they are too well known to need repetition here. "L.'s" argument about India being protected from a general fall in prices proceeds on the belief that her silver currency has not lost efficiency from the decline in the value of silver. Not only must this, as a fact, be accepted with the greatest amount of qualification, but as a theory of practical application to trade I think it was disposed of by Mr. Fawcett asking the late Mr. Bagehot a single question, when he was under examination before the Silver Committee (Question 1,377), and by Mr. Bagehot's answer. This, and the two preceding points in "L.'s" letter, along with other criticisms on my plan, I intend to examine in a short time in another form and place, when I hope to do more justice to the gravity of the silver crisis as it affects India, and to the ability of my critic, than the necessary brevity of this letter permits me to do here.

I am, SIR, yours, &c.,

CLARMONT DANIELL.

THE CASE AGAINST BIMETALLISM.

From the *Fortnightly Review*, August, 1879.

The fall of silver during the last few years has produced a large crop of that dismal currency literature which has brought almost all writing on currency into disrepute. The distinguishing feature of this literature is the constant assumption that some small defect in a currency which has all the recognised essentials of a good money—a basis in one or other of the precious metals, identity of the standard coins with a certain weight of that metal, and security for free coinage with only a small seignorage, or with no seignorage at all—may be productive of monstrous evils; or that a small manipulation of the currency, even at the risk of violating one of the essentials, may have some vague and indefinite advantage. It would be useless to enumerate the various schemes, of which the most prominent has perhaps been the proposal, generally known as Colonel Smith's, to raise or restore the rupee coinage of India to a level in value with gold. They are sufficiently answered by the common sense of the monetary world, which demands, in this question, merely that a government should authorise a coinage having the essentials above described, arrange for the coins being legal tender and receivable in taxes, and for the rest leave the matter alone. But there is one theory or system which has to a certain extent commanded more respectful attention than the others—viz., the theory which is known by the name of bimetallism. In its best form this theory is not open to the charge of artificiality, and of being inconsistent with free mintage, to the degree that some of the other schemes are open to the charge. The idea is that a State, instead of having the basis of its money in one of the precious metals only, should declare money obligations to be solvable by either of the two metals, silver and gold, in prescribed quantities, still permitting free coinage. The theory, therefore, has gained adherence even from people who have little enough sympathy with the way in which currency writers exaggerate the possible evils of slight derangements in the currency, and look for impossible advantages from currency changes. I wish, then, to put together some observations on this bimetallist question, and account if possible for the dislike of bimetallic theories which is entertained as a rule by those who have carefully studied the English monetary system. Bimetallists are often treated like other currency prophets, as inventing or grossly exaggerating the evils produced by the choice of monometallic systems in preference to theirs, and as aiming at benefits which cannot possibly be derived from any currency change. Is there real cause for this dislike or for the contumelious treatment which bimetallist advocates, who comprise among their number not a few men of real eminence as economists and statisticians, not infrequently receive?

It will be expedient to begin with a short account of the bimetallist arguments. Up to a certain point monometallists and bimetallists—at least the more able of the latter—are really agreed. They hold to the common sense doctrine of currency already referred to—that it is not an arbitrary thing to be regulated at will, but that a government fulfils its duty in selecting one or two of the metals as money, receiving all that is brought to them, impressing upon them certain stamps denoting their weight and fineness, and declaring them receivable for taxes, if not legal tender in release of all obligations expressed in money. Where they part company is on the point whether

Mr. R. Giffen.

a government should have one metal only, or two or more metals for its standard. Monometallists affirm that there should only be one, and even that there *can* only be one; bimetallists that there may be two, the law establishing the indifferent employment of certain prescribed quantities of one or the other, and that it is desirable two and not one should be so used. In support of the view, bimetallists maintain that legalising the use of both metals as a standard will procure certain advantages which are not procurable with one metal only. Such a regulation, it is said, would have the effect, first of all, of keeping more money in use than would otherwise be the case. Money would be more abundant than with one metal only, and abundant money is good for trade.* It is no doubt admitted now that unless all governments and communities have the same money regulations, the legalisation of the use of both metals will not have the effect of keeping both in use at one time in a particular State. On the contrary, the debtor will always pay in the metal which it is easiest for him to obtain; a very slight fraction of difference in procuring the prescribed quantity of the one, as compared with the prescribed quantity of the other, will drive the dearer metal out of use. But any inconvenience arising from this alteration, it is said, is amply compensated for by the greater abundance of money generally in which all countries participate.† Another alleged superiority in the

* See Wolowski's *L'Or et l'Argent*, pp. 331–2, where M. Wolowski quotes Count Daru's argument for the famous law of 1803, giving France the system of bimetallic money, which it retained till within the last few years. Daru says: "En réduisant l'or à n'être qu'une "marchandise, en diminuerait la masse du numéraire, on gênerait le "commerce," &c., &c. And this language is still of the essence of the bimetallist argument.

† This is the modern account of the argument. But so far as I can judge, the authors of the French bimetallist law, as of former bimetallic experiments, really hoped to retain both gold and silver in use in their own country. They thought they had found a ratio from which the metals

use of the two metals as compared with the use of one only is the increased facility of exchange between different countries. The legal ratio of use, it is said, tends in fact to keep the metals nearly at the corresponding relative value, so that exchanges between countries not bimetallic themselves, but some of them having gold and others having silver, become almost as steady, through the help of the bimetallic regulations of other countries, as if only one metal were universally in use. This facility would be enhanced by several nations becoming bimetallic, and still more by all nations adopting that system. This is the general theory of bimetallism, and it is supported by practical arguments from present circumstances. The depression of trade of the last few years is by some held to be accounted for by the scarcity of money due to the demonetisation of silver, and greater pressure upon gold; and by the confusion introduced into the exchanges by France (which has played the *rôle* of intermediary between gold and silver countries during the present century) abandoning its bimetallic regulations. By others who do not go so far, the actual evils of the last few years, especially through the derangement of the exchanges, are said to be so great as to require a special remedy such as bimetallism would give. Finally it is held by some ardent enthusiasts in the cause that there is a providence in the matter; that not only have two metals adapted for use as money been provided, but that a certain ratio, viz. 15½ to 1, tends naturally to be established between them. A bimetallic law fixing this ratio of 15½ to 1, merely confirms an ordinance of nature! Such is a fair account, I believe, of the bimetallic argument, and the last point in it, I may observe, is not inserted by way of caricature, but in order not to leave out any principal argument on which leading bimetallists lay stress.

would not vary for a long period, and in the original draft of the law a revisal of the ratio was contemplated. See Wolowski, *L'Or et l'Argent*, p. 295.

Mr. R. Giffen.

What we have to inquire into, then, are the objections of monometallists to this argument. Is there any real foundation for the superiority to monometallism alleged? and are there no counter-considerations? How far is bimetallism even a practicable scheme? I would begin by saying that the whole onus of proof is on bimetallism. Not only is the opposite system installed, but that system has the merit of simplicity. No one can say that if only one metal had been in existence suitable for use as standard money, the world would have been badly off because there were not two. The controversy is also a comparatively modern one. What governments had to debate before the present century was not any real choice between one or several metals for use as standard money, but how to get a sound metallic currency of any sort. Their difficulties were the temptation to make a profit for themselves at the expense of their subjects by debasing the coin or "raising its denomination" (which comes to the same thing), and the natural difficulty of keeping the bullion contents of a coinage up to the nominal value assigned to it. It is only since 1696 in England, and since the beginning of the present century elsewhere, that governments have learnt the wisdom of resisting the temptation to debase—if even yet the lesson has been perfectly learnt; and the effectual method of meeting the difficulty caused by wear and tear is of equally recent discovery. The alleged advantages of bimetallism therefore are supplementary only to the primary advantages aimed at by a good currency. A people afflicted with debased coins, whether the debasement was due to natural or artificial causes, would plainly be only too glad to get a good metallic currency of any sort. This of itself is almost enough to prove that there is a fundamental exaggeration in the bimetallist argument. Why is there so much importance attached to matters which could not have been thought of when nations were struggling with the real difficulties of coinage?

Even when these real difficulties existed, it may be remarked, though the social misery and nuisance were intolerable, and there was some hindrance to trade, it was possible for countries to make great advances in material prosperity. Speaking of the seventeenth century, when, as we shall see, the country was afflicted with debased and constantly changing coinage, and when there was besides a long period of civil war and confusion, Lord Liverpool who was above all statesmen alive to the evils of a bad currency, remarks: "It is certain, however, that during "the whole of this period, when our coins were in so great "a state of confusion, the commerce of the kingdom was "progressively improving, and the balance of trade was "almost always in favour of this country."* It seems impossible, therefore, that bimetallic money can be so necessary to the world as is alleged, when countries got on so well as they did with money so inferior, that the question between bimetallism and monometallism could not arise, attention being absorbed in more serious matters.

But let us examine directly what the argument comes to. One of the two points of superiority alleged may, I think, be passed over as hardly counting, or rather as counting against those who use it as an argument for bimetallism. This is the allegation that bimetallism increases the quantity of money in use as compared with the opposite system. It cannot be true that it will have that advantage necessarily, that is if there is any advantage in the matter. Clearly as much gold and silver may be in use as money throughout the world, if some nations have gold and others silver, as if some or all were bimetallic. The quantity of money in use might be diminished by all nations becoming monometallic, and using the same metal; and were this to be done suddenly, great evils might ensue. I believe evil has ensued from the haste to introduce gold in place of silver in some countries, which prevailed ten

* Lord Liverpool on the *Coins of the Realm*, p. 120.

or fifteen years ago under the influence of eager advocates of a universal gold money. But this diminution of the money in use is obviously not a necessary consequence of monometallism. It would be rather the result of an injudicious application of the principle which the nations of the world are not now likely to be guilty of.

And the argument turns against bimetallists in this way, that by attaching such great importance to keeping money abundant, they ally themselves with the most vicious of currency theorists. It is not true that the quantity of money, apart from the possibly mischievous effects of any sudden change, socially and otherwise, can affect materially the real wealth and welfare of an industrial community. It is a mere truism to say that while it may be useful to the world for other purposes to have gold and silver more easily obtained than they are, yet, so far as their use as money is concerned, they would be equally serviceable if they were only half as abundant. The bimetallist argument is accordingly tainted, and this accounts very much, I believe, for the extreme disgust and dislike of the theory which economists and statesmen have shown. The prophets who prophesy that the world is to be enriched by abundant money are the detestation of men of sense.

Has not the scarcity and appreciation of gold, it may be rejoined, something to do with the present depression of trade? To this I would reply that the depression is mainly traceable to many other well-known causes of such phenomena, so that the scarcity of gold can only have been a contributory cause. In any case, moreover, the temporary effects of a change in the supply or demand for a particular kind of money, causing a general change in the level of prices, are not to be confounded with the permanent effects of scarce or abundant money. At the new level of prices established, the scarcity and abundance of money may become what they were before. However much, therefore, the scarcity of gold may have contributed to the recent fall of prices, and through that to the depression of trade, it does not follow that the effect will be continued, or that trade will be permanently contracted. A less number of gold and silver pieces at low prices will serve for the same exchanges as a larger number at higher prices. It may be added that it was never proposed by the great English writers on currency—Locke, Harris, Lord Liverpool—to prevent the fluctuations of one of the precious metals in reference to itself at different periods. If other fluctuations were got rid of, those in the metal itself were not reckoned as of great importance, while they were considered to be inevitable. It may be said, perhaps, that abundant money is of more consequence now than it was a century or two ago, because the effect of any given quantity of money is now multiplied by our system of credit. But I fail to see how the constitution of our system of credit makes any difference adverse to the conclusion of Lord Liverpool and the old authorities. Rather we have now a constant demonstration that moderate changes in the quantity of money in use, unless they are suddenly made, are not material. In consequence of changes in credit alone, the serviceableness of the same quantity of money varies indefinitely in comparatively short periods; the scale of prices is in constant oscillation; no conceivable changes in the quantity of money itself could at all have the effects which are constantly being produced by changes in credit alone.

To come to the other alleged superiority of bimetallism, the facility of exchange, we find there is again a good deal of exaggeration. The benefits of great facility of exchange may themselves be readily exaggerated. We may look only how trade has been carried on with inconvertible paper countries, and with enormous fluctuations in exchange. The fluctuations are no doubt an evil, and a serious one, but in a question of the relative advantages of two systems of money, we must see exactly how great the evil is. Even serious evils may have to be endured, because relatively they are unimportant compared with the great objects proposed in a sound currency. Moreover, the question of exchanges concerns only the foreign trade of the countries affected, that trade being at most a fraction of their whole trade. Whatever injury great fluctuations of exchange may inflict, they can only do so by hindering the development of a part of the whole trade of a country—even in this country perhaps only a sixth or an eighth part of its trade. Naturally, and in the long run too, it results from the nature of gold and silver as money, and the magnitude of the stocks in existence, that exchanges between countries using gold and silver will be steady without bimetallism. There may be rapid fluctuations at particular periods, as there have been lately, and as there were in 1850, when great changes in the supply of particular metals and in the demand for them occur. But such great changes, unless all nations lose their senses, are not likely to be of frequent occurrence, and in ordinary times exchange will be steady. The reason is that as neither gold nor silver is likely to change greatly with reference to commodities in general, this being the cause of their selection for use as money, they are not likely to change with reference to each other. Accordingly we find that in past times, without bimetallism, exchanges have been steady for long periods together. I would refer especially to the course of exchange between France and England from about 1820 to 1850. During all that period France was practically a silver-using country. Silver being cheaper than the legal rate, and tending to become cheaper still, had expelled gold from circulation, till, in 1848, the Bank of France had hardly any gold left in its till. French bimetallism, therefore, could not have prevented a further fall in silver. "Ten years ago," says M. Leon Faucher, writing in 1852, "every one was frightened at the prospect

" of the depreciation of silver." But notwithstanding this inoperativeness of bimetallism, the price of silver and rate of exchange between France and England remained almost as steady as they have done since, although bimetallism afterwards came into operation through gold becoming cheaper than the legal ratio fixed, and the bimetallic countries having a great quantity of silver to be exchanged for it. Thus fluctuations in exchange are neither so formidable to trade as they are frequently represented, nor are the exchanges so likely to be unsteady as a rule without bimetallism, as its advocates have been in the fashion of maintaining.

The fluctuations with bimetallism may also be considerable. Bimetallism of some sort was the attempted practice of the world for centuries, but this did not prevent great fluctuations in exchanges or the price of silver. Lord Liverpool, writing in 1805, says—

> " The price of silver in dollars has varied in twenty-two years, " that is, from the end of the year 1774 to the 31st of December, " 1797, 11$\frac{113}{117}$ per cent., and even in the course of one year, that " is the year 1797, no less than 9$\frac{1}{6}$ per cent. The variation in the " price of silver bullion appears to have been still greater, by another " account, with which I have been favoured, by the late Mr. Garbett, " an eminent merchant and manufacturer at Birmingham ; it there " appears that the silver purchased by him, as a refiner, with bank " notes, varied, according to his calculation, in the course of ten " years, to 1793, more than 19$\frac{1}{4}$ per cent., and in one year only " more than 13$\frac{1}{3}$ per cent." *

Apart from its bearing on the particular point in hand, this quotation may, perhaps, be useful in convincing people that great fluctuations in silver or in exchange with silver-using countries, are not so novel as they have lately been assumed to be.

What, then, is the increased steadiness of exchange

* Lord Liverpool on the *Coins of the Realm*, p. 150.

Mr. R. Giffen.

which bimetallism can give? And of what advantage will it really be? The answer to the first question appears to be that, in certain circumstances, in some countries, bimetallic regulations would help to steady the exchanges. When a change in the relative value of the two metals is occuring *in the direction of making the less valuable the more valuable,* and when the bimetallic country possesses the metal which is becoming appreciated, bimetallism may help to steady the exchanges. The metal becoming cheaper pours into the country to be exchanged for the metal becoming dearer, and so the rise in the latter and fall in the former are arrested. Of this the world had a conspicuous illustration after the Australian and Californian gold discoveries. Silver, from being cheaper, became dearer than what was fixed by the legal ratio between silver and gold in France; and as France had much silver to be exchanged for gold, the rise in silver and fall in gold relatively to each other were arrested. Gold was poured into France and exchanged for silver, the process continuing for many years. More lately an opposite process was beginning, silver, as it lately fell, being sent back to France in exchange for gold, when a stop was put to the proceeding by France suspending the free mintage of silver. But it is only in such transition periods that bimetallism can have any effect. Suppose a change, not in the direction of making the cheaper metal dearer than the other, but in the direction of making it cheaper still (the chances of the one event being exactly equal to the chances of the other), bimetallism, it is plain, can have no influence of any sort. It is powerless to arrest the fall, because the bimetallic country has *already* got the cheaper metal, and has none of the metal which is becoming dearer to exchange. As already mentioned, this was precisely the case in France for many years before 1850. If silver had become abundant then as now, as there was at one time, it appears from the above-quoted statement of M. Leon Faucher reason to think it would be, there was no gold in France to be exchanged for it to arrest the fall. It is not true, then, that bimetallism has a general effect in steadying the exchanges. A country which adopts it must expect that it will only operate in that way in certain special circumstances, and those circumstances may never occur.

It may be said, perhaps, that if many countries were bimetallic, the steadying effect would be greater. But this is clearly not the case. If all bimetallic countries had the same ratio, and the cheaper metal tended to become still cheaper, they would simply be as one country. The fact of their being many would give them no more power over the exchanges than if they were one country, and their power would be precisely that of monometallic countries. Of course, if all countries were bimetallic, supposing that to be a possible arrangement, exchanges would be steadier, just as they would be if all were monometallic upon the same basis. So much may be granted on this head to the bimetallist argument.

But what would be the advantage of this increased steadiness of exchange? As we have seen, the exchanges in any case are likely to be fairly steady; great fluctuations, when they do occur, are not so harmful to trade as they are often supposed to be, while foreign trade, after all, is only a fraction of the business of great countries. In any case, unless there is universal bimetallism, bimetallism will only help to steady the exchanges in certain circumstances, and will have no effect in other circumstances which are just as likely to occur. Can the increase of steadiness which bimetallism may give, therefore, be worth any great price, so long as there is no universal bimetallism? Is universal bimetallism worth aiming at for the sake of mere steadiness of the exchanges? I cannot but think that, when really looked at, the alleged superiority of bimetallism in this respect, as in regard to its promise of more abundant money, amounts to very little.

Mr. R. Giffen.

But what of the great evils sustained by the Indian Government through the fluctuations of silver and the exchanges? by Anglo-Indians who receive salaries in India and have to remit in gold? and by banks, insurance companies, and others who have invested in Indian securities? Is it not desirable, to obviate these evils, that bimetallism should be made to operate as far as possible—that is, in the circumstances when it will steady the exchanges—and that there should also be universal bimetallism? To this I would reply that, so far as the Indian Government is concerned, and the Indian community generally, the evils of the fluctuations which have occurred have been enormously exaggerated. The difficulty of the Indian Government and people, so far as it is a real one—that is, so far as the changes between silver and gold impose any additional real burden on the Indian community, which can only be if gold has appreciated—will not be affected at all by India becoming bimetallic. The Indian Government would receive silver just as they now receive it, and this would not help them with the increased real burden of their gold payments. England might help India by becoming bimetallic, and so arresting the rise in gold or fall in silver, because England has much gold to exchange for silver; but this would be gratuitously altering our monetary system for the sake of a temporary advantage to India. If gold, on the other hand, has not appreciated, and silver has really depreciated, the difficulty even of the Indian Government can only be transitory, pending the adjustment of all prices and payments in India. As to Anglo-Indians who receive salaries in silver and have to remit in gold, their case is no doubt a hard one, though to some extent the hardship is exaggerated. They are not worse off than annuitants were in this country after the gold discoveries, when all prices rose and their salaries or annuities did not. Here, again, to introduce bimetallism would be to make a permanent alteration in a monetary system to meet a temporary evil.

Much the same may be said of the question of investments by banks, insurance companies, and others in silver securities. They had suffered a temporary loss at a time of great fluctuation, and at the present moment there is a difference of about three-eighths in the rate per cent. which the Indian Government has to pay on its rupee compared with its sterling loans, showing the premium which investors here charge for the additional risk of an investment in a silver security compared with a gold security. But as the exchanges become steadier even this premium will, no doubt, diminish. It cannot be said that the flow of capital from gold to silver countries is seriously checked by the want of bimetallism.

Yet another advantage is alleged for bimetallism, viz., that the standard of value set up by it will probably be more stable from period to period than a standard of one metal only. And on the doctrine of chances it would seem there is, perhaps, some foundation for this statement. There is some probability that the chances of one metal fluctuating in value in reference to itself from period to period, will be partly compensated in a double standard system by the chances of the two metals not fluctuating in the same direction. But in this matter, it seems to me, the doctrine of chances is not a sufficient guide for action. The preponderant probability, on one side or the other, is not very great—it appears something like two to one in favour of bimetallism; whereas, for a guide to action, the probability should be so great as to amount almost to certainty. The assumption on which the doctrine of chances is appealed to is, moreover, not quite warranted. In real life, it may be assumed, nations will not be constant in their monetary arrangements. In the future, as in the past, changes of price, political aspirations, the love of imitation, and hundreds of other motives, will induce one nation to change gold for silver or silver for gold, or to give up bimetallism for one or the other metal. The result may

Mr. R. Giffen.

well be that, after a long lapse of years, the change of one metal in value in reference to itself will be no greater than the change in the combination of the two. In any case the differences over long periods in the relative stability of monometallic and bimetallic standards of value, hardly seem an object worth any great concern to a State.

So much for the negative criticism of the alleged superiorities of bimetallism to the opposite system. But there is another side to the criticism. May there not be positive defects in the bimetallic proposal, which would counterbalance even greater advantages than any that seem to be promised?

As far as what may be called particular bimetallism is concerned, that is, the bimetallism of one or two countries only, as distinguished from universal bimetallism, there can be little dispute, I believe, of the existence of such great defects. For particular States to be bimetallic is, in fact, to condemn themselves to the misery and nuisance of constant alterations of the money in use. M. Wolowski argues that this is a minor matter, alleging that a country like France suffers nothing by constantly changing its money in use; but history is against him. Since he wrote, France has shown its practical fear of the consequences of bimetallism by suspending its silver coinage, and this was only in accordance with the previous experience of other countries. Lord Liverpool dwells upon this misery at certain periods in English history, as one of the reasons which decided him against a Double Standard. Those who have any curiosity in the matter may be referred to Lord Liverpool's treatise (p. 57 *et seq.*), but the following summary may give some idea of his argument:—

" The evils resulting from the fluctuations in the relative
" prices of these metals do not appear to have shown themselves in
" any great extent, or at least to have been the subject of general
" complaint, till the reign of James I. At this last period these
" evils were felt in a most alarming degree. . . . . In the first

"years of the reign of this monarch, the complaints of the expor-"tation of the gold coin, on account of the low value at which gold "was then estimated at the English Mint, compared with the value "at which silver was then estimated, were great and incessant. "To remedy this evil, King James raised the value of gold in his "coins by successive proclamations, but he at last raised it beyond "the due proportion; so that during the remainder of his reign, "and the whole of the reign of Charles I., the silver coins were in "their turn exported, and a very small quantity of these last "remained in circulation. The complaints of the want of silver "coins were then as great as the complaints of the want of gold "coins have been before. During a short period in the middle of "the seventeenth century, the relative prices at which the precious "metals were estimated at the Mint in our coins, appear to have "been in a sort of equilibrium, or to have maintained a due pro-"portion with the prices at which they respectively sold in the "market. But in the fifteenth year of the reign of Charles II., "that is, in the year 1663, when a new estimate was made of the "relative value of gold to silver at the English Mint, that of gold "was underrated. . . . . A general coinage took place by the "advice of Parliament in the reign of King William III. After "this recoinage the gold coins passed in payment at a higher value "than that at which they were still rated in the Mint indentures, "or than the relative value of gold to silver at the time would "justify; not, however, by authority of Government, but by the "general consent of the people. The consequence was that the "new silver coins began immediately to be melted down and "exported, notwithstanding the very great charge which the public "had incurred in recoining them. A very considerable part, in the "course of not more than seventeen years, had disappeared, and "there was found to be a want of them in circulation. The same "deficiency in the number, as well as the weight of the silver coins, "has remained to the present day, to the great inconvenience of "your Majesty's people. From the beginning of the reign of "James I. to the period of which I am now speaking, gold and "silver coins were alternately exported, for the reasons just stated, "to the great detriment of the public, as often as individuals could "profit thereby." *

* Lord Liverpool on the *Coins of the Realm*, pp. 117, 118.

Mr. R. Giffen.

These were the practical reasons given at the beginning of this century for adopting a single rather than a double standard, and the mere statement, confirmed as it has been by the subsequent experience of France, is enough. No country will endure the misery and nuisance of the incessant change, and M. Wolowski's allegation to the contrary is singularly unfortunate. In England especially there is a special reason against the alternation in its expense. There is no seignorage on the standard coin at the English Mint, a feature of importance in our monetary system. Whether it is good or bad, it would have to be abandoned in a bimetallic system. It could not be proposed that the expense of an incessant recoinage should be thrown on the country.

To some extent the misery inflicted by these alternations appears to arise from their depriving the people of the peculiar sort of money they want, so that bimetallism really thwarts the natural inclination of communities in choosing their money. It is a procrustean rule under which the State forces, or attempts to force, an overrated metal into use, so that a country wishing to have gold may be made to take silver, and *vice versâ*. That nations have their wishes in such matters is not only proved incidentally by the continual outcries in England in the seventeenth century, but by numberless facts, such as the difficulty Germany now experiences in keeping the gold it has acquired at so much expense and disturbance to the money market, the refusal of California to take greenbacks in the American Civil War, the liking of the Americans and of almost all English-speaking communities for gold rather than silver, the difficulty of floating a note-circulation in India, the preference in Scotland and Ireland for £1 notes to sovereigns, and other phenomena of a similar kind. The most significant event of the sort, however, was perhaps that adoption of gold by England after 1696 in place of a new silver coinage by the free choice of the people without its being legal tender, described in the above quotation from Lord Liverpool. Those who talk of legislation being able to constitute a demand for money, and being all that is necessary to do so, may be referred to such facts as these. Bimetallism, proceeding on the same assumption, also stands condemned by the facts.

It may be urged that now it cannot matter to a nation which metal it employs for a standard, because the real standard is now bullion only, and all the coins in use are substantially token coins, used only for small change, whether they are of gold or silver. Mr. Lowe's scheme, as described in the *Fortnightly Review* of last month, also assumed that standard coins of gold could be dispensed with. But it may be doubted if, even in England, we have yet got to the stage of wholly dispensing with coins in use of the standard metal. For travelling, and for settling minor balances between countries, gold coins and not gold bullion are only still useful, as silver coins or silver bullion would not be. Apart from this, the greater convenience of gold for storage and for the handling of banks and other institutions which have to deal in it, would make it naturally to be preferred by the richer countries; and whatever may be the case here, it is quite certain that many nations are still in a state to require coins of the standard metal in use, and particularly the silver-using countries. So far as such preferences still exist, bimetallism would tend to thwart them. It would at times create in a country which naturally likes silver a premium on the export of that metal; and at other times, in countries which preferred gold, a premium on its export. This would be obviously a daily and hourly drawback to bimetallism, if any country thinks of adopting it, to be set against the possible advantages it may confer. It will be answered that under universal bimetallism nations will be able to use whichever metal they want, and to what extent they want; but so far as they do so, and do not use both equally, bimetallism will be inoperative. If they are not to have both metals in use as standard money, they might as well be monometallist at once.

Having mentioned these drawbacks, we need not dwell on others. It is plain that bimetallism, if it does any good, will have many counterbalancing disadvantages, whether it is particular or universal. But the catalogue is far from exhausted. For instance, the difficulty of making such subsidiary arrangements as the exemption of standard money from seignorage, now so conveniently made in a monometallic system, would soon be felt. There would also be an obvious difficulty, under particular bimetallism at least, in finding a means of bullion remittance as compared with the present system. In remitting now to a country where gold is used, any one at need can draw a cheque on his bankers and get the gold he wants. Under bimetallism he might be offered silver, and consequently have to purchase gold in the market. Under universal bimetallism the difficulty would be the same. Gold and silver *ex hypothesi* would be equally available in paying debts, but money is not wanted exclusively to pay debts with; a particular sort of money is wanted for special purposes, and all choice of this sort would be at an end. In effect, also, the use of either silver and gold in prescribed quantities in paying debts, though it avoids in appearance the fixing of a legal ratio, does fix a ratio in reality. It alters the demand for gold and silver from what it would be if communities merely selected the money they wanted according to their convenience, and *pro tanto* diverts and hinders the natural development of the industry of working the precious metals. It is not to be assumed certainly that this interference with natural taste will be more successful with gold and silver than it has been with other commodities. But passing over all this catalogue of objections, let me only urge that, as a practical measure, proposed to a country like England, bimetallism will be objectionable, because it is an alteration of a system rooted in our habits, to which we have become accustomed as the air we breathe, and which we have acquired with much cost and effort after long experience of many bad systems. Even if the other advantages of bimetallism very much outweighed those of the opposite system—and the exact contrary is the case—would not the mere trouble of alteration be an overwhelming disadvantage? The old authorities on English currency might be invoked to bring even stronger arguments. The emphatic protests of Locke and others against *any* alteration of a standard once chosen, as necessarily involving injustice and a violation of contracts, are not to be forgotten, though it is not necessary to our argument here to dwell upon them.

Finally it remains to be urged that bimetallism, admitting the balance of advantages to be in its favour, and that all other objections are got over, is not practicable in any proper sense of the word. Of course theoretically any particular government adopting bimetallism, and willing to force its subjects to endure the nuisance and misery of incessant changes in their money, which always occur when bimetallism is really operative, may introduce a bimetallic law. But to have such a law is not to have the two metals actually in use, which is the object aimed at, or to obtain for a country most of the other alleged advantages of bimetallism. The advantages it procures will be for others, and sooner or later, therefore, any single country trying bimetallism will abandon it, as France has so lately done. Nations are not philanthropic to the extent of sacrificing themselves for the good of others. A group of nations trying bimetallism will experience the same results and follow the same course. The only chance for bimetallists then is the possibility of their scheme of universal bimetallism being tried. But can any one dream of such a consummation? Who is to draw the treaty?

Mr. R. Giffen.

What power of persuasion will bring all countries and governments to accept this gospel? The initiative must clearly come from the great governments, those of England, France, Germany, Austria, Russia, and the United States. But only a dreamer could imagine such governments agreeing on the principle, on the ratio to be fixed, and on all the subsidiary arrangements necessary; and then uniting to persuade their smaller neighbours, the dissent of almost any of whom would be fatal. So strong has this objection seemed that, for no other reason, Mr. Bagehot and other monometallists have steadily declined to discuss bimetallism. Their reluctance is surely not to be wondered at. Even if there were no other difficulty in the way of universal agreement, there is one which would probably be fatal— the risk of particular countries over-issuing paper. The Latin convention has been a practical failure as regards Italy for this reason, so that universal bimetallism to be really effective must regulate paper as well as coin issues. If it does not, the world will be no more bimetallic than it is now.

What may be urged more strongly, however, on the score of the impracticability of universal bimetallism, is the probability that great mercantile communities may have a mind of their own in the matter, and may not accept bimetallic money. It is amazing to see how the discussion is carried on, as if a government had only to issue its fiat, and bimetallism would come into use. Enough facts have been stated in this paper to show that mercantile communities themselves exercise choice in this matter, as England did after 1696; and that bimetallic legislation would not necessarily be followed by corresponding practice. Have bimetallists then any reason to believe that England, which freely chose gold in place of silver in 1696, would now reverse its choice, now when it is so much richer and so much more a centre of international payments than it was two centuries ago? Have they reason to believe that the Californians who rejected greenbacks would submit to take any money the legislature chose to give them; or that the New York Banks would reconsider their late decision not to accept any of the silver coins which Government had just issued as full legal tender? These and other questions must be answered in the affirmative, and with conclusive facts in support of them, before bimetallism can be talked of as a practicable scheme. And no one who knows the business world of London will fancy that, as regards this country, the question would be answered in the affirmative. Leading exchange brokers and bullion dealers have bimetallist leanings; they would like if it could be introduced in any country. There is a half-notion at this moment among some merchants, especially in the Eastern trade, that as bimetallism has so much said for it, it might be tried, though it may be doubted how far this notion would stand the test of actual experiment; but so far as I can judge of City feeling in general, the attempt to force bimetallism on the mercantile and banking world of this country would produce an instant revolt. The slightest approach to "actuality" which bimetallic theories may attain, would soon bring out the real strength of the feeling or prejudice in favour of the present system which exists throughout the City.

The case against bimetallism thus appears to my mind overwhelmingly strong, and the dislike manifested towards it seems accounted for. Its boasted superiority over the single standard consists in the promise of abundant money, which it does not and cannot fulfil, and which its advocates give in a way that taints their entire argument with unsoundness; in the promise of greater steadiness in the exchanges which it will only keep in certain circumstances, while it does not really matter whether the promise is kept or not, as the exchanges in any event will usually be fairly steady; and in the promise of greater stability in the

Mr. R. Giffen.

standard of value from period to period, which it may fulfil in certain circumstances, but where, again, the alleged advantage seems really immaterial. On the other hand, whether particular or universal, the system will be attended with no small inconveniences, such as incessant change of the money in use, and interference with the natural taste of communities in the choice of their money, which have formerly caused great outcries; and in England it would have the undoubted evil of altering a long-established and excellent system, which is based on experience and has answered in every particular the ends of its designers. Bimetallism, moreover, is really impracticable. If one or two or even more nations try it, they do not succeed in getting the two metals in use, and it is not even conceivable that all should agree to try it. Moreover, whatever governments may say, it does not follow that great mercantile communities will be obedient, and the chance of their preferring monometallism is an element of difficulty to be reckoned with. Such a scheme does not seem entitled to any favour. As founded on the assertion of vague and indefinite evils, which cannot exist in a community possessing a sound metallic currency, as promising vague and indefinite advantages, and as utterly and hopelessly impracticable, even if it should be tried, it seems really liable to all the dislike which sober business men entertain towards flighty currency projects. Matters in its favour are not needed by the talk which I have not thought it worth while to discuss, about the ratio of 15½ to 1 being the result of providential arrangement. If bimetallists are sometimes reviled as lunatics, and economists like Mr. Bagehot can hardly be brought to overcome their disgust at the argument for bimetallism, so as to turn aside even to discuss it, they are surely not without excuse. Mathematicians do not stop to argue with squarers of the circle, or with reasoners that the earth is flat.

One more remark, by way of supplement. A former controversy on this subject arose out of the suggestions for an international money, which were so common ten or fifteen years ago. Those who attach great importance to the world having such a money, will regret that the case against bimetallism is so strong, as it is only in such a scheme they can at present see a way to their end. To attempt to reach it by means of the opposite system implies an extensive demonetisation of one metal or the other, which is not to be thought of at present. But the idea of an international money, in the present stage of the world's economic progress, is really premature. Nations generally are not yet so closely inter-connected as to make it worth while that all should have the same money, to which there are many other obstacles—such as over-issues of inconvertible paper—as well as the differences between gold and silver. We may well leave future generations, therefore, to deal with this question, content to do the best we can with the monetary arrangements in our power. As the need for international money increases, the means for introducing it may also be prepared, as they would be prepared, for instance by the gradual introduction in all countries of the use of gold for large payments, the general use of silver in token coinage only, the increasing wealth of the world causing a great increase of the demand for token coinage, and the extension of economising expedients, so as to lighten the strain upon the dearer and standard metal. An international money upon a monometallic basis is thus a possibility of the future, and there is no need for precipitating matters by impracticable schemes.

ROBERT GIFFEN.

BIMETALLISM.*

From the *Contemporary Review*, May, 1881.

It may be safely said that the question of bimetallism is one which does not admit of any precise and simple answer. It is essentially an indeterminate problem. It involves several variable quantities and many constant quantities, the latter being either inaccurately known or in many cases altogether unknown. The present annual supply of gold and of silver are ascertained with fair approach to certainty, but the future supplies are matter of doubt. The demand for the metals again involves wholly unknown quantities, depending partly upon the course of trade, but partly also upon the action of foreign peoples and governments, about which we can only form surmises.

The question is much complicated, again, by presenting a double problem—that regarding the next decade of years, and that regarding the more remote future. Possibly, a step which might be convenient during the course of the next five, ten, or fifteen years, would prove subsequently to be the mere postponement of a real and inevitable difficulty. When we pursue an inquiry of this complex and indeterminate kind, it resolves itself into endless hypotheses as to what will or will not happen if something else happens or does not happen. Nevertheless, it does not follow that, because statistical science fails us, we can

* Reprinted, with other Essays on the same subject, in a volume of papers by the late Professor Jevons, on *Currency and Finance*, and published by Messrs. Macmillan & Co.

come to no practical conclusion; on the contrary, from the very vagueness and uncertainty of the subject may emerge a conviction that it is best to do nothing at all. A party of travellers lost in a fog will probably indulge in a great many speculations and arguments as to the possible paths and turnings they might take; but the wisest course may, nevertheless, be to stay where they are until the air becomes clear.

Looking at the question, in the first place, as a chronic one, that is, as regarding the constitution of monetary systems during centuries, it is indispensable to remember the fact, too much overlooked by disputants, that the values of gold and silver are ultimately governed, like those of all other commodities, by the cost of production. Unless clear reasons, then, can be shown why silver should be more constant in its circumstances of production than gold, there is no ground for thinking that a bimetallic gold and silver money will afford a more steady standard of value than gold alone. The common argument that there will not be enough gold to carry on the trade of the world with, does not stand a moment's examination in this aspect. In the first place, if the value of gold rises, more gold will be produced, and the great number of gold-mining enterprises now being put forth may have some connection with this principle. In the second place, so long as sudden changes of supply and demand can be avoided, it is almost a matter of indifference, within certain limits, whether there is much gold or little. Prices having once settled themselves, it is only a question of carrying a little more metal or a little less in your pocket. As Cantillon, and subsequently, but independently, Hume, remarked, if the money in the world were suddenly doubled or halved trade would go on as before, all prices being approximately doubled or halved. But, of course, the interests of creditors and debtors would be affected while the change was in progress.

Professor Jevons.

Now, as regards the *chronic* question, it is probable, though not certain, that the establishment of the bimetallic ratio of 15½ to 1 would give a worse rather than a better standard of value, because the momentary standard is always the over-estimated metal. The double-standard system gives an option to the debtor, so that if either gold or silver were in future years discovered in large quantities, the debtor would have the benefit. In the monometallic system there is no option, and all parties stake their interests on the single metal. To these considerations must be added the historical fact that silver has during the last thousand years fallen in value more than gold. The ratio of values in the Middle Ages was about 10 to 1, fluctuating at times to 12 to 1. Later on silver became comparatively cheaper, and in the latter part of last century, 15½ to 1 correctly represented the natural ratio. For some fifty years it was held pretty steadily at this point by the action of the French Currency Law. The unprecedented discoveries of gold in California, Australia, New Zealand, and elsewhere, reversed the course of prices for a time, but more lately the tendency to a preponderating fall of silver has reasserted itself. No doubt the events here so briefly recapitulated admit of endless discussion, and it would be impossible even to mention the volumes which have been written since the time of Locke upon the comparative steadiness of value of gold and silver. There emerges a certain degree of probability that silver is more subject to depreciation than gold, although both have, in the course of a thousand years, been very greatly depreciated in comparison with corn and the chief kinds of raw materials.

If this may be assumed to be the case, it follows that an attempt to re-establish the ratio 15½ to 1 would tend to discourage the production of the dearer metal, gold, and to encourage the production of the more depreciated silver. We should be filling our pockets and our strong boxes with a metal 15½ times as heavy and 28½ times as bulky as gold, proportionally to value, in order to get a worse medium of exchange, and a probably worse standard of value. Nor should we be approximating towards a better state of things. If gold is destined ultimately to be the general standard of value of all civilized nations, we must let it take its own natural value, and must allow the appreciation, if any, to tell upon the profits of mining. But the arbitrary reduction in the value of gold, involved in the present bimetallic project, would tend constantly to replace gold by silver; and unless it were desired actually to take silver as the medium of exchange, the last state of things would be worse than the first. It thus becomes plain that a bimetallic *régime* is not the means of approximating to a gold *régime*. On the contrary, it must either be a permanent *régime*, or it will, sooner or later, leave us with a vast stock of silver, liable to sudden depreciation, and a diminished stock of gold. In short, the project of M. Cernuschi is not a real panacea for our present troubles; it is only a mode of postponement leading to eventual aggravation.

When we turn to the *temporary* view of the subject, by which I mean the circumstances and interests of the next ten or fifteen years, the difficulties increase, chiefly because the data become wholly uncertain and contingent. The great principle of the cost of production fails us, because in the case of such durable commodities as gold and silver, the accumulated stock in hand is immensely greater than the annual production or consumption. It stands to reason, of course, that if several great nations suddenly decide that they will at all cost have gold currencies to be coined in the next few years, the annual production cannot meet the demand, which must be mainly supplied, if at all, out of stock. The result would, doubtless, be a tendency to a fall of prices. M. de Laveleye, in one of the able articles which he is contributing to the *Indépendance Belge*, as an advocate of Cernuschi-ism, points to a fall of 30 per cent., which he thinks has already been occasioned by the demand for gold currency. He excites our imagination as to what may be expected to happen should Italy and other countries need gold for coining. But he omits to observe that the fall of 30 per cent. is probably due for the most part to the collapse of credit and speculation, a periodic event of which we have had many prior instances. The period of 1833 to 1844, especially was one when no great wars and monetary operations were in progress; it was a period of active industrial and commercial progress. Yet the tables of prices given by Tooke, in his *History of Prices*, and reduced in my paper on the Variation of Prices, communicated to the Statistical Society in May, 1865 (vol. xxviii. pp. 294–320), show that the average prices rose by 22½ per cent. between 1833 and 1839, and fell 25 per cent. between this last year and 1844. So far as I have been able to discover, this great oscillation was entirely due to the general expansion of trade and credit, and to its subsequent collapse. Like causes have certainly been in operation in the last ten or twelve years; and if, as seems probable, we are now getting round by the lapse of time to the period when trade naturally revives, experience would prevent us from imagining that the late fall of values will be continued or repeated without an intervening rise. I am far from denying that if the Italian Government decide to carry into effect M. Luzzatti's threat of buying gold at all hazards, and if the like course be taken by the United States and France, not to speak of Germany, then there might be a considerable disturbance of values for a time. But is it likely that such proceedings will be taken by rational statesmen and rational parliaments? It is really too absurd to suppose that any country will insist upon immediately having a gold currency at any cost, regardless of the fact that it will thereby injure its own trade and commerce in the getting. The position is simply this. We have had for fifty years or more an abundant currency of gold. Italy and some other countries have a paper currency. Suddenly becoming disgusted with paper, they say that unless we consent immediately to abandon our gold to a great extent, and take silver instead, they will insist upon buying our gold from us at whatever price we like to ask for it. We have so good a currency that, unless we consent to give it up willingly, they will insist on borrowing it from us. But surely in this case, possession is nine points of the law. The largest stock of gold in the world is to be found in England, and many of the great gold-producing districts are to be found in the English colonies or dependencies. If these foreign nations insist upon having gold currencies, they must pay our price for gold, and they must in raising the price benefit us and our colonies, comparatively speaking.

When we consider what are the difficulties put forward as the ground of this bimetallic crotchet, we find that they arise either out of the sudden issue and withdrawal of paper money, or else out of the efforts of certain governments to get rid of silver. If the Italians suddenly want fifteen or twenty millions of specie, it is because they allowed their specie to be replaced by paper in former years, and they now discover the evils of a variable paper currency. Germany wants gold, because Prince Bismarck and his economists recognised the soundness of the principles on which Lord Liverpool fashioned our metallic currency. But because Germany has met with a temporary check in striving after a gold standard, is there any reason that we, who have had a gold standard with little interruption since the time of Sir Isaac Newton, should throw it up at the demand of M. Cernuschi? The difficulties of France simply consist in the fact that, having had the law of the double standard previously in operation, she suspended the action of the law as soon as it began to occasion a return of silver. If all civilized countries were to adopt the double standard, they would just be inviting the growth of a silver currency, which France, with full experience of the use of silver, has practically decided to avoid.

Much that has recently been published on this subject,

including the official text of the draft resolution to be submitted to the Conference in Paris, implies that the French law establishing the double standard was intended to act as a regulator of the values of the metals according to the ratio of 15½ to 1. The fact, however, is that no such idea seems to have prompted the law. Gaudin, who in the ninth year of the Revolution proposed the ratio of 15½ to 1, did so upon the ground that this ratio was sufficiently near to that of the market values to allow coins of gold and silver to circulate side by side indifferently. In case the market ratio should alter after a time, he thought that the gold pieces could be melted and reissued. Sir Isaac Newton, again, when in 1717 he fixed the guinea at 21*s.*, did so upon the ground that this was the closest convenient approximation to market rates. Only four months ago I quoted in the *Contemporary Review* (January, 1881, vol. xxxix. p. 73) the remarks of Cantillon upon this decision of Newton. Cantillon says:—

"It is the market price which decides the proportion of "the value of gold to that of silver. On this is based the "proportion which we give to pieces of gold and silver money. "If the market price varies considerably, it is necessary to "alter the proportion of the coins. If we neglect to do this "the circulation is thrown into confusion and disorder," &c. There is, in fact, no precedent for the views now pressed upon us. It is not even proposed to accept the prevailing ratio of the markets, but by an arbitrary convention to raise up silver to the place it held in the markets before, which involves bringing down gold so as to meet it about half-way. I do not undertake to deny that if a convention were agreed upon, and carried into formal effect, it might possibly raise silver to its former price of 59*d.* per ounce. The measure is one of so novel a character that it is almost impossible to say what would or would not happen. The attempt to force silver dollars into use in the United States has entirely failed, and it might fail even under a convention. It is quite conceivable that in the United Kingdom and the colonies the scheme would be defeated by the tacit refusal of the people to accept silver legal tender. A bank or a tradesman might try to stand upon his legal rights, but the result would be a kind of commercial "Boycotting." Some formula would probably be discovered for contracting affairs out of the Double Legal Tender Law. At present there is no law to prevent people from making contracts in terms of gold or silver bullion, or tin or copper or corn, or whatever else they like, which is capable of precise definition. Even if the law were not thus circumvented, it might still be possible to make payments in gold a point of honour.

Then, again, the perpetual maintenance of this supposed convention is the only safeguard against the most serious inconvenience to some of the parties to it. The convention would resemble a chain, the breaking of each link of which would throw an increased strain upon the other links. There exist, indeed, a good many international conventions relating to postal intercourse, extradition of criminals, copyright, and so forth; but in none of these cases would the breaking or suspension of the convention result in any ruinous consequences. There would be suspension of benefits rather than occasion of evil. But should war break out among some of the countries involved in the monetary convention, the probable effect would be to throw the mass of silver coin upon neutral nations. This might be done without any express breach of the convention, simply by the issue of paper money, a measure which we cannot pretend to consider unlikely, seeing that the chief difficulties of the present monetary situation arise out of efforts for the withdrawal of recent paper-money issues. It is true that the 8th Article of the proposed Convention enacts that "the fact of issuing or allowing to be issued paper money, "convertible or otherwise, shall not relieve the State issuing "it, or allowing it to be issued, from the above stipulated "obligation of keeping its mints always open for the free "mintage of the two metals at the ratio of 1 to 15½." But, as far as I can understand this "keeping of the mints open," it seems probable that this article would be quite nugatory in time of war. If silver were depreciated 5 or 10 per cent., paper legal tender might easily be depreciated 20 or 30 per cent., and nobody would think of coining silver to pay their debts, when they could pay them so much more cheaply with paper. The issue of paper legal tender forms then, to the best of my belief, an indirect mode of abrogating the convention without a distinct breach of faith. No government has ever yet resisted the temptation of resorting to paper under serious stress of war, and therefore, until a wiser and better state of things is brought about in the long course of time, it would seem impossible to fulfil the first condition of the bimetallic project—the making of an indefeasible convention.

When a measure is so clearly undesirable, it is hardly needful to point out the many difficulties which would arise in its operation. But there is one which presents itself to my mind as almost insuperable—namely, the confusion which would be produced in the masses of national and other debts contracted in terms of gold money. Silver is now about 13 per cent. below its old customary value, compared with gold. If, then, debts contracted formerly in gold could be paid in silver, by the option of the bimetallic system, the claims of all creditors would be endangered to this extent, and in all probability would be depreciated to half that extent. Nor would the matter be much improved by enacting that old debts should be paid in gold as contracted, because gold, being forced into a fixed par with silver, would be depreciated, say, six per cent. The adoption of the bimetallic *régime* would be a *coup d'état* affecting the value of all past monetary contracts in a degree incapable of estimation; and although such a *coup*, or almost any other *coup*, might be advisable under certain circumstances, according to the maxim, *salus populi suprema lex,* yet it would be clearly impossible to unsettle the whole monetary contracts of the British nation and the British race, to the extent of some six per cent. or more, for the sake of the exceedingly problematic, if not visionary, advantages to be derived from this proposed convention.

Though it thus appears to be altogether out of the question that the English Government should contemplate the abandonment of the gold standard, there are two or three minor measures of a temporary nature which might perhaps be adopted to relieve the disturbed relations of the precious metals. There would probably be little or no inconvenience in raising the limit of legal currency of silver coin in the United Kingdom to five pounds instead of two pounds as at present. This change would probably prove to be merely a nominal one, unless bankers and others could be induced to pay out silver coin more largely than at present. The Mint gains so handsome a profit upon the coinage of silver money at present that the opportunity might well be taken to throw as much silver into circulation as possible; but unless the habits of the people be changed it would not stop in circulation. There is, in fact, at present a very clear disinclination on the part of the public to take any larger amount of silver money than is necessary. It is an almost unknown thing in England for any tradesman to give as much as two pounds in silver change. No customer is expected to take more than ten, or at the most twenty shillings in silver, and any surplus of silver receipts is paid into the banking account, and the general balance of the district is eventually returned to the Bank of England. It is very doubtful whether Mr. Seyd's scheme of a four-shilling piece or any other scheme would overcome this fixed habit, which is moreover a reasonable habit.

A good deal has been said about the expediency of bringing into operation the Third Clause of the Bank Charter Act, which is supposed to authorize the issue of notes upon a reserve of silver bullion to a certain extent. That Clause reads as follows :—

"And whereas it is necessary to limit the amount of silver "bullion on which it shall be lawful for the same department of "the Bank of England to issue Bank of England notes; be it "therefore enacted, that it shall not be lawful for the Bank of "England to retain in the Issue Department of the said Bank at "any one time an amount of silver bullion exceeding one-fourth "part of the gold coin and bullion at such time held by the Bank "of England in the Issue Department."

It is obvious that this clause is solely a restrictive one; that which authorizes the holding of silver bullion is the preceding clause, far too long for quotation. It states, however, that it shall not be lawful to issue notes in excess of the securities allowed to be transferred to the Issue Department, "save in exchange for other Bank of England "notes, or for gold coin, or for gold or silver bullion received "or purchased for the said Issue Department under the "provisions of this Act," &c. It is curious that, although the second clause thus seems to speak of silver bullion being "received or purchased under the provisions of this Act," there are no provisions in the rest of the Act relating to the purchase of silver. The fourth clause defines the price at which all persons may demand notes for gold bullion, but there is no like definition as regards silver. The result seems to be that the Bank of England buys and sells silver bullion as an ordinary dealer or speculator. If, then, the Bank Directors think that it will conduce to the interests of their shareholders that they should lay in a stock of three, four, or five millions of pounds' worth of silver, as the case may be, let them do so. They will gain or lose according as the value of that stock rises or falls; but who can say how that will be? In any case, the effect of such an operation upon the silver markets of the world must be inappreciable.

There is one further measure which might well be

adopted at the present conjuncture, namely, the alteration of the Bank Act so as to allow of the issue from the Bank of one-pound notes. Now that Parliament has authorized the circulation in England under very questionable conditions of a fractionable paper currency, the last shadow of reason has disappeared why one-pound notes, so long current in Scotland and Ireland, should be unknown in England. If we could suppose that thirty millions of such notes were put into circulation eventually, about twenty millions might be issued on Securities, giving a profit to the Government of nearly half a million a year. The margin of ten millions more or less of gold added to the specie reserve of the Issue Department would be ample to meet any conceivable demand for payment of such notes, the circulation of which would probably be more constant than that of the larger notes. Thus a supply of twenty millions of sovereigns would be opportunely thrown upon the markets of the world, which might be scrambled for by the various nations now wanting gold currencies.

It will easily be seen that in this article I do not pretend to enter into the complexities of the subject, nor to answer the numerous arguments adduced in favour of the bimetallic project. The literature and statistics of the subject are of an almost interminable extent. If any reader wants to learn what he has to read before he can be considered to have mastered this subject, let him refer to *A Partial List of Modern Publications on the Subject of Money*, prepared by Mr. Horton, and printed among the Appendices to the Official American Report on the International Monetary Conference, held in Paris, in August, 1878. This volume is replete with information on the subject. But my contention is that to wade through the interminable discussions on bimetallism is about as useful as to wander through a forest in a mist, the happiest result of which is usually to find yourself back again at the point you started from.

W. STANLEY JEVONS.

WHAT IS A POUND?

From the *Nineteenth Century*, June, 1881.

THIS old question, which Sir Robert Peel so much rejoiced in, has once more cropped up, and in the remarks I wish to make upon it I desire to say a few words upon what *was* a pound and what *may be* a pound.

In his speech on the Bank Act of 1844 he says of the principle of the metallic standard: "It must at the same " time be admitted that it would be quite consistent with " that principle to adopt some other measure of value than " that which we have adopted. It would be consistent with " that principle to select silver instead of gold as the " standard, or to have a mixed standard of gold and silver, " *the relative value of the two metals being determined*, or to " dispense with gold coin altogether, and regulate the " amount and value of the paper currency by making it " convertible only, according to the proposal of Mr. Ricardo, " into gold bullion of a given minimum amount."

The authority of this great financier may therefore be cited as showing that bimetallism as now proposed is not otherwise than in accordance with the principle of the metallic standard.

The Earl of Liverpool made his proposal for a gold standard on the ground that Great Britain is "so dis- " tinguished for its affluence and for the extent of its " commercial connections, that gold coins are best adapted " to be the principal measure of property."

The monometallists in the present controversy maintain this doctrine, and assert that the superior wealth of England enables her to keep her gold standard, while less wealthy nations, such as Germany, Italy, &c., could not do so. On the other hand, the bimetallists declare that this supremacy would continue and even increase if England submitted herself to a general law agreed on in concert with other nations. The Americans believe that their wealth, intelligence, commercial activity, and undeveloped resources will enable them, if they are forced into a gold standard, to outstrip England in the race for wealth, and to draw from England's store of gold a sufficient amount to place them in the foremost rank.

The present controversy dates from the first monetary conference in Paris, which sat in June, 1867, and which was called for the purpose of "appreciating more earnestly "the advantages which would be derived from the unifi- "cation of coinages."

At the very first meeting the question of standards arose, and on its arising the existence of the double standard seemed so little understood that the delegate from Russia, having been placed among those representing the double-standard countries, declared that there was only one standard in Russia, that of silver; but he was corrected by Monsieur de Parieu, the French delegate, who informed him that both metals were legal tender in both countries.

On the 20th of June, at the third sitting, the proposition "that the desired result, namely, monetary unification, "is attainable on the basis and condition of adopting the "exclusive gold standard," was carried with one dissentient voice.

In 1871 the German demonetisation of money commenced, and in 1873 an Act of Congress was passed by which silver was legally demonetised in the United States, which act was, however, corrected by what is called the Bland Bill, enforcing the coinage of a certain amount of

Mr. H. R. Grenfell.

silver monthly. In 1878 another international monetary conference assembled at Paris, at which the German Empire was not represented, but, notwithstanding the absence of that important element, the European States, through their delegates, agreed "that it is necessary to maintain in the "world the functions of silver as well as those of gold," thereby coming to a conclusion at variance with that at which the previous conference had arrived.

A third conference is now sitting. Since the demonetisation of silver in Germany, a change which was the legitimate consequence of the verdict of 1868, a continued fall of prices has taken place, and one of the subjects of dispute between those engaged in the battle of the standards is, whether that depreciation of prices and the existing depression of trade are due to the usual ebb and flow of commercial life caused by bad harvests and the cupidity and folly of man, or whether they are due in a great measure to the currency revolution of 1873.

The English system of metallic currency is founded on Lord Liverpool's letter to the King on coins, on the report of the Bullion Committee of 1810, and on the various Acts relating to the resumption of what were called cash payments, or the right to receive standard coin in exchange for bank-notes.

Most people are aware that previous to 1819 our circulation was a paper one, but few are aware that, previous to the suspension of cash payments, it was bimetallic, and not measured by a gold standard. Of this fact it must be supposed that Sir Robert Peel was not conscious when he made his famous speech on the resumption of cash payments in 1819, the peroration of which contains the following sentence: "Every consideration of sound policy and every "obligation of strict justice should induce us to restore the "ancient and permanent standard of value."

Now, this is precisely what he did not do, but what the bimetallists are now advising. What they wish for is a return to the "ancient standard of the realm" in common with the rest of the nations of the earth.

The fall of prices which took place after the institution of the modern, not ancient, gold standard of 1816, and that which has taken place since the demonetisation of silver in Germany, have both been the subject of a most voluminous literature.

The evils connected with the fall in prices are disputed by some economists, so in alluding to them I prefer to quote the remarks of those whose orthodoxy is undoubted. Mr. Giffen said in 1879 :—

"I have come to the conclusion that not only is there a "decline of prices at the present time from the high level estab-"lished a few years ago, but that this decline is more serious "than the downward fluctuations of prices usually exhibited in "dull times, and that it may be partly of a permanent character, "unless some great change should occur in the condition of "business at an early date. . . . .

"The reason is that a sudden pressure on the precious metals "at a given period tends to disturb the money markets of the "countries using them. . . . .

"Altogether, during the last six years, Germany has coined "84,000,000; the accumulation of gold in the United States "amounts to 30,000,000 sterling."

A falling off in the supply of gold, as well as the increased demand, is then described.

Now, if these things are admitted by the monometallists, the question arises to what extent is the fall in prices an evil? and what is evil, and what is good, to a writer on political economy?

In my humble opinion, violent, sudden, and frequent oscillations in the price of commodities are an evil. A long continuance of the inability to obtain the due return for their labours, be they what they may, is an evil to ordinary men. It is an evil for those who have made fair and honest

Mr. H. R. Grenfell.

calculations, founded on a belief in a continuance of steady returns of any kind, to find them permanently falsified to their loss and detriment. It is bootless to tell us that we must consider this as a chronic question, irrespective of the immediate effect of such sudden changes. If an enormous depreciation in prices of all things produced in England be not an evil, then I admit the bimetallist would be very wrong to press his views on the public notice.

The inflation of prices in 1872 was felt to be a most undoubted evil to consumers; to those who produced nothing it was an unmixed evil To these same persons the state of commercial depression is rather a good than an evil. They receive as much now as they did before, and they pay less for what they consume. But to those who are neither enthusiasts nor doctrinaires the sudden inflation of prices which went by the name of the coal famine was a great evil, though perhaps not so great as the present depression, which, though less sudden, appears more lasting, and therefore may be more mischievous in its results.

Consumers may be the better for this state of things, but it must be allowed that if the interests of consumers who have produced nothing are to be weighed against those of consumers who have produced something—that is to say, the drones against the working bees—these working bees always have been, and always must be, the objects of first consideration.

Philosophers tell us to postpone all thoughts of the interests of producers, in the hope that fifty years hence all things may be set straight again and trade go on as before, even though "all prices be approximately doubled or halved, "the interest of creditors and debtors being affected to that "extent while the change was in progress." Neither creditors nor debtors would bear the doubling their property with modesty, or the halving it with equanimity, even though the operation might vindicate the perfection of the doctrines of Locke and of Lord Liverpool.

Having stated the extent to which I believe certain evils exist, I proceed to say what bimetallism is and what it is not.

The bimetallism proposed is the free mintage of the two precious metals at a given fixed ratio of 15½ to 1 in all countries agreeing to a convention for the establishment of the principle. It naturally would entail the legal tender of either metal at the option of the debtor for the payment of all debts.

Bimetallism is not an attempt to make silver or gold, or both together, the currency of any country, the probability being that under such an arrangement no alteration would take place as to the coin in which the ordinary transactions of life are carried on. Bankers would; as they do now, hold in their tills just such notes, coin, or change as their customers require, and would not, any more than they do now, force their creditors or depositors to take away sacks of five-franc pieces or crowns when they want cash with which to pay their wages or bills. Legally, of course, this could be done; but as the habit now is to keep precisely that form of currency which depositors require, so would it be under a bimetallic system. The example of this is to be found in England in the last century. The law was bimetallic, but the practice was a gold currency. In India, if a bimetallic law were promulgated to-morrow, in practice silver would continue to be used.

Bimetallism existed in this country from 1717 to 1778, during which period an Englishman could pay his debts either in gold or in silver to the amount of £25 in tale and any amount in weight. Bimetallism existed in France from the beginning of this century to 1873, during which period it is not denied that both gold and silver have been the prevailing currency of that country, though not both at the same time; nor is it denied that during that period the relative prices of gold and silver were kept almost exactly at the legal rate of 15½ to 1, not only in France, the bimetallic country, but in the markets of the world, or that England, having been bimetallic previously, returned to cash payments in 1819 in gold alone, thereby causing an important loss to debtors and gain to creditors.

The following may be shortly stated as the fundamental propositions of bimetallists, which they assert have not been answered :—

1. That the precious metals used for circulation are so large a proportion of the existing mass that the amount in use for any other purpose is too small to have any influence on their value.

2. That the amount used by the larger States so far exceeds that of the rest of the world that any agreement made by them for the regulation of the relative value must of necessity fix it to the world at large.

3. That there is nothing impossible or impracticable in an international agreement for the fixing of the rate.

4. That the ratio of 15½ to 1 having been maintained for nearly the whole of the present century by the French bimetallic arrangement, it would be the best ratio at which to fix it.

At the present moment it is of paramount importance that these propositions should either be answered or proved to be beside the question. Those who are occupied in discussing it are apt to treat it as if it were only a chronic question, and not one requiring immediate attention. If it had not been the subject of attention in 1868, it is quite true that no one would have dreamed of stirring it in 1881. Both parties to the controversy are agreed that it would have been far better if Germany had never followed up the conclusions of 1868.

To those who argue that this is a chronic question and

not necessary to be immediately considered, the following facts are not unworthy of attention.

It has been shown that by the admission of the advocates of monometallism the evils of trade depression are to be traced to the diminution of the supplies of gold, and to the increased demand for it, and it is now proposed to show that the latter cause is likely to be increased if Germany throws her silver on the market, if Italy resumes cash payments in gold, and if America completes her gigantic task of resumption and recall of her bonds by resorting, as many of her financiers wish to do, to a monometallic gold currency.

Mr. Jevons admits this when he says:—

> "It stands to reason, of course, that if several great nations "suddenly decide that they will at all cost have gold currencies "to be coined in the next few years the annual production cannot "meet the demand, which must be mainly supplied, if at all, out "of stock. The result would be a tendency to a fall in prices."

The question, then, is not whether a change in currency is a good thing or a bad thing, because we are all agreed that it is a bad thing, but whether the change of England to bimetallism or that of the Latin Union and the United States to a monometallic gold standard would be the greater evil.

Some of the adherents of the single standard assure us that it is an error to suppose that it is possible to make such a change as this at all, and, granting that possibility, that we insure greater steadiness in prices than at present. Again I prefer to quote Mr. Jevons rather than to express my own opinion.

In his work on *Money and the Mechanism of Exchange* he says:—

> "I have no doubt whatever that M. Wolowski is theoretically "quite correct in what he says about the compensatory action of "the double-standard system. English writers seem to have com- "pletely misunderstood the question, asserting that the system

" exposes us to the extreme fluctuations of both metals. . . . Nor " is this the whole error of English writers. A little reflection " must show that MM. Wolowski and Courcelle Leneuil are " quite correct in urging that a compensatory, or, as I should " prefer to call it, equilibratory action goes on under the French " currency law, and tends to maintain gold and silver more steady " in value than they would otherwise be.

" Imagine two reservoirs of water, each subject to variations " of supply and demand. In the absence of any connecting pipe " the level of the water in each reservoir will be subject to its " own fluctuations merely, but if we open a connection, the water " in both will assume a certain mean level, and the effect of any " excessive supply or demand will be distributed over the whole " area of both reservoirs."

From this it will be seen that the more serious of the monometallists admit the superior steadiness of the bimetallic system.

One of the objections to bimetallism is that it would vitiate contracts and alter prices. I have shown that in these respects we cannot shut ourselves up in our insular security. There is no "silver streak" in commerce; prices have been disordered by German demonetisation, and the perfection of the English system no longer carries with it the success which was supposed to attend it. Prince Bismarck, who administers the affairs of Germany, and who adopts the traditional policy of Frederick the Great, to attain the glory by following every road which leads to it, desired to confer upon his country something of the commercial supremacy of England. He believed, or rather his economical advisers believed, that the metropolitan position of England in commerce was due to her single gold standard, and not to her vast capital, her ships and colonies, and her industrial resources. He acted on this opinion, and widespread ruin has been the consequence.

Giving full credit to Lord Liverpool for the perfection of his treatise and for the completeness of his system, I am led to examine, as he would have done, under what circumstances his so-called infallible dogma originated. His letter was written when England was struggling for existence with the rest of the civilised world, and in like manner, in the reign of King William the Third, when Locke was writing, England was engaged in a war for the defence of the liberties and independence of mankind, and neither of these writers had any idea of cosmopolitan agreement upon such matters.

What Lord Liverpool said was, that in a given country it was better to have a single metal made into coins, which should be the standard of value and national legal tender, but he cites as an example of that necessity the practice of the commercial states and countries on the Continent making foreign bills of exchange, and sometimes other bills exceeding a certain amount, payable in what is usually called bank money.

Now this important example is to me the most telling argument which can be used in favour of bimetallism by agreement. That bank money which is described by Lord Liverpool as being a necessity in Venice, Genoa, Amsterdam, and Hamburg in past days, seems to me to be more required in London than in any place in the civilised globe. London is now to the world what all those places put together were in other days, and if we strip the bimetallic discussion of all extraneous matter, I should be content to see it argued upon the question of whether bank money could not be made of two metals, either of which would pay a bill of exchange.

If silver were money nowhere, either in the Latin Union, India, Russia, China, or America, it would certainly be better that all things should be reckoned by the London gold standard; but as it is a fact that several of these countries are wholly silver, that the United States is trembling in the balance, and that Italy is desirous of resuming cash payments in the best possible metal, we

Mr. H. R. Grenfell.

have to face, as usual in this nether world, the facts as they stand, and not as we wish them to be. And this is precisely what Lord Liverpool did. He examined carefully and exhaustively every fact of past history, and surveyed every circumstance which surrounded him, and his decisions are based upon those facts and upon his personal experience. Viewed in this light, his term of bank money as an expression for convention currency is of paramount importance to the discussion. He described this bank money as being used to pay bills of exchange in certain limited places, and the necessity for it arose from the debased state of the coins in those places, as well as from the variety of them current for ordinary transactions in such centres of commerce, where anything but the payment in a perfect currency would produce great embarrassment in all commercial dealings, and would render the exchange very much against such state or country.

If then the bank money, that is, gold or silver or receipts for them at a fixed relative value, is the same in New York, Frankfort, Vienna, Rome, Paris, and London, and is of a greater certainty and more steady in its value as regards the mass of commodities than either gold or silver separately, then such bank money would approach more nearly the ideal standard of Lord Liverpool than gold bank money alone.

But Mr. Jevons himself has demonstrated that although the variations of the two precious metals measured in commodities would be perhaps more frequent, they would be less violent, and seeing that we have the example of France before us, where a single bimetallic country not only obeyed the above law, but actually kept the relative prices between the precious metals themselves without any important change, how can it be doubted that if the transactions of all Europe, the United States, and India were added to those of France, the functions of bank money could safely be entrusted to both gold and silver?

Measuring the value of Lord Liverpool's doctrine and his matchless treatise, we must not forget who and what Lord Liverpool was. He was an official mainly occupied with the phenomena which he watched from an official standpoint, and, though practically conversant with almost every branch of official life, he had no real knowledge of the cosmopolitan commercial machinery which it is our business now to discuss.

Monometallists seem to think that the subject has received its last touch from Lord Liverpool's mind. Against his authority I cannot help quoting that of Alexander Baring, first Lord Ashburton, who lived a generation later than Lord Liverpool. He had perhaps the largest and most complete experience of affairs of every kind, except military affairs, of any man of his day. Before he was forty he was the confidential intermediary between Napoleon and the English Government, and shortly afterwards he was the rival of the first Rothschild in financial operations. Subsequently he was the Cabinet friend of Peel and Wellington, and he finished his career by a treaty with America, which still goes by his name.

I find that he gave evidence in 1828 as to the consequences which had followed a blind adherence to Lord Liverpool's doctrines, in which he said—

" he had always thought that it was possible and desirable to " maintain in this country a silver currency as a legal tender " founded on the proportion of silver to gold established in the " currency of France, or something very near it."

And he gives as a reason for that opinion—

" that a sudden change from peace to war, a bad harvest or a " panic year arising from over-trading and other causes, imposes " upon the Bank of England, which is the heart of all our " circulation, the necessity, for the purpose of protecting itself, " to stop the egress of specie, sometimes even to bring in large " quantities into the country.

Mr. H. R. Grenfell.

"Now it is evident that the Bank wishing to reinforce its "supply of specie can do so with infinitely increased facility "with the power of either drawing in gold or silver than if it "were confined to only one of the metals."

These opinions of Lord Ashburton were given without any wish to stir in the matter, but merely as a contribution to the mass of knowledge in the possession of the Government on the subject.

It may now be well to notice some of the objections that have been made by those who have frankly admitted the superior steadiness of the proposed system over that now in existence. I will take those which seem to me to be perhaps the most important.

One is that it is a direct attempt to force the stream backwards; that the tendency of all the wealthier and more civilised nations of the world is towards a monometallic gold standard, the superiority of which is so clearly established by the commercial supremacy of that country which for a long time was the only one which had succeeded in enforcing it; that it is idle and impossible to attempt any arrangement founded on another system; that as the experiment made to force silver dollars into use in the United States has failed and might fail under a convention, it is possible that payments in gold might be made a point of commercial honour.

A great many things are possible, but as it has never been found that in commerce or in any other profession people pay more as a point of honour than they are bound to do, and as all payments are made, with the exception of unimportant balances, by paper currency, book transfers, or cheques, it must be clear to every one that that metal or those metals which are the legal security for the ultimate payment of papers in various countries would be the foundation of all legal as well as honourable payment.

I confess, then, that I am not alarmed at this objection. It is founded, without doubt, upon a review of what has taken place in the United States in the eagerness which her citizens have displayed to seize the foremost place both as to national and commercial credit.

Another objection made by a very able writer is that, whatever may be the evils connected with the depreciation of prices and the depression of trade in England, the damage done to India by the fall in the exchanges is wholly imaginary. He states that it "is political economy of the "most elementary description, that the low rate of exchange "ruling between England and India has the effect of "checking exports to India, and of stimulating imports "thence, and that this is precisely what is wanted if India "is to pay her obligations here in any shape, and that "without such fall in the exchange her financial straits "would be much worse than they are."

There is some truth in this assertion, but then it is utterly incompatible with the arguments generally used by the monometallists, that to raise the value of silver and to depreciate that of gold to their old ratio would inflict a loss upon gold-using countries and confer a great benefit upon those using silver.

One writer has estimated the loss of England by such a transaction as £8,000,000 on her stock of gold, and the profit of France on her stock of silver as £16,000,000.

Nothing can show more clearly the divergence of opinions held by monometallists as to the practical effect of the carrying out of their doctrines to their legitimate conclusion than these two surmises, made by equally competent thinkers and writers.

The next objection which I am bound to notice is the fear which exists in the minds of monometallists as to what would happen in time of war. We are told that a war-making nation would necessarily break the convention and refuse free minting: that is to say, that if Russia or Chili go to war and issue a forced paper currency, this act would be in breach of the bimetallic convention.

Mr. H. R. Grenfell.

Now, what really happens on such an event taking place is that a belligerent nation does not increase the volume of its own currency by using pieces of paper instead of metal, but by exporting its own metal it increases the volume of the currency in the world at large. Its pieces of paper being discredited, it is obliged to use the precious metals for the payment of everything to be bought abroad, and for its belligerent operations, and it can and does enforce upon its subjects the duty of receiving and paying in pieces of paper at home.

The monometallist seems to imagine that at the same moment when a belligerent is by a natural process exporting its precious metals, some other country or body of merchants, either from mere curiosity or from a desire to test the convention, would send precious metals back into that belligerent country and have them minted. This proposition is so absurd that it need only be stated clearly to secure its refutation.

The issue of paper by a belligerent would have, under a bimetallic convention, precisely the same effect which it has now. The explanation of the operation would, however, lead me into a too lengthy paper. I content myself, then, with stating my belief that the temporary effect of war and of forced paper currencies would be somewhat the same as a large discovery of the precious metals, and would be spread over a larger surface and more evenly under an international bimetallic convention than with the present separate national standards.

Having answered some of the most recent objections started to bimetallism, I approach the consideration of certain remedies which have been suggested in substitution of it. One proposal is to permit the raising of the limit of legal currency of silver coin to five pounds, instead of two pounds as at present. Considering that any one may, if he like it, pay forty shillings in discharge of a debt, and that, as far as my experience goes, it is never done, it is highly improbable that anyone would dream of carrying about sums of two, three, or four pounds in his pocket in silver for the purpose of vindicating the rights of that beautiful metal.

Another plan is to issue twenty or thirty millions of one-pound notes, of which twenty might be on securities. Thus we find men who are aghast at the notion of a currency which, though it does not rest upon gold alone, is yet founded upon a metallic basis quite ready to increase the circulation by emitting a large amount of paper, having no tangible metallic basis at all. If this proposition means anything, it means that in England, as is now the case in Ireland and Scotland, every one would use one-pound notes instead of sovereigns. Those who are in favour of this proposition would do well to read the chapter in Lord Liverpool on paper currency, in which he says :—

"It is certain that the smaller notes of the Bank of England, " and those issued by country bankers, have supplanted the gold " coins, usurped their functions, and driven a great part of them " out of circulation: in some parts of Great Britain, and especially " in the southern parts of Ireland, small notes have been issued " to supply the place of silver coins, of which there is certainly " a great deficiency.

"I will first observe, that if this practice is suffered to con- " tinue, as at present, without any limitation, there can be neither " use nor advantage in converting bullion of either of the precious " metals into coins, except so far as it may serve for the conveni- " ence of your Majesty's subjects in their most private concerns; " that is, no greater quantity than many of the writers who have " of late speculated on this subject will allow to continue in " currency: the bullion of which these coins are made had better " be exported in its natural state, like any other unmanufactured " commodity, for the use of which the trade of the country has " no occasion. The coins of your Majesty when carried into " foreign countries, will only be valued as bullion; and the pre- " cious metals, whether exported in coins or in bullion, will

" equally serve the purpose of a commercial capital; and it is " useless and absurd to impose upon the public the expense of " making coins, merely for the purpose of sending them out of " the kingdom."

I have now endeavoured to show that international bimetallism would be in accordance with the opinions and principles of some of those who are looked up to by economical writers with profound and deserved veneration; that Sir Robert Peel admitted bimetallism to be in accordance with the principle of the metallic standard; that Lord Ashburton had good reason for thinking that it would have the effect of facilitating the return to commercial calm after ordinary stormy weather; and that the views of Lord Liverpool as to the value of bank money would be more nearly acted upon by creating an international measure of value than by adhering to a separate national standard.

The most singular part of the whole controversy is that both this country and the United States seem to have abolished the silver element in their standard accidentally.

It has already been shown that in 1819 the question of silver hardly found a place in the resumption discussion in England, and with regard to the United States, Mr. Groesbeck, the delegate of that country at the conference of 1878, stated that the demonetisation of silver in 1873 was passed "through inadvertence," and on being asked what he meant by it he said that it had occurred when the Government was in a state of suspension, and when public attention was not sufficiently directed to the subject, and further that a number of members of Congress had confessed to him that they had not known what they were doing.

The Conference of Paris has now been adjourned till the 30th of June, in order that the delegates may receive fresh instructions. The opinions of most of the governments were already so well known that, beyond bringing the questions at issue into a still more definite and condensed shape than they were before, there is little fresh to remark upon except the important propositions made on behalf of the Indian Government by Sir Louis Mallet, and by Baron de Thielmann on behalf of Germany.

The former is simply a promise not to demonetise silver. The German proposition is founded on the admission that £87,000,000 of gold had been coined, that £54,000,000 of silver had been demonetised, and that the expenses of this operation had amounted to £2,200,000, while £25,000,000 of silver still remains in Germany.

To enable those countries where silver had not been demonetised to carry out the reforms which the Conference had met to consider, the German Empire is willing to abstain from all sales of silver for a fixed period, and to confine itself afterwards to such a limited amount as would not encumber the general market.

Thalers might be forbidden to be sent to the mints of the bimetallic union, or those mints might refuse to take them, so as to make the operation of selling them too costly.

Germany would also be willing to recall the gold pieces of five marks, and the treasury notes of the same value, and to re-issue five and two mark pieces to the amount of about £8,000,000, taking as a base a ratio between the two metals as near as possible to 15½ instead of that which, according to the present law, equals a ratio of about 1 to 14.

Having heard the above propositions from Germany, the energies of the Conference were devoted on the one hand to the persuasion of the English delegates to make some concessions, and on the other to induce France and the United States to proceed to a practical solution in case England should be unwilling to accede to their wishes.

It would be obviously improper for me to offer any opinions of the projects submitted or to be submitted to

Mr. H. R. Grenfell.

our Government in furtherance of the common object which all parties have in view—namely, the steadying of the prices of the precious metals in relation to commodities.

In this discussion my wish has been to keep clear from anything like zeal and enthusiasm. I am absolutely without any prejudice in the matter, and I have confined myself, in the evidence I have quoted, with the exception of that of Lord Ashburton, to the facts honestly brought out by those from whom I differ, so that I may say that the small bias which exists in my mind upon the subject is almost entirely due to the study of my opponents' opinions.

If, then, I am forced to answer the question "What "is a pound?" I incline to answer it in the words of Sir Robert Peel—namely, that we ought to return to "the "ancient standard of the realm," or, as the Americans call it, "the dollar of our fathers," rather than to adhere to the measure carried by that statesman, and founded upon Lord Liverpool's letter.

H. R. GRENFELL.

IS THE VALUE OF GOLD AND SILVER MONEY ARTIFICIAL?

To the Editor of *The Times*.*—May 7, 1881.

SIR,—Gold and silver have real and artificial values—real and natural, as for gilding, for use in surgical appliance, forks, spoons, and other things; artificial, for money, for circulating mediums. Owing to their real and natural value and the easy way in which that value can be stamped on them, and other considerations, every civilized nation takes gold and silver as representatives of value, and uses one or both metals as its money or circulating medium.

This artificial value is much greater than the real. If some substitute for gold and silver were found which could be used more advantageously as money and displace them, their exchangeable values would be vastly less than at present. That is, if an ounce of gold exchanges for two quarters of wheat now anywhere, it would, if it ceased to be used as money, exchange for much less—how much, is beyond speculation. New uses would be found for the two metals as they became cheaper, and they might retain a considerable proportion of their exchangeable value.

But does it not follow from the value of these metals being mainly of this artificial character and used mainly

* These Letters, by the Right Hon. Lord Bramwell, Mr. T. H. Farrer, Mr. H. H. Gibbs, Mr. H. D. Macleod, and M. Cernuschi, are reprinted from *The Times*.

by few consumers, that their value relative to each other can be kept practically at a definite ratio?

If all the Governments of the world determine that they will give "A" ounces of gold for "B" ounces of silver and "B" ounces of silver for "A" ounces of gold, and no more nor less, will not "A" ounces of gold always be worth "B" of silver?

For suppose, it having been so determined, very productive gold mines, as they are called, are discovered, what will happen?

This: the less productive gold mines will cease to be worked, and the less productive silver. There will be more gold and less silver. For suppose the same labour and capital before the discovery of the new mines produced "A" ounces in gold and "B" ounces in silver, no rent being paid, better mines of each metal paying rents where more of either was produced, and suppose, owing to the discovery, the capital and labour which produced "A" ounces in gold produces five-fourths "A" ounces in gold, paying no rent, all gold mines producing less will cease to be worked, and all silver mines producing less than five-fourths "B" ounces of silver. Of course, not at once nor immediately, but in time, in the long run.

The same thing would be true if the discovery were of new mines of silver. The same also would be true if either metal became more difficult of production from exhaustion of the mine. So that if gold mines became productive we should have more gold money, if silver mines more silver money. It will be asked what would happen, if, for example, gold became so abundant that no silver mine could be worked at the same ratio—*e.g.*, if twice "A" ounces of gold could be got for the labour and capital formerly required to get "A" ounces and no silver mine would for that capital and labour produce twice "B" ounces?

One answer to the case supposed is, that it is impossible.

Another is, that if it were possible, we should in time have all gold money. A third is, that after a time the gold mines would be exhausted and silver would come in again. The same reasoning is true if silver increased in productiveness. The world would have a period of heavy, clumsy money. But the thing is impossible.

I have suggested this would be true if all civilized nations would agree to the ratio of "A" to "B," or any other. But would it not also be true if the greater part of them would—the great consumers of the two articles, the great minters: all Europe and America, perhaps, without England?

It may be asked, Could they make gold and silver of equal value, or gold 50 times the value of silver? I am not sure; I doubt it. I should think they must adopt a ratio as near that of the cost of production as can be arrived at. But this may be shown. The relation of value of the two metals, both being money, must be between the relations of value they would have to one another if each were exclusively money. For suppose gold, and gold only, is used for money, and that silver is produced to supply the demand for the use for purposes other than money. Suppose that being so, that one ounce of gold equals "A" ounces of silver; next suppose silver the only metal used for money, and that then one ounce of gold equals "B" ounces of silver, "B" will obviously be less—less in number—than "A"—that is to say, gold will exchange for less silver when silver alone is money than when gold alone is. Now, suppose an attempt is made to use both metals as money, and it is determined that for this purpose one ounce of gold shall equal "C" ounces of silver, "C" in amount in number must be between "A" and "B."

For the use of gold for ordinary purposes would cause it to be absorbed at the rate of one ounce equal "B"; and if "C" is less than "B" no gold will be taken to the Mint; on the contrary, gold in circulation would be withdrawn and melted down. So if "C" is more than "A" no silver would even be minted.

It may be asked, could iron or copper be dealt with in this way—*i. e.*, a fixed ratio established between them? I say no; nor beef and mutton. Their values are not at all artificial, but wholly natural; and the consumers could not be got to agree on a ratio.

Is not bimetallism then a possibility? It would be attended with this consequence—if either metal or both became more abundant, the exchangeable value of both, not *inter se*, but in relation to other commodities, would be lowered. If either or both became less abundant, the exchangeable value of both, not *inter se*, but in relation to other commodities, would be raised. The world, therefore, would have its circulating medium liable to more frequent fluctuations in value than if it was monometallic. On the other hand, as both gold and silver would be raised or lowered at the same time, those fluctuations would be less in extent. The cause of change would be spread over a larger area.

If bimetallism is adopted, the ratio of gold and silver apparently should be 1 to 15½, for the reasons given by M. Cernuschi in his last pamphlet—viz., it is practically the ratio of the world; the ratio or nearly of four five-franc pieces to the napoleon, of thalers to marks in gold, of rupee to sovereign, and so on. If a higher ratio were adopted—say, one of gold to 20 of silver—some silver mines would be abandoned; if lower—say, one to ten—some gold mines would be. It might, however, be worth while to see what could be said to some other ratio. If this ratio, 15½ to 1, was adopted, gold would fall in value and silver would rise. For the circulating medium would be made up of both metals instead of one, as it is now throughout Europe. For Europe is either monometallic in gold or bimetallic with silver when coined, appreciated by a limitation of the coinage. But it is obvious that if two metals are used for the circulating medium instead of one, and the added metal is appreciated, the other will be depreciated.

Supposing bimetallism established, what good would it do to the world? I have shown it would make fluctuations less in extent, but more frequent. Would this be a benefit on balance? Some people suppose that because there would be more money the world would be better off. An utter mistake. It might as well be said that the world would be richer if bank-notes were printed on larger pieces of paper. It is a paradox, but the world has enough money and so has every country.

Suppose by some magic all the gold coins and all the silver, and all the bullion were doubled in size, what would be the effect? The world would be richer, because it would have more of an article of real value and could afford to turn more of its coin or bullion into spoons, &c.; but, allowing for that, the quarter of wheat which sold for £2 would still sell for £2, only each sovereign would be twice as big as before. Similarly, if by some magic all coin and bullion was made half as big only as it was, some gold and silver would be turned into coin; but, allowing for that, prices would be the same.

The truth is, the world uses gold and silver as circulating medium, only taking from it so much for other purposes as it is worth while to take. It does not make its saucepans of silver, because people would rather have what can be got by the material turned into money than have silver saucepans. So of each country. It parts with its precious metals to foreigners for something it values more, where by so doing it has raised their value it retains them. Scarcity of money rarely means scarcity of coin or bullion. No doubt the discovery of new and productive mines is a good thing for the country where they are and a great stimulus to trade and movement, but a very doubtful good to the world at large, perhaps even a harm. For it takes its capital and industry from the production of what the world wants to the production of what it does not want. If it were discovered that hammering gold for 24 hours doubled its size and weight, there would be a great deal of hammering and a great deal more gold; but the world, instead of being richer, would be very much poorer.

But then it is said that the burden of national debts and other obligations would be less than with a monometallic circulation of gold. Certainly. So it would be if the sovereign was alloyed with half silver. So it would be by any other contrivance that wronged the creditor. It is strange that they who advocate bimetallism on this ground do not see they are advocating wronging the creditor.

True it is that gold is appreciated at this time, at least I believe so; but the creditor runs the risk of its being depreciated. Why is he not to have the benefit of his bargain to be paid in gold, because that is appreciated? But then it is said, "See how the demonetization of silver "by Germany has lowered its value, and what will happen if "Germany goes on with the process and demonetizes its "thalers, and if France does the same with its silver?" Silver will fall to half its present value or less. Perhaps, and this furnishes an excellent reason why nations with a stock of silver should be bimetallic, or monometallic with silver; but, at the same time, it furnishes an equally strong one for a nation with a stock of gold like England not to be so. If bimetallism is adopted at the ratio of 1 to 15½, silver will rise in value as compared with gold, say, in round figures, from 52 to 60, or about 16 per cent. I say as compared with gold, not generally, because gold, as I have shown, will fall in exchangeable value with other things.

Let us halve the percentage and say that the real fall in the value of gold is 8 per cent., the rise in silver 8 per cent. Suppose we have a stock of gold of £100,000,000. We lose £8,000,000. The French, it is supposed, I

Lord Bramwell.

believe, have £200,000,000 of silver; they gain £16,000,000. The Bank of France would be straightway £4,000,000 richer.

But it is said "consider India. That country has a vast "stock of silver which would be appreciated." I doubt it. I doubt if the depreciation has reached there. The thing is most mysterious. Great mistakes are made about India. People talk of a loss by the Indian exchange. That is wrong. A loss by exchange is always of small amount and temporary character, and is a loss on gold against gold, or silver against silver. It is no more a loss by exchange than it would be if India paid its tribute to us in silk, and silk would not fetch as much in the European market as formerly. A loss by exchange ought never to be greater than freight, insurance, and other expenses.

This is not a question of words, but of substance. India has to pay us so much in gold. It may buy that gold here, or at home, or anywhere else. The thing it has to buy gold with is silver. The same silver would not buy as much as it would formerly. India, therefore, has to find more silver. If silver has not fallen in price and India exacts more from its taxpayers, it adds to the tax on them; otherwise if silver has so fallen, for then the taxpayer would get more silver for the same produce of indigo, rice, or wheat. They would have risen in price. But it is said they have not. If so, the depreciation of silver has not reached India. Still, it cannot be denied that in time it must. In time the stock of silver in India will be of less value, and India, to have enough money, must deprive itself of things which it has, and so be a loser. It must export more, as Mr. Bagehot showed. Is it worth England's while, then, to forward bimetallism? It is said it will be done without us. Perhaps, but should we help?

In considering the question, the effect of the change on debtors and creditors should be borne in mind. It is, perhaps, incorrect to say that the creditor would be wronged.

He has bargained for payment in gold, and will be paid in gold or what will purchase that gold, and there has been no bargain with him not to improve the currency by making it bimetallic. But would it be just to make it bimetallic, not to improve the currency, but to diminish the burden of debt?

B.

(BRAMWELL.)

April 28, 1881.

To the Editor of *The Times.*—May 21, 1881.

SIR,—May I be allowed to appeal to history on a subject which is generally treated as a matter of scientific deduction, and to state one or two matters of fact which appear to me to have an important bearing on this question? The arguments put forward in favour of bimetallism constantly assume that the value of gold and silver coin is artificial. Value, it is justly said, depends on supply and demand; if either of these is within the absolute control of law, law can, it is said, regulate values. The supply of the precious metals is admitted not to be within the control of law. But it is alleged or assumed that the demand for gold and silver coinage is a matter which depends upon and is regulated by law. It is the use of coin as money which creates the demand for it; and it is the Government which says what shall constitute money. The action of Government, therefore, gives money its value; and if all Governments agree, they can, at least, go so far in determining the value of money as to fix the ratio of value between gold and silver money.

Such, as I understand it, is the contention, and the question I wish to ask is whether the history of our own

Mr. T. H. Farrer.

coinage bears out this view; and for this purpose I will refer shortly to the facts of that history as given in the first Lord Liverpool's well-known letter on the coins of the realm.

It is unnecessary to go back farther than the reigns of Charles II. and James II. At that time silver had for centuries been the money of account and the standard of value. Gold coins had from time to time been introduced, and efforts had been made by different kings to determine the relative values of the gold and silver coin. But these efforts were unsuccessful; the attempt to determine these values had been abandoned, and at the time of the Revolution of 1688 silver alone was the money of account and legal tender. Gold guineas were issued and were in use, but there was no law fixing the price or value of the gold coin; and the guinea, which was originally supposed to be equal to 20*s.* in silver, circulated at the value in silver which the people chose to give for it, and rose in value as the value of gold rose.

In the early years of William III.'s reign the silver coins had become clipped and defective to the extent of nearly half their weight; prices at home and exchanges abroad were thrown into confusion; the evil became insufferable; and at last, under the guidance of Montagu and by the advice of Locke, the old silver coinage was called in and good silver coins were issued, at a loss to the nation of about £3,000,000. It was expected, on the faith of theories which, taken by themselves, were perfectly sound, that things would return to their previous condition; that silver, being the money of account of the country, or, as we should term it, legal tender, would resume its place; and that the gold coin, to which no definite value was attached by law, and which was not legal tender for the payment of debts, would circulate, if at all, at a price in silver corresponding to the value of gold in the market. But none of these things happened. The newly-coined silver was exported; little or no fresh silver was brought to the Mint to be coined; the gold guineas took the place of the silver coinage, and continued to circulate at a price, in silver, higher than the intrinsic or market value of the gold contained in them. They did this without any law fixing their value, and in spite of the law which made silver the legal tender and money of account. In spite of law, in spite of deficiency of intrinsic market value, people preferred the gold coins, and kept to them. The guinea had become a token coin, not by law, but by habit and inclination. Lord Liverpool says (p. 92):—

> "The high rate of the gold coins to which the people then "voluntarily submitted can only be ascribed to the preference "which at that time began to be given to the use of gold coins in "all payments, at least of considerable amount. It is evident "that during the late re-coinage the common people had become "accustomed to the use of the gold coins, and the reason which "induced them still to prefer them was, perhaps, the convenience "of making large payments in coins of that metal. This change "from what had been the case in the reign of Charles II. was "probably owing to the great increase in the commerce of the "country, and to an augmentation in the price of every commodity, "so that payments in general required coins made of the most "valuable metals. The fact certainly is that from this period the "gold coins began to take the ascendency, and to become the more "usual instrument of commerce and measure of property, in pre-"ference to the silver coins. In the reign of King William, when "the silver coins were so very deficient, Mr. Locke had said:—'It is "'no wonder if the prices and value of things be confounded and "'uncertain when the measure itself is lost.' To restore this "measure the public had expended £2,700,000. But, notwith-"standing so great an expense, this measure of property in the "lapse of a very few years was a second time lost, and had again "no existence unless it had passed into the gold coin."

In this state of things the Government of George I., on the advice of Sir Isaac Newton, determined to fix by law

Mr. T. H. Farrer.

the value of the gold guinea, wishing apparently to prevent the exportation of the silver coin. They did not, however, reduce it from 21*s.* 6*d.*, the then current value, to 20*s.* 6*d.*, the actual value, but only to 21*s.*, leaving it still above the market value of the coin in silver. The effect was to confirm the tendency of the people to pay in gold coins, and gold has ever since, by law as well as habit, been the current money of the country. Silver coins ceased to be used in large transactions; various statutes, commencing in 1774, deprived it of its character of legal tender, except for payments of small amount, and it was ultimately reduced to its present condition of a token coinage.

The interesting point in this history is to see that we have obtained our present gold coinage, not by law, but to a great extent in spite of law; that law was powerless to force upon the country a currency which it did not want, but all-powerful when it followed and stereotyped the practice of a people; that this practice was suggested by motives of convenience and inclination differing from and counteracting the motives which arose from a mere consideration of market values; and that, even in such a matter as currency, speculations founded on the effect of law, or even on mere considerations of value, have been and are likely to be at fault unless corrected by a careful consideration of special wants and circumstances.

Political economists ought to be well satisfied with these results. They illustrate and confirm the position that the value of coined money is, like that of other things, a question of supply and demand; and it depends on human wants and habits; and that if law is to be effectual, it must follow and consult these wants and habits; in other words, that the value of gold and silver money is at bottom "natural," just as other values are natural.

These words will not have been useless if they call attention to Lord Liverpool's celebrated letter, republished last year by the Governors of the Bank. The way in which he collects and states actual facts before generalizing from them, and in which he corrects logical deductions by reference to experience, may well afford a valuable lesson to many modern economists, and especially to those advocates of currency reform who appear to think that they have solved a practical question when they have stated it in the clear and definite form of an algebraical problem, and who prophesy the results of their schemes with as much confidence as if they were getting out the values of x and y. What the effects of bimetallism would really be I will not venture to say, but I will venture to say that they are much more doubtful than its advocates suppose.

F.

(T. H. FARRER.)

To the Editor of *The Times*.—May 26, 1881.

SIR,—Your correspondent "F.," in *The Times* of yesterday, says that the value of gold and silver money is at bottom natural, as other values are natural, and that it depends, not on law, but on wants and habits.

Permit me to observe that the facts quoted by him in proof of his statement really turn against him. "F." says:—

> "The Government of George I., on the advice of Sir Isaac "Newton, determined to fix by law the value of the gold guinea, "wishing to prevent the exportation of silver coin. They did not, "however, reduce it from 21*s.* 6*d.*, the then current value, to "20*s.* 6*d.*, the actual value, but only to 21*s.*, leaving it still above "the market value of the coin in silver."

Now, this so-called market value was nothing else than the legal ratio between gold and silver on the Continent.

Had the reduction to 20*s.* 6*d.* been made, the exportation of silver would have been prevented and international bimetallism established. Sir Isaac Newton thoroughly explained this matter (see Cobbett's *Parliamentary History*, vol. vii., 525). The habit of the people as regards coins is nothing else than the inevitable result of a monometallic legislation, or of a difference of ratio between the national bimetallic legislation and a foreign one.

I am, Sir, yours obediently,

HENRI CERNUSCHI.

7, Avenue Velasquez, Parc Monceau,
Paris, *May* 22.

To the Editor of *The Times.*—May 26, 1881.

SIR,—A writer in *The Times* of Saturday, who appends the signature "F." to his very able letter, attacks what he apparently conceives to be a position of the bimetallists—that, whereas it is the use of certain metals as money which gives them their value, and whereas it is the Government which says what shall constitute money, it is the action of Government which gives money its value. But where is the bimetallist who has said that the value of certain metals springs entirely from their use as money?

It is true that the use of a metal as money, like any other use which may be discovered for it, gives additional value to that metal, but, speaking as a bimetallist, I deny that the money-metals have no value but what the action of Government gives. But it is true that the greater part of the value of νομισμα (money) is given it by νομος (law), to which it, as Aristotle says, both etymologically and actually owes its origin.

It is, as Aristotle again says, consent which establishes its use as money, and law springing from consent. And this is, in fact, the gist of "F.'s" historical argument. Consent, he says, in King William's reign made gold the money of common use in England, and law, beginning in King George's reign, ratified that consent.

In "F.'s" statement, again, that "the value of gold and "silver money is natural, just as other values are natural," I fully agree. What, then, is the value of silver, for instance, as measured in gold? That which the market price demonstrates? Yes, the value at any given moment, but not the value in the abstract.

What really defines the value of the commodity silver as expressed in the money gold is the cost of production (expressed, for convenience, in terms of that money). But has the cost of production—the real cost, the labour at the mines, altered since 1872, so that the cost of the mass of silver is absolutely less than it was when the market price of the metal was 60*d.* an ounce? Not, I think, in any appreciable degree.

It may be said, and truly, that by the demonetization of silver a vast mass of the metal has been "produced"—as really produced as if, silver not having been demonetized, a vast increase of mine-yield—such an increase as was vainly predicted of the Comstock Mine—had taken place. So, by this means, the cost of production of the mass is appreciably less.

That is very true; but the increased mine-yield would be permanent and substantial; the increase caused by throwing some of the stock of silver out of work is of a very different character. Demonetization has produced it; remonetization of the metal would in one moment undo what had been done—would un-produce the additional stock; and then the true measure of the decrease (if any) in the money value of the commodity silver would be the addition to the mass made by the late discoveries in

America, an addition of no moment when compared with the quantity of the pre-existing mass.

I quite admit "F.'s" suggestion that no agreement between Governments and no law promulgated by any Government for the adoption of a double standard of value can so far affect the matter as to prevent people from making separate bargains to be paid in this or that preferred metal. But, as he shows, it is not the market value (however clearly proved) existing before such an agreement or such a law which would determine its acceptance by the people, and my contention is that, even if there had been some insignificant difference in market value between the two metals, people would soon be tired of making stipulations which would prove of no real advantage to them, and that convenience would soon produce that consent which is necessary for permanence.

It suits, indeed, the argument of the writer of the Money Article in *The Times* of the 7th inst. in his comments on an able letter signed "B." to assume that those who advocate the double standard contend that it is the arbitrary will of princes which gives value to money, and "F.," in his present letter, seems, as I have said, moved to combat some such imagination. But "B.'s" letter said no such thing, nor does any one else so far as I know.

What I have asserted above is, that the use of silver as money gives additional value to the stock of that metal in existence, just as the use of wool for clothing gives additional value to the stock of wool in existence. If man were suddenly endowed by nature with a coat of fur, the demand for woollen clothing would diminish and the market value of wool would fall. So if another substance —gold—is found more suitable to serve as money than silver is, the demand for silver diminishes and the value of silver falls, and the more so if its value is measured in that metal—gold—of which, by the hypothesis, the value has risen in proportion as the demand has increased.

That demand is the immediate creation of consent and law (though springing from intrinsic qualities existing, or supposed to exist, in the metals), and it cannot, therefore, be denied that consent and law—sometimes, as "F." shows, consent without and even in spite of law—give value to the commodity; but that differs widely from the belief which the above-mentioned Money Article in *The Times* attributes to "B."—"that the value of the metals used as "money is wholly artificial and dependent on the will of "Governments."

In *The Times* of to-day, again, the writer of the Money Article uses the same kind of method in combating a belief which he attributes to bimetallists, that the adoption of their system will make prices steady. I am not aware that any bimetallist has expressed such a belief. The use of silver and gold as money cannot influence the cost of production of the commodities which they have to measure, and cannot, therefore, make their prices steady or otherwise. What bimetallists assert is that, so far, and only so far, as prices of commodities depend on the greater or less quantity of the mass of money in the world they will be steadier (as Mr. Jevons, himself no bimetallist, clearly shows in his *Money and Mechanism of Exchange*, p. 138) when two metals form the measure of value than when one forms it.

Yours faithfully,

CHRYSARGYROS.

(HENRY H. GIBBS.)

May 23.

To the Editor of *The Times.*—May 27, 1881.

SIR,—M. Cernuschi draws strange conclusions from my facts. I showed that when the Government attached no value to gold, and did all that a Government could do, by law and by good coinage, to attach value to silver, the people of this country rejected the silver and kept the gold, though they had to pay a fancy price for it; and, further, that the law was then made to follow this practice of the people, by attaching to gold a greater proportionate value than to silver, and that it was then, and not till then, obeyed.

M. Cernuschi draws the conclusion that if the Government, instead of following the practice of the people, had attached a higher value to silver, the law would have been obeyed, English people would have kept their silver, and England would now be a bimetallist country.

My conclusion, if I were to draw one, would be that if the Government had done as M. Cernuschi suggests they might have done, the English people would have disregarded the law, would have rejected the silver, and would have kept the gold, even if they had had to pay an agio for it.

But I am not strong in "would have beens." The object of my letter was to draw attention from the "would "be's" and "must be" of which, it seems to me, many bimetallists are too fond, and to direct attention to what "has been" and what "is."

F.

(FARRER.)

May 26.

To the Editor of *The Times.*—May 28, 1881.

SIR,—In the very able letters of "F." in your Saturday's issue and of "Chrysargyros" in your issue of to-day there is some misapprehension of the way in which gold became the sole legal tender in this country, which I request you to allow me to correct.

Both writers seem to think that gold became sole legal tender by law in the reign of George I. This, however, is an error.

The real facts are these. Both gold and silver were unlimited legal tender in the beginning of the last century. Guineas were current at 21*s.* 6*d.* But the ratio of the English Mint being different from the ratio of foreign countries great disturbance ensued. On the question being referred to Sir Isaac Newton, he showed that the true value of the guinea was 20*s.* 8*d.* But in December, 1717, the guinea was fixed at 21*s.*; and then, in the language of the Mint, the price of gold was fixed at £3 17*s.* 10½*d.* per ounce.

Gold and silver continued equally unlimited legal tender; but gold, being thus overrated by 4*d.* on the guinea, was gradually adopted by mercantile custom (not law) as the understood medium of payment in the course of the last century. Silver being underrated by law, in accordance with what is now recognized as Gresham's law, all the good silver was exported, and none but worn, clipped, and degraded coin remained in circulation. This became so intolerable that in 1774 an Act was passed limiting legal tender of silver to £25. And so the law remained till the great re-coinage in 1816, when silver, which was then coined as a token, was further reduced to 40*s.* as legal tender.

I regret to see that "Chrysargyros" still sticks to the exploded cost of production theory of value. Nothing can be more erroneous. To show its fallacy, it is only necessary to state the well-known fact that even inconvertible paper may be maintained at the value of gold, if only it is rigorously limited in quantity. In 1874 the inconvertible notes of the Bank of France circulated at par with coin. How could this be if their value depended on cost of production? Value depends purely on intensity of demand and limitation of supply.

Your obedient Servant,

H. D. MACLEOD.

Oxford and Cambridge Club,
May 26.

To the Editor of *The Times.*—June 1, 1881.

SIR,—In his second letter "F." contends that in reducing the legal silver valuation of the gold guinea to 21*s.* the Government in 1717 did all that a Government could do. I cannot agree to this. Why could not the same Government reduce the silver value of the guinea to the point suggested by Sir Isaac Newton, the point which would have established in England the same legal ratio between silver and gold as on the Continent, and thus prevented all temptation, as Newton had said, of importing or exporting one metal rather than the other?

"F." thinks that English people would reject silver and prefer to keep gold even if they had to pay an agio for it. I answer, England possesses 30 millions of gold sovereigns lying permanently in the banks of England, Scotland, and Ireland, and 30 millions in the hands of the public, together with 20 millions of debased silver coin. People's habits are the same in England as in France.

In both countries the small payments are made with silver, gold, and notes, the large with notes, cheques, and clearances, without handling any metal. When international bimetallism is adopted by England there will be in the Bank of England, side by side, gold bars and silver bars, the latter to be the first employed for paying all foreign countries except Scandinavia and Portugal. But no change will be imposed on people's habits. The bimetallic reform will not even be visible to the naked eye.

Paid in specie or by cheque, money is not received to be kept, but to be spent immediately, or to be credited in the banker's books. Nobody consents to pay, nobody dreams of asking, an agio above the level par either on gold or silver, if not induced to do so by a foreign monetary legislation different from his own.

Yours obediently,

HENRI CERNUSCHI.

7, Avenue Velasquez, Parc Monceau,
Paris, *May* 29.

To the Editor of *The Times*.—June 2, 1881.

SIR,—Mr. Macleod, in *The Times* of last Saturday, attributes to me the opinion that gold became sole legal tender by law in the reign of George I. This is, however, not what I said.

What I said was that gold was not legal tender at all in the reigns of James II. and William III., because there was at that time no law fixing the value of gold coins in silver, which was the money of account; that gold coins circulated, to use Lord Liverpool's words, as a commodity;

that, notwithstanding this, the gold coins were given and taken by the people at a fancy price, and silver was expelled; and that the law became effectual only when it followed the habits of the people, and fixed the value of the gold coin in silver at a rate corresponding to those habits. I am quite aware that silver, which had always been unlimited legal tender, remained so until 1774. It was expelled from circulation, first by the practice of the people, and afterwards by the change in the law made on the advice of Sir Isaac Newton in the reign of George I., which followed and confirmed that practice. The law of 1774 and the subsequent laws which have limited the functions of silver as legal tender have still further followed and confirmed that practice, and are consequently effective. All these facts confirm my original position that the value of money is not artificially created by law, but it is natural in the sense in which other values are natural.

M. Cernuschi's letter in your paper of to-day (June 1) calls for no reply from me. I have been dealing with what "has been," not with what "would be."

F.

(FARRER.)

June 1.

THE DOUBLE STANDARD.*

FROM THE RIGHT HON. EARL GREY, K.G.,
TO MR. H. R. GRENFELL.

HOWICK,
May 31, 1881.

DEAR MR. GRENFELL,—

I have just been reading the pamphlet by Mr. Gibbs on *The Double Standard*, with an introduction by yourself, and I should feel much obliged to you if you would consider the following remarks which it has suggested to me.

Mr. Gibbs has, I think, succeeded in showing that the existing arrangements restricting the use of silver as an instrument of exchange are even now a source of great inconvenience to the whole commercial world, and threaten to produce still more serious evils unless some change should be made in them. But while I concur to this extent with Mr. Gibbs and yourself, I must confess that I cannot believe that the inconvenience he describes could be cured by the means he recommends of establishing a Double Standard of value by the consent of the principal commercial nations of the world. Mr. Gibbs admits the force of the objections to the adoption of a Double Standard of value by a single nation, which since the days of Locke have been generally

* Correspondence between the Right Hon. Earl Grey, K.G., and H. R. Grenfell, Esq., Governor of the Bank of England.

recognized as insurmountable, but he urges that these objections to the system would not apply if it were adopted as generally as he desires. His argument in support of this view of the subject is exceedingly ingenious, but without attempting to answer it in detail I must say that it does not appear to me to be satisfactory. I cannot believe that any agreement among nations, however general it might be, or any laws they could make to give effect to it, could prevent the relative value of gold and silver from being determined by the supply and demand, and ultimately by the cost of producing the two metals. If both were made equally available by law for the discharge of debts, that which was at the moment obtainable at the least cost would be chosen by debtors to meet their obligations. This would not happen the less because the mode in which the cheapest metal would be made to supersede the other would be somewhat complicated, and the result would in the end be the same in the whole body of nations united by the proposed agreement, as in the case of a single nation, though they would not, perhaps, be arrived at so quickly. If there should be an increase in the quantity of either gold or silver produced annually, together with a diminution in the cost of producing it, I can see nothing in the plan proposed by Mr. Gibbs which could prevent the metal which had thus become the cheapest from being brought in increasing quantities to the mints of the various nations included in his proposed union, and thus gradually bringing down the value of the circulation in them all to the level determined by the greater cheapness of one of the metals.

Inconvenience would thus arise from having a Double Standard, even if, in the first instance, the relative values assigned by law to gold and silver coins were accurately adjusted to the natural prices of the two metals in the markets of the world. But far more serious difficulties must be anticipated if the various nations that are to be parties to the proposed agreement are freely to open their mints, as Mr. Gibbs desires, for coining both gold and silver into coins which are to be a legal tender in payment of all debts, while the value assigned to silver coins is to be far higher than that borne in the market by the bullion they contain. Should this arrangement be sanctioned by Parliament, every person would be entitled to carry as much silver as he pleased to the English mint, and to receive it back in coins of which 15 pounds and a half in weight would be a legal tender in payment of the sum represented by one pound weight of our present gold coinage. But we are told by Mr. Gibbs that at the present price of silver the intrinsic value of these coins would be 15 per cent. less than the sum for which they would be a legal tender; that is to say, all debtors would have the right of paying their creditors in a currency which, if the price of silver remained unaltered, would be worth 15 per cent. less than that in which their debts had been contracted.

Of course it is not intended by Mr. Gibbs that such a gross injustice should be committed, and if I rightly understand him, he trusts that it would be averted by the effect the arrangement he proposes would have in making the comparative values of gold and silver correspond in fact with those assigned to them by law, so that it would become immaterial to those to whom money is now due whether they receive it in gold or in silver. I am not prepared to admit that even if the expectations of Mr. Gibbs on this point should be realized, the change he recommends could be introduced without injustice unless some further provision were made for the protection of existing interests. I acknowledge that so long as the existing standard of value is maintained unaltered, any regulations having for their object to economize the use of gold and thus limit its value, might be introduced without giving any claim for compensation to those to whom money is due, but it would be a very different matter to make silver a measure of value concurrently with gold.

Mr. Gibbs holds that if this were done in the manner he recommends, gold and silver coins would be enabled to circulate together at the relative values he would assign to them, partly by a rise in the value of silver, partly by a fall in that of gold, which he anticipates as a consequence of the measure, so that the general value of the metallic circulation of the world would be established at a rate intermediate between the higher or the lower one it would bear, if gold on the one hand, or silver on the other, were to become the accepted medium of exchange at their present prices. Should this anticipation prove correct, would not an injustice be inflicted on creditors by requiring them to accept payment of what is owed to them in a currency thus depreciated, even though they might still be able to obtain the same weight of gold coins they could have claimed before? Without, however, dwelling upon this point, I have to remark that it would be unsafe to rely on the expected rise in the price of silver in consequence of its having the character of money available for paying all debts conferred upon it by most of the commercial nations of the world. Probably the first effect of that change would be to raise the value of silver, but whether to the extent expected by Mr. Gibbs is uncertain, and it is still more uncertain whether such a stimulus might not be given to the production of silver that the supply would speedily become equal to the increased demand, and bring back its price to the present level. Mr. Gibbs, in a very ingenious and elaborate argument, endeavours to show that there is no reason for entertaining any apprehension on this score, and says that "the words 'price' and 'value' "are misapplied in describing the mutual relation of the "metals forming together one metallic standard of value, "that is to say, forming inseparable parts of one monetary "system." I will not attempt to follow Mr. Gibbs through this argument, but I would ask him whether he doubts that the command which money, whether it be of silver or of

Earl Grey,

gold, has over commodities is in the end determined by the greater or less abundance of the metal and the cost of its production? He clearly agrees in the received opinion that the value of silver or of gold in the market of the world determines the value of the currency of every nation which adopts the one or the other as its standard, and that this value depends in the first instance upon the proportion between the demand for the metal and its supply. But unless I misunderstand his argument he does not equally admit that ultimately the supply, and therefore the value of the metal, will be regulated by the cost of producing it. Yet surely it must be so, since according to the return they yield, a greater or a less amount of labour and of capital will be applied to the production of the precious metals. We continually hear of enterprises in gold and silver mining being abandoned because they do not pay; no doubt a rise in the value of the metal produced would enable some of them to go on and thus maintain the rate of production. Variations in the price of silver are known greatly to affect the extent to which it is worked, and with regard to gold, though its *price* cannot alter in this country since it is itself the measure of value, variations in its value may and do take place with a like result. If gold becomes scarcer and more valuable, the prices in gold of other things (including labour) must fall and diminish the cost of producing it. On the other hand, an increased abundance of gold diminishes its value,—in other words, raises the price of everything else. In the last 30 years these effects of variations in the supply of gold have been well exemplified in Australia. When the gold diggings first grew into prosperity, wages and all articles of consumption rose there to extravagant rates, which necessarily increased the cost of producing gold, and tended to limit the quantity produced. Afterwards, when the exhaustion of some of the richest diggings, and the flow of gold to other places, had corrected its local excess, its value on the spot was reduced, that is, wages and prices in general became lower, reducing the cost of production, and checking the decrease of this branch of industry.

For these reasons I must adhere to the opinion so long and generally maintained by the highest authorities, though now as it seems rejected by Mr. Gibbs, that the value both of silver and of gold, whether in the form of coin or bullion, ultimately depends on the cost of producing them. It is true that variations in that cost do not cause rapid fluctuations in the value of these metals because they are so durable, and the total mass of them available in the world at any one time is so large as compared with the produce of a single year, that it is a good while before a reduction in the cost of producing either metal, and an increase in the amount produced, can cause any sensible variation in its value as compared to the other, or to commodities in general. Still it is proved by experience that variations in the supply and in the cost of producing the precious metals do sooner or later tell upon their value. Such being the case it is at least not impossible that if, as Mr. Gibbs recommends, all the great commercial nations were to concur in passing laws assigning to silver as money a higher value than the metal now commands in the market, this measure instead of producing the effect he anticipates of enabling gold and silver to circulate together at the rates proposed, might give such a stimulus to the production of silver as to increase the supply as much or more than the demand, and leave its value as compared to gold, the same as it now is. This I contend is at least a possible result of the change of system recommended by Mr. Gibbs, and it would therefore be unjust to pass a law compelling those to whom money is due to accept payment in silver coins at the rate of 15½ pounds of these coins for every pound weight of sovereigns they are now entitled to. Mr. Gibbs seems to feel this, for he says (p. 50) that he "presumes the law "would provide that debts or other payments falling due "under contracts dated before the law came into operation "might be demanded in gold." Such a provision would undoubtedly be necessary, but has Mr. Gibbs considered that it must include all payments of interest on the national debt, and on the enormous sums lent on mortgage or on other securities, and what confusion must arise from issuing silver coins which would be a legal tender in settling recent transactions, but would not possess that character with regard to the vast mass of older ones? It seems to me impossible that Parliament should be persuaded to create such confusion for the sake of abolishing a monetary system which has worked well for many years, in order to substitute for it one which is untried and apparently dangerous.

I therefore regard the arrangement recommended by Mr. Gibbs as impracticable, but I concur with him (as I have already said) as to the importance of the object it was intended to accomplish, nor do I see any reason for assuming that some better means of effecting it might not be discovered. Mr. Gibbs believes that unless something is done to check the prevailing tendency towards an increased use of gold, this metal will more and more supersede silver, and become the chief instrument of exchange for nations, both in their internal trade and in their commerce with each other. He also believes that the supply of gold will be insufficient to meet the demand thus created for it, that its price will consequently rise, or in other words the price of all commodities in gold will fall, and that great commercial difficulties must ensue. So far as I am aware no successful attempt has been made to answer the arguments advanced by Mr. Gibbs in support of these conclusions, and if they are accepted as correct, it follows that he must also be right in contending that it is desirable that silver should be used to a greater extent than it seems likely to be as an aid to gold in carrying on the transactions of commerce. The question then arises whether it would not be possible to secure this advantage by some arrangement that would be free from the objections to which the scheme of Mr. Gibbs is open? My object in writing this letter is to ask you to consider whether, so far as our own country is concerned, this might not be accomplished by a very simple change in our monetary system, involving no departure whatever from its principles.

By the existing law a part of the bullion which the Bank is required to hold as against its issues of notes may be silver. But as this silver cannot be used in payment of its notes it is of little real use. I would ask what valid objection there would be to providing that when notes are presented to the Bank for payment in sums exceeding £500 the Bank should be at liberty to make the payment one-half in sovereigns, the other half in silver, coined or uncoined, at the market price of the day; while it should also be authorized to keep in silver instead of in gold one-half of the bullion against which it is entitled to issue notes? There would be no difficulty in finding some trustworthy authority to ascertain and declare the market price of silver which should be regularly published in the *Gazette*, as the price of corn used to be to determine the duty payable upon it, while the sliding scale was in force. The *Gazette* price of silver published twice a week in the *Gazette* would in like manner determine the rate at which silver would be received or given by the Bank in exchange for its notes.

You will perceive that the alteration in the law I have suggested would be merely the adoption, with modifications, to make it suit the circumstances of the present day, of the plan long ago proposed by Ricardo for a "Secure and Economic Currency." I would remind you (though it is hardly necessary to do so) that in his admirable pamphlet on this subject, he has shown the value of paper money issued by the authority of the State to depend upon its amount as compared to the wants of the State in which it circulates. No one, I believe, now doubts this to be true,

Earl Grey.

and experience has proved that inconvertible paper-money will circulate not only without depreciation, but even at a premium, if the issues are sufficiently limited. Ricardo also explained that the real use of insisting upon the convertibility of paper-money, is to secure that its amount like that of a metallic currency should be self-regulated by the action of the exchanges, and that this object would be equally attained whether the paper-money were convertible into bullion or into coin. On the same principle, I hold that silver taken at the market price of the day might be used in conjunction with gold as the basis of our paper circulation without in the slightest degree disturbing its value. Large amounts in notes are usually presented to the Bank for payment less with the view of using the sovereigns received for them at home than for exportation, because the state of the exchanges makes a remittance of gold abroad profitable; and the practical effect of demands of this sort upon the Bank is to contract its paper circulation and thus maintain its value. Precisely the same results would follow if notes presented for payment in large sums were paid as I have suggested, partly in gold and partly in silver at the market price. The dealers in money would receive in exchange for the notes they carried to the Bank gold and silver (the last having been received at the market price would, if necessary, be converted into gold, though this could seldom be required) for remittance abroad, and the circulation of the Bank would be contracted exactly as it now is. The money in ordinary use would still consist of small silver, of sovereigns, and of Bank notes, the value of the latter being maintained in the same way as at present.

I have suggested that the rule of making the notes of the Bank payable half in silver and half in gold should only apply when considerable sums were presented for payment. When the demand came from money dealers, in consequence of the state of the exchanges, small sums would not be asked for, and it would be inconvenient that bankers and other traders, who require sovereigns for carrying on their business, should be compelled to accept silver bullion for part of the notes they might present at the Bank for payment. Probably it might be convenient to name a larger sum than I have mentioned above as that which should give the Bank the right of paying partly in silver. The point, however, is not one of much consequence, for the Bank, if asked to give sovereigns for the whole amount of notes brought to it for payment, would seldom refuse the request, if there were good reasons for making it.

The arrangement I have now suggested would be free from all risk of producing the inconveniences I believe to be inseparable from any attempt to maintain a double standard of value; yet it could hardly fail, even if adopted by England only, to be of considerable service in averting the difficulties which are now feared with respect to the employment of silver as a medium of exchange. The advantage would of course be much greater if this system should be adopted by other nations as well as ourselves, as it probably would be if we set the example. The Monetary Conference, now being held in Paris, proves how strongly the nations that invited it to assemble feel the inconvenience of the present state of things. If they should fail, as they most likely will, in gaining the general assent required for trying the experiment of a Double Standard, it may therefore reasonably be expected that they would agree to a measure of which the general adoption would be at least a step in the direction they desire to move in, and which would afford no small part of the facilities they think are wanting for the use of silver in making payments among nations. Some countries would find additional motives for introducing the proposed change in circumstances peculiar to themselves. Thus, in France, it is well known that the Bank is encumbered by having a large stock of five-franc pieces

Earl Grey.

which it is at a loss what to do with, since it cannot use them at their nominal value to pay its notes without depreciating the currency. Making them available for this purpose, at the market price of the silver they contain, would render the large capital locked up in these coins again available to the Bank. If it were at the same time provided by law that silver should be a legal tender only for sums not exceeding 50 francs, the circulation of France would be placed on the same footing as our own. The United States and Italy might derive perhaps even greater advantage from acting on the same principle, since it would enable them to dispense with the adoption of measures for substituting gold coins for the paper circulation they are now actually using. The "greenbacks" of the United States are now equal in value to gold, and seem to be accepted in that country as convenient in the transaction of business. If a law were passed requiring the Government to give these notes to all who applied for them in exchange for gold, or for silver at the market price of the day, and also to take them back in return for gold coin and silver bullion in equal proportions, when presented for payment, the country would continue to enjoy the convenience which has arisen from the use of the greenbacks, while the value of the currency would be self-regulated by the exchanges, precisely as if there were a purely metallic circulation.

To Italy the gain would be still greater. That kingdom is about to raise a large loan to meet the cost of substituting gold coins for its present paper-money. Why should this burthen be incurred when the paper-money now in circulation might be made, by the means I have pointed out, to perform all the functions of a metallic currency, with the same security against mischievous fluctuations in its value, and without expense? Though the financial situation of Italy has been wonderfully improved, and the nation deserves high praise for the sacrifices it has submitted to for the purpose of effecting this improvement, all must agree that the burthens pressing upon the people are so heavy that it is most desirable to relieve them from every unnecessary charge. But if gold coins are to be substituted for paper all over Italy, a large capital will have to be provided by the State to supply these coins, and the interest upon this capital, which will yield no return, will be a charge on the national revenue. If, as I believe, the paper-money now in circulation could be given the same steadiness of value which belongs to a gold currency, it would surely be far better for a nation, which has such urgent demands for all the capital it can command for many important improvements that would increase its resources, to avoid the unproductive employment of capital in using for its ordinary business so costly a medium of exchange as gold, instead of the cheap one of a well-regulated paper currency. At the same time, if the statesmen of Italy think it expedient to adhere to their intention of providing a gold circulation for the country, the adoption of the arrangement I have suggested would not impede but would, on the contrary, facilitate their doing so.

Pray excuse me for troubling you with these suggestions, but, from so long ago as the time of the discussions which followed the panic of 1825, I have taken much interest in the subject of our currency, and I confess that I now observe with regret that what I regard as the very unsound doctrines on which the scheme of Mr. Gibbs is founded, are apparently beginning to be received with more favour than formerly, and that the scheme itself has obtained the powerful support of your approval.

Believe me,

Yours very faithfully,

GREY.

H. R. Grenfell, Esq.

FROM MR. H. R. GRENFELL TO THE RIGHT HON. EARL GREY, K.G.

BANK OF ENGLAND,
9th June, 1881.

DEAR LORD GREY,—

The objections which Locke felt to be insurmountable in a Double Standard, arose from the certainty that a country with such a standard would inevitably be left with the cheaper metal.

Cernuschi, the apostle of the new creed, declares that France, notwithstanding that objection, gained by the system. Mr. Gibbs, in his pamphlet, neither admits nor denies the inconvenience to a single nation of being bimetallic. He admits that certain effects were produced, and that those effects are stated by one set of men to be evil, by others to be good. He then states that he does not accept Cernuschi's conclusion, or deny that there may be some considerable disadvantage, but doubts it to be so great as is commonly supposed. (Page 17.)

As you say, there would be nothing in the proposed plan to prevent "the cheapest metal from being brought in "increasing quantities to the mints of the various nations" —gradually bringing down the value of the circulation in them all. Neither is there now. When silver is the cheapest it goes to silver mints, and gold to gold mints, bringing down the value of the circulation in each. Under the proposed plan, the change of value would be over the world at large.

The proposed relative value at which the two metals are to be coined is, approximately, the one which was kept in force for the whole of the present century up to the demonetization of Germany. (See table, on page 27, from 1827, in Mr. Gibbs' pamphlet.)

With regard to the injustice, it is hard to see where it would be. All debtors are mulcted, to the same extent as it is now proposed to mulct creditors, simply by the change in Germany but eight years ago. Mr. Gibbs does not say that gold and silver would in any currency circulate together. He says that in gold-using countries gold would still be used, and silver in silver.

Then as to the relative price being brought back again to its present state by the extra demand for silver, Mr. Gibbs' contention is that there could not be any other relative price than the legal one, because to suppose otherwise would be to state that a full-weight sovereign could have any other value than a sovereign.

He does not doubt that command of money over commodities is determined by the greater or less abundance; but he says that the variations of production would engender less important oscillation owing to the larger area which those variations would affect. There would be the effect produced by the alteration in the cost of production of gold and that produced by the alteration in that of silver, making the oscillation, perhaps, more frequent, but less violent. This is now admitted by the monometallists.

If gold cannot alter its price now in England, neither could silver or gold when bimetallic agreement was carried out. Neither did they when France enjoyed solitary bimetallism. What France did was to have its prevailing currency in the cheapest metal, but its price written in francs in France was the same as that of the dearer. The variation was in francs translated into rupees or pounds sterling.

At page 158, you say Mr. Gibbs admits that present contracts ought to be exempt; from what I have already said I think you will see that in this point I hardly concur myself with Mr. Gibbs. If such were really necessary I agree with you the arrangement would be impracticable.

I now come to your remedies: Sir Robert Peel, in

bringing in his Bank Act, permitted ⅕th of the whole bullion to be silver, leaving ⅘ths to be gold. He assigned as a reason "that a stock is convenient to our trade, and "that merchants often require that metal as a remittance." It is, however, a fact that since silver, on the discoveries of gold, became at the French mint price the rarer metal of the two, the Bank have never held any except on one occasion for a very short while. To have the power of paying one-half of the Bank's notes in silver, and to hold one-half of its bullion in that metal, would, I submit, be practically an admission of bimetallism; since, of course, this would only be done on condition of France and the United States agreeing to bimetallism. If France, being bimetallic, kept the prices so near to 15½, *a fortiori* would it if agreed with the United States; and then, although France and the United States might suffer either of the inconveniences already discussed, it is quite clear England would enjoy the advantage of both systems—her own monometallic gold system, and the fixity of the French bimetallic silver price. The question is, will France and the United States consent to pull the chestnuts out of the fire for us?

Ricardo's proposal is particularly discussed in Lord Liverpool's letter, in which he points out that coining would be unnecessary if all the one pound circulation in the country was in notes. It would be a useless expense since for all foreign remittances of bullion, bars would do just as well. Paper is just as convertible when a large stock can be exchanged by large bullion merchants for bars for export, as if one five pound note can be exchanged for small milled discs with the Queen's superscription on them. This I think would, however, raise a separate question.

It appears to me then that your proposition would be nothing more nor less than bimetallism. You qualify it by saying "at the price of the day;" but the price of the day would be the mint price of France and the United

States. It is true that you speak of it as adopted by England only, but if other countries are suffering from the contraction of the favoured metal, and are expecting to suffer still more, then there cannot be a doubt that the very first effect of such a proposal would be the immediate adoption of the 15½ to 1 bimetallism by the two States who have convened the present congress.

The further contraction expected is from Italian resumption and American repeal of the Silver Coining Bill, which goes by the name of "The Bland Bill."

The finances of America, her wealth and prosperity, would enable her to repeal that Bill whenever she likes. A few owners of silver mines might suffer, but the remainder of the citizens not engaged in silver mining would be indifferent to the loss, while their vanity and ambition would be flattered by the notion of being important enough to have a gold currency. Their power to draw as much gold as they like from Europe is disputed by no one.

With regard to Italy the circumstances are somewhat different. But Italy is also actuated by a rage for being of importance in the world at large; and just as Bismarck altered the currency of Germany with a *cœur leger*, so an Italian statesman would be capable of it. Moreover they could raise a loan in England at a high price only if it were a gold loan. Therefore if bimetallism were not carried anywhere, they might have, out of self-defence, to make a gold standard as well as a gold loan.

The "well-regulated paper currency" you speak of, must have a metallic basis, and if so, Italy would have to get metal somewhere. The Latin Union arrangement lasts four years longer. By that she cannot coin more than a given amount of silver yearly; but with bimetallism she would at once use in her resumption of metallic payments a large portion of the Italian currency now lying in the

Bank of France which could not be better employed than in taking in her small note circulation.

I have endeavoured very hastily to answer your letter, but my views on this vexed question are expressed more clearly and at length in an article I have just contributed to the *Nineteenth Century*.

I remain,
Yours very faithfully,
H. R. GRENFELL.

The Earl Grey, K.G.

FROM THE RIGHT HON. EARL GREY, K.G.,
TO MR. H. R. GRENFELL.

Howick,
June 13, 1881.

Dear Mr. Grenfell,—

I am much obliged to you for your answer to my letter. I have read it with great interest, and also your article in the *Nineteenth Century*, which I was not aware that you had published when I wrote to you. I am now anxious to offer a very few rather desultory observations on one or two of the points you have touched upon in your letter and in your article.

In the first place, I do not think that either you or Mr. Gibbs sufficiently recognize what I believe to be the fact, that the relative values of gold and silver currencies will ultimately be determined by the comparative cost of producing the two metals, in spite of any laws which may be enacted (either by a single nation, or by several nations acting in concert) for the purpose of declaring what is to be considered the equivalent in one metal for a given weight of the other, and that either shall be a legal tender at the rates assigned to them. Changes in the comparative cost of producing the two metals will not immediately alter their relative values, for the reasons I mentioned in my former letter, but by degrees that which is most cheaply produced will become the cheapest in the market of the world, and drive the dearest out of circulation in a number of nations, just as it is admitted to do in a single nation.

You tell me that, supposing his plan to be adopted, "Mr. Gibbs does not say that gold and silver would in any "currency circulate together. He says that in gold-using "countries gold would still be used, and silver in silver." I cannot understand how this could be. In the present state of the world, and with the existing facilities for communication among nations, it appears to me that if the proposed arrangement were made, the metal which could be obtained at the smallest cost of labour and capital would be the only one sent to the mints of all the nations which had agreed to open their mints freely to both metals at a fixed rate; none of the other metal would be coined, and after a time the circulation would practically consist everywhere of the cheapest metal. Under the system of legal bimetallism has it ever happened that the two metals have really been both available as currency at the rates assigned to them by the law? I remember, as I think you must also, that formerly in France nobody ever received gold without paying for it. If one changed a circular note or a draft on London in Paris, one's banker always gave one for it either bank notes (of which in those days there were none for less than 500 francs) or a sack of 5-franc pieces. If one asked for gold one had to pay for it, generally, I think about 10 francs for 50 napoleons. In England, at one time, the case was reversed—the legal value of silver coins was lower than the market value of the silver they ought to have contained. The consequence was that they were clipped or melted down, and there were no silver coins of full weight in circulation; the currency practically consisted of guineas, with light silver for small change, gold being the real standard of value. Among the united nations, in the same manner, the cheapest metal, if both gold and silver were made legal tenders at a fixed rate, would drive out the other. If, therefore, the increased demand for silver (which would, of course, be at first created by the adoption of the plan of Mr. Gibbs) were so to stimulate the production of that metal that its relative abundance as compared to gold were restored, its value, as I observed in my first letter, must likewise fall back to what it now is in comparison with gold. The inevitable consequence would be that silver only would be taken to the mints of the united nations, sovereigns and 20-franc pieces would be melted down, and silver would become the general currency. Of course when silver became a legal tender in this country, the Bank of England must have the same right of using the new silver coins in paying its notes, as other persons would have as to the money they owed. This right would not be refused to the Bank, and would necessarily be used, for otherwise there would be a constant drain from the Bank of sovereigns, which it would be unable to replace, except by buying gold at its price in the market in order to issue it again at its legal rate. An end would thus be put to the circulation of sovereigns, and our circulation would be depreciated accordingly. Mr. Gibbs denies that this could happen, and contends that between gold and silver "there could not be any other relative price than "the legal one, because to suppose otherwise would be to "state that a full weight sovereign could have any other "value than a sovereign." I do not quite understand this argument, but I would ask why should a sovereign not bear a *higher* value in the market than its legal one? The napoleon in France 50 years ago was worth more than 20 francs; a hundred years ago a new British shilling was worth more than a shilling, and in both cases the result was that these coins were not received by creditors in payment of money due to them, and that a less valuable description of coins became the real standard of value. I can see no reason why in the same manner, under the proposed arrangement, gold coins should not disappear by degrees from the circulation of the united nations, if the comparative cost of producing the two metals should continue to be such that a given weight of silver could be produced by a smaller expenditure of capital and labour than the quality of gold for which it would be a legal equivalent. And we can have no assurance that this may not happen, or even that the comparative cost of silver might not fall still lower.

Mr. Gibbs will, I am sure, admit that it is not the law but the intrinsic value of the metal they contain that determines the value of coins, as has been very clearly proved by the result of a diminution of the weight or purity of the metal contained in their coins to which nations have so often had recourse for relief from financial difficulties. Nor will it, I think, be disputed that the intrinsic value of gold arises from the great demand there is for it for other purposes besides coinage, and from the cost of producing it. This value has been, and I believe would be again under the proposed arrangement, sufficiently high to prevent gold coins from circulating.

You say that the measure I have suggested would be practically an admission of bimetallism. No doubt it would be so in this sense, that it would make silver as well as gold available as an instrument of exchange among nations. But it would be directly opposed to bimetallism, as the word is commonly understood, inasmuch as it would not attempt to establish two independent measures of value, but would on the contrary leave our existing standard of value altogether undisturbed. This last is a consideration of supreme importance; any tampering whatever with our

Earl Grey.

standard of value would work so much injustice, and would so entirely derange all private contracts, that it ought to be firmly resisted.

You assume that the measure I have suggested could only be adopted "on condition of France and the United "States agreeing to bimetallism." I cannot admit this to be the case: on the contrary, I hold that our action on this question ought to be entirely independent of what they may do. Neither this nor any other country can, without imprudence, make the regulation of its currency a matter of negotiation with other nations. Each nation should, without being trammelled by any agreement with another, keep itself free to deal with the subject as it may think fit. We ought therefore neither to bind ourselves by stipulations respecting our currency with other states, nor seek to obtain any from them. But whatever may be the policy of other nations, I believe that very great advantage would result from this country's making greater use of silver by accepting it at the market price of the day as the basis, in conjunction with gold, of our paper circulation. At the same time I am far from denying that as we have an interest in everything that tends to give increased facilities to the trade of the world, it would be for our advantage, as well as for their own, if other commercial nations were to follow the example I desire that we should set in this matter. And if we led the way I think it probable that they would follow, because it would be for their interest to do so. Suppose we were to take the course I have suggested, how would it affect France, and how would France be likely to act? As far as it went, our making more use of silver would clearly be of advantage to France, since it would tend to diminish the quantity of silver now pressing upon the market by creating a new demand for it. And what would France do? There seem to me only two courses she could reasonably take. She might determine to maintain her existing law (thus allowing both gold and silver to continue to be legal tenders at their present rate), while at the same time she made this law effective by removing (as soon as she is free to do so) the existing restrictions upon the coining of silver. This would of course drive out gold from her circulation, and would be equivalent to a depreciation of her currency unless the price of silver should rise. But she has a strict legal right so to act, and I am not prepared to say that her creditors would have any ground to complain of injustice if she were thus practically to reduce the amount of her obligations and pay the interest of her debt in a currency of a lower value. Whether this would be for her real advantage is another question which I need not discuss. Or if she decided against adopting this course, she might so far demonetize silver as to make it no longer a legal tender at its present rate for large payments, declaring that gold should for the future be the standard of value. If she did this she would obviously incur a heavy loss by the depreciation of the silver coins now held by the Bank and by the nation. Now this loss and the inconvenience she would incur by making gold the basis of her circulation, would be greatly diminished by her adopting the same rule I have suggested for this country, of allowing bank notes to be paid in equal proportions in gold and in silver by weight at the current price of the day.

I cannot see any course which France could follow with any expectation of placing her currency upon a secure and permanent basis except one of these two. She might indeed go on for a time nominally maintaining the system of bimetallism, while it is really in abeyance, by declining to alter her law, but continuing to suspend the coinage of silver; but the inconvenience of this would be so great that before long she would practically be driven to choose between the two courses I have mentioned, and it would be entirely for herself to determine which she would adopt. To us it would be of comparatively little importance what her decision might be.

Similar reasoning would apply to the cases of the United States, of Germany, and of Italy. All these nations would find that our taking the course I have suggested would not only leave them perfectly free to choose the policy they might think best for themselves, but would tend to diminish the difficulties they may have to encounter whatever that policy may be. Our example might probably have a good deal of influence on their decision, but we have no business to interfere with it.

The question as to the use of £1 notes in this country is, as you say, quite a distinct one from that which I have been considering, and it is quite needless now to discuss it. I must, however, confess that I have never seen any reason for altering the opinion I formed at the time that the abolition of small notes after the panic of 1825 was a mistake. Notwithstanding the high authority of Huskisson on such a question, I thought then and I think still that no sufficient answer was given to the arguments against the conclusion he had come to which were urged in very able reviews that were published of the proceedings of the sessions of 1825 and 1826. But be this as it may, the country has so long been accustomed, and attaches so much importance to the use of sovereigns, while the expense of our gold currency is one that we can so well afford, that, although I believe it to be needless, I should not recommend any attempt to get rid of it. Nations in which small notes now form a principal part of the circulation, and where coin could only be substituted for these notes at a very heavy expense, stand in a very different position. In their circumstances it seems to me that the wisest course would be not to abolish small notes but to give them steadiness of value by making them convertible into bullion.

Yours very faithfully,

GREY.

H. R. Grenfell, Esq.

FROM MR. H. R. GRENFELL TO THE RIGHT HON. EARL GREY, K.G.

BANK OF ENGLAND,
17*th June*, 1881.

DEAR LORD GREY,—

Mr. Gibbs and I fully recognize that the value of the precious metals in relation to commodities will be determined by the cost of producing them, subject to the following qualification of that proposition:—

That in the case of consumable commodities, the yearly production being often greater than the existing stock at any moment, the effect of an alteration in cost of production is, comparatively speaking, immediate; while in the case of the precious metals, the annual production being so small a proportion of the existing stock, a falling off is scarcely felt.

With regard to the relative value, the same rule would hold good unless Governments step in and, by opening markets—that is mints—at a given fixed ratio, create a steadiness not otherwise attainable.

It is quite true that a napoleon in France 50 years ago bore a premium. But nobody paid the premium in order at once to pay away the napoleon for a debt. People paid their debts in that which would at once procure a release from them. A napoleon was an article of luxury as much as a comfortable carriage or a fast horse.

You are quite right in saying that there would be no reason why gold should not disappear from the circulation of the united bimetallic nations as it did from single ones, but where would it go?

Monometallists have suggested that if the United States, India, and Europe entered into the suggested monetary league, some outside nation, such as China, Japan, or Brazil, might take it into its head to erect a gold standard for the same reason which induced Germany to try it. But it would very soon prove, as it did in Germany, a most costly and ruinous operation.

Lord Liverpool says that a gold coinage is fitting for England on account of her commercial activity, not that her commercial activity and pre-eminence spring from her gold coinage or standard.

I now notice your objection that nations should not negociate with each other on such a subject.

It seems to me that if there is one subject more than another on which a good understanding ought to exist, it is in the value and measure of those commodities which by the agreement of all ages and nations are made the means of balancing international accounts. We have arrangements for lights at sea, for signals, for many other tools of commercial life, and why not for money? Such international regulations would not interfere with the right to make laws for interior currency.

I now return to your scheme for enabling the Bank to pay half its notes in silver above £500.

The objection which presents practical difficulties to my mind is that the person sending, say £10,000 of notes into the Bank, and receiving £5,000 in silver, would either want that silver or he would not. If he wanted the silver, the operation would be much the same as it is now. If he did not want it, he would send the silver back to the Bank for notes the next day, and he would be in the same position as the man who had got £5,000 gold for his notes under the present regulations.

You then ask what the effect of the alteration would be on France and Italy? Any alteration which did not entice the Latin Union and the United States to keep open their mints for silver would, in my opinion, be inoperative to "rehabilitate" that metal. I see then no other course possible but for all those nations to go to a gold standard and regard silver merely as a commodity useful for subsidiary coins, which the Monetary Conference of 1878 declared would be fraught with incalculable disasters to the commerce of the world.

With regard to the one-pound notes, the policy of returning to them depends on whether it would be economical to use paper instead of gold for those small amounts. Calculations have been made, and are now before me, showing that it costs more than 20*s.* to keep a £1 note in circulation with the regulations we now enforce as to registration, non-reissue, and forgery prosecutions. I confess I don't believe in the accuracy of these calculations.

My reason for preferring sovereigns is that a large amount of gold exists in the country in the pockets of the lieges, which, in case of war, such as in 1797, is a practical reserve which could be got at by suspension of cash payments.

I hope you will excuse this rather hurried answer to your most interesting letter.

I am,

Yours faithfully,

H. R. GRENFELL.

The Right Hon. Earl Grey, K.G.

FROM THE RIGHT HON. EARL GREY, K.G., TO MR. H. R. GRENFELL.

HOWICK,
June 24th, 1881.

DEAR MR. GRENFELL,—

I will not trouble you with any further arguments in reply to your last letter, but having had a good deal of conversation with Lord Halifax while I was at Hickleton on the subject of our correspondence, I write a few lines to tell you that I think he quite agrees with me in coming to the following conclusions:—

1st. That the objections to bimetallism are insurmountable; bimetallism being understood to mean a system under which the character of money is given to both silver and gold coins, and either at a fixed rate is made a legal tender in the payment of debts.

2nd. That the present standard of value in this country ought to be strictly maintained, and that no departure from it or from the principles of our existing monetary system ought to be made.

3rd. That if, in consequence of our determination to adhere to our present monetary system, France, the United States, Germany, and Italy, were to resolve that they also would maintain gold currencies, and should make such changes in their existing laws as to the use of silver as would be necessary to keep the gold coins they might issue in circulation, the demand for gold must be so increased as, for a time at least, materially to raise its value, and thus occasion much commercial embarrassment and very serious pressure on all branches of productive industry in most nations.

4th. That authorizing the Bank of England to use silver *at the market price* together with gold as the basis of its issues might avert this evil, by leading other nations to adopt similar arrangements, and would, at any rate, mitigate the evils that would arise from a great extension of the use of gold in the circulation of those countries, by diminishing the amount of gold required by England, and affording facilities for the employment of silver as an instrument of exchange between nations.

5th. That this measure would not involve the slightest departure from our present standard of value, or from the principles of our monetary system.

I do not gather from your letters that you would seriously dissent from any of these conclusions, except the first. And with respect to this (if I am not mistaken), in holding that bimetallism would be of advantage if the system could be adopted with the general assent of all the great commercial nations, you are aware that the assent of this country could not be obtained, and that without its concurrence the measure would be impracticable.

Such being the case, the suggestion I have offered with the view of averting, or, at all events, mitigating the evils to be apprehended from the course other nations may adopt in consequence of the determination of this country to abide by its present system of currency, seems to me to deserve to be at least fully considered.

I have been writing in such haste, to save the post, that I fear my letter will hardly be legible.

Yours very truly,

GREY.

From Mr. H. R. GRENFELL to the Right Hon. EARL GREY, K.G.

Bank of England,
28*th June*, 1881.

Dear Lord Grey,—

Without saying anything more on the subject of your three first conclusions, I merely desire to point out with reference to the fourth, that while your proposition gave the right to the Bank to pay its notes one half in silver at the price of the day, I could only assent, during the continued existence of the present standard of value, that it should hold a portion of its bullion in silver without infringing the right of all holders of notes to receive gold for them at all times.

I remain,

Very faithfully yours,

H. R. GRENFELL.

The Earl Grey, K.G.

WHAT IS MONEY?

From the *Nineteenth Century*, April, 1882.

The wisest course which can be taken with popular delusions is very often found to be to treat them like raging waves of the sea, and let them foam out their own shame. More especially is this the case when the delusion in question touches the verge of abstruse and difficult subjects, with which the mass of mankind are content not to meddle at all. Such has been to a great extent the treatment which has been experienced by the promoters of the doctrine and discipline of bimetalism. The answer appears to most minds so complete and so crushing, that it has been thought unnecessary to give it at any length. It was supposed by those who examined the subject that, like the mother of Sisera, it would make answer to itself. Too much confidence has perhaps been reposed in the doctrines inculcated by the standard writers on political economy and the success that has hitherto attended obedience to their advice, and too little allowance has been made for the power of fear and of interest to warp and obscure the clearest intelligence. Now, however, when we find the Governor of the Bank of England coming forward as a bimetalist, and recommending a general committee in order to promote the adoption of the double standard, and when we find the meeting at which this remarkable proposal was made presided over by a gentleman of the ability and authority of Mr. Cazalet, it is time to point out what certainly appear to be the gross and obvious objections to the admission of bimetalism in any shape and under any conditions. In accordance, I presume, with the suggestion of the Governor of the Bank of England, the *Bullionist* newspaper has been enlisted as the organ of bimetalism, and those who adhere to the doctrines of Smith, Ricardo, and Mill are put upon the defensive. It is not wise to trust entirely to great names and works that have been for a long time before the public; and even if little can be added to them that little should on no account be omitted, lest arguments which have hitherto appeared to be unanswerable should be supposed to have lost anything of their force.

Being anxious to inform myself as to the very latest phase of the doctrine and discipline of bimetalism, I have carefully perused the proceedings of the meeting in November last of persons interested in the silver question, most appropriately held at the India Office, where silver reigns supreme, in hopes to extract from their consultation a clear statement of what they desire, a complete explanation of what is meant by the highly ambiguous term of bimetalism, and a distinct description of the manner in which the union of the two metals, should it be effected, is expected and intended to work. I supposed that an assembly of so many able and experienced men, gathered together to take counsel on a subject with which they were all thoroughly conversant, could hardly separate without leaving behind them a perfectly clear and distinct outline of their proposals, and an equally clear and decisive answer to the difficulties and objections which might present themselves. Never was an expectation more delusive.

"The feeling (says the chairman) that appears generally to
"prevail among the public in connection with this question of
"bimetalism is, that bimetalists are prognosticating dangers and

"difficulties without any good and sufficient grounds for their doing "so. The question we have to deal with is not so complicated as "some people suppose. It is simply this: Can silver be eliminated "from use as currency in Europe and America without enormously "increasing the value of gold and depreciating the value of silver? "It is not a speculative theory which we enunciate, when we say "that the withdrawal of any portion of the active currency of a "country must enhance the value of what remains in proportion "to the amount withdrawn."

This is really all the argument which the chairman produced in order to show that we ought to adopt bimetalism. He did not even condescend to tell us what meaning he attaches to the word bimetalism, or give us the least intimation what is the measure which will avert the evils which he apprehends. His speech resolves itself into a mere lamentation over the scarcity of gold, and leaves us absolutely in the dark as to a remedy, except that it is to be found in bimetalism—a word which neither he nor any of those that followed him have taken the trouble to explain. This gave the tone to the whole discussion; speaker after speaker rose and lamented in piteous terms the dangers and difficulties that would arise from the continuance in England of a monometallic standard, but no one from first to last ventured to say what he meant by bimetalism, or in what sense that highly ambiguous word was to be applied. The discussion amongst so many eminent persons, from whom we had a right to expect at least a clear and distinct definition of the remedies which ought to be applied, resolved itself into a mere lamentation over existing and apprehended evils, which were to be remedied by a nostrum which everybody carefully avoided defining or explaining. I may so far anticipate as to point out that the word that everybody agreed to employ, and everybody was anxious not to define, the word bimetalism, is a highly ambiguous term, and may mean either a forced currency, in which, for instance, a seller is bound to accept either one ounce of gold or fifteen and a half ounces of silver at the option of the buyer, or it is left to the option of the buyer to pay in silver or gold at his pleasure, without any attempt to establish a fixed relation between the two metals. It is a singular instance of the degree in which the minds of those who originate this movement have been occupied, to the exclusion of all other considerations, by the terror inspired by the apprehended scarcity of gold, that though they have taken unto themselves a name under which to unite, they have carefully shrunk from defining what that name means, and shelter themselves behind a mist of unmeaning words. It is also curious that they write and speak as if a drain of gold, however caused, were a permanent and durable calamity, whereas, while nothing is more likely to occur, nothing is more certain to be redressed.

If the whole monetary system of the country is to be overthrown, we have at any rate a right to require that it should perish in the face of day, and that our future fate should not be concealed from us under dark and dreary ambiguities. We do not want to be told—what of course is obvious enough—that the substitution of gold for silver in Germany, for instance, must raise the value of that metal all over the world, and therefore in England. We want to know what is the precise remedy that is proposed, and whether it is possible, and, if possible, whether desirable, that that remedy should be applied. Utterly failing in our effort to obtain from the meeting of bimetalists in November last any information as to what is really meant, or anything, indeed, except a lamentation over the dearness of gold, we turn to the pages of the *Bullionist*, which, in pursuance of the resolution of November last, has become the chosen organ of bimetalism, whatever that may mean. But here we are encountered by precisely the same difficulty. The *Bullionist* carefully avoids any authoritative statement as to the real meaning of the term bimetalism. The most which it ventures to do is to quote with approval a passage from the *Journal of the Institute of Bankers,* in which it is stated that

"the object of the association is to be the promotion of the stability "of values, by establishing the free coinage of silver and its use "as money under the same conditions as gold, by advocating and "furthering an international agreement, whereby a fixed relative "value between gold and silver may be established, and the two "metals may jointly form the currency of civilised nations, thus "facilitating the adjustment of international balances and lessen-"ing the excessive and needless risks which have now become "attendant on home and foreign trade."

It is added very appropriately that

"it is well that those who hold the views advocated by the asso-"ciation should more distinctly declare themselves, and whether "they fail or succeed in obtaining assent to those views, nothing "but good can result from their being more clearly enunciated."

In this sentiment at least I can most fully concur. Let us have done with vague generalities, and call to mind the memorable aphorism of Mr. Lowell, that it jerks one terribly to kick at nothing.

One would suppose that we were about to undergo some unheard-of plunder, some cruel and unjust humiliation; one would suppose that we were about to be stripped of our property by the violence and wickedness of some unjust and overbearing rival; certainly one would suppose that the possession of a certain quantity of gold had been secured to us by some solemn contract which lawless violence was about to cancel and overthrow, and that the Germans were guilty of an unpardonable crime in seeking to despoil us of our ancient and undoubted possessions. But what is the tenure by which we hold our possession of gold? Instead of being, as these gentlemen seem to suppose, our undoubted right, the possession of gold is of all things the most liable to change masters. By what tenure do we hold it? Simply by the conviction of its possessors that it is more profitable for them to employ and use it in England than elsewhere. This is a question which is decided not by any regulation or any compact, but by the feelings and wishes of mankind. If a certain quantity of gold remains in England, it is because its possessors believe that it can be more profitably employed in England than elsewhere. Show them a place where gold will command more of the necessaries and luxuries of life than here, and gold, which is perfectly cosmopolitan in its ideas, will fly at once to that favoured region. It is, if we may use the metaphor, a coy beauty, and will fly all the faster from any attempts to retain her by force. If a certain quantity of gold is found to command more of the necessaries, and conveniences, and pleasures of life in England, it will remain there, and as soon as it ceases to do so it will find for itself a more congenial home elsewhere. Bimetalists seem to think that they possess some power of checking or destroying this tendency of gold to wander, but the only real security is to be found in such a state of prices as will enable gold to command more here than elsewhere. So far from retaining gold by these artificial and bungling contrivances, they would only make the flight of the metal more certain, and its return more difficult.

The speaker at the meeting to which I have alluded seemed to treat the probability of the transfer of a certain quantity of gold from England to Germany as an irreparable loss, but nothing can be further from the truth. Gold is always to be had by those who will pay the price necessary for its possession, and that price is cheapness. The more of the necessaries and luxuries of life gold can obtain the more firmly is it held. One would suppose from the language that has been used in the alarmist meetings to which we have referred, that if gold was attracted elsewhere

Lord Sherbrooke.

there was no hope of its return; but nothing can be further from the fact. Once proved to its possessor that it is more fruitful in one place than another, old grudges are at once forgotten, and it returns to its former home without shame or hesitation. Everybody knows how gold can be got—that is, by paying the best price for it—and it really passes the bounds of patience when we hear its possible diminution spoken of as an irretrievable calamity.

I have hitherto treated of what appeared to me to be on general principles the exaggerated apprehensions inspired by a temporary failure of gold; it remains to consider the nature of the remedies which are most likely to be proposed for an evil which the desponding votaries of bimetalism seem to believe to be inevitable. I have already pointed out the real remedy, which is, if I may so speak, offering gold better terms—that is, giving in exchange for it a better value; in other words, a reduction of prices. It is a disagreeable remedy, but perfectly efficient, and of course much easier to be practised by a wealthy than by a poor nation. In these matters every day brings its changes, and a wonderful self-acting machinery cures defects and compensates errors.

It remains for us to put aside all these considerations, to assume our case to be absolutely hopeless, and to examine the remedies which may be applied by way of palliatives. In this undertaking we may naturally expect to receive every possible assistance from the fervid votaries who harangue our men of business, and hire our newspapers in the cause of bimetalism. But here we are confronted by a serious difficulty, and one which we know not how to overcome. Bimetalists are ardent and eloquent in their cause, but they scarcely admit of an answer, for a simple reason, that they have hitherto abstained from telling us what bimetalism is. We are summoned in the name of our bleeding country to do something to save her from an impending calamity; but when we ask how this is to be effected, we are paid by a barbarous word, which no one apparently has the heart to define. Like Joseph, we have first to discover the riddle and then the interpretation thereof. Perhaps this little difficulty may be removed by some revelation from the higher powers before this essay sees the light, but it is somewhat strange, when a new and most important step is recommended, to find ourselves obliged to guess at that to which we are called upon to agree. I am even exacting enough to think that we ought not only to be told what is the plan, but also the reasons which have led to the adoption of whatever form it may assume. Not being among the initiated, however, I must even be content to draw such inferences as I may from the single word bimetalism, and to state objections which possibly a further explanation, if ever it shall arrive, will show to be unfounded.

Having delivered myself of this protest, I will proceed to answer as well as I can what I suppose will turn out to be the proposals of bimetalism. I presume it is intended that, instead of basing our currency upon gold of full value and upon silver which is made much less valuable by means of the alloy than the metal it personates, we are for the future to have two standards; and this, as it appears to me, can only be done in one of two ways. We can arbitrarily select a certain value of silver—say, for instance, fifteen and a half times the weight of a single ounce of gold—and declare the two metals bearing such relation to each other as above stated to be to all intents and purposes of precisely the same value; or I can suppose that we may make two currencies, one of silver, the other of gold, to divide the patronage of the country between them, both being made legal tender, and no attempt being made to establish any fixed relation between them, an attempt which if made must necessarily fail. There may be some other method of satisfying the conditions of the bimetalists' problem, but I at least am perfectly unable to conceive what it may be, and must content myself with deploring the unhappy fate of the other metals, which, without any fault of their own, are excluded from their right to take a part in the metallic congress of which they also are members. In the total absence of any information on the subject, I should have thought that if safety is to be found in numbers, and if two metals are better than one, three must be better than two and four better than three.

Being left, however, totally without any information on this subject, I will venture to ask one or two questions which seem never to engage the attention of bimetalists; and first I should like to propound the question, With what object was money, which is a pure and absolute creation of man, invented? It was not certainly for the purpose of creating value, for value exists independently of any fiat or ordinance of man. As soon as a man appropriates any object of desire to himself, the notion of value is firmly established in his mind. The animal that he has tamed, the field that he has cultivated, the game that he has caught, all give him a notion of property, which he is ready to defend for himself and to respect in others. All these things are far anterior to the idea of money. Bimetalists argue as if money and wealth were identical, whereas nothing is more certain than that the existence of these two phenomena is separated by an indefinable period. What, then, is the want which money was invented to supply, and which has become so ingrained in our minds that our bimetalists seem quite unable to see any distinction between money and wealth? I will answer this question in the language of an author who seems to have had a far clearer idea of the real function and duty of money than the bimetalists, who apparently see no distinction between money and other kinds of wealth. The writer I allude to is Aristotle. It is curious to observe how much more clearly the ancient philosopher appreciated the real function and duty of money than the modern bimetalist.

"Intercourse" (he says) "takes place between people having "different objects of desire. In order that they may be exchanged "with each other it is necessary that they should be compared, for "which purpose money came forward, and is as it were a medium, "for it measures everything, both the excess and defect; as, for "instance, how many pairs of shoes will be equal to a house or to "food, for if this is not done there will be no exchange or inter- "course. All things, therefore, must be measured; but it is, in "truth, want which holds all things together: for if persons "wanted nothing from each other, or not equally, there would be "no exchange. Money, then, has been made by agreement as it "were a substitute for demand, and is so called because it exists "not by nature, but by law, and it is in our power to change it and "make it useless for the purpose. If it were not possible to ex- "change there would be no commerce. If a man requires nothing "at the present time, money is as it were a surety to him for a future "exchange that it shall be made when he wants it. But money "itself is not always of the same value, but yet it has more tendency "to remain fixed; wherefore everything ought to be appraised, for "so there will be exchange. Money, like a measure, makes things "equal; for if there were no exchange there would be no inter- "course, nor any exchange if there were no equality, nor any "equality if there was no common measure. In truth, it is im- "possible that things differing so much should be commensurate, "but for practical use it is sufficiently possible. Money makes all "things commensurable, for all things are measured by money."

It is extremely interesting to see how clearly Aristotle apprehended the great truth that the original and principal use of money is not the hoarding of treasure, but the providing a means of exchange, and that the fact that money possesses generally a certain value of its own is not part of its nature. The original use of money was to determine prices; that it possesses itself value of its own is a mere incident. All that is required in order to enable

Lord Sherbrooke.

us to determine the value of an article is a common measure with which we may compare it; that measure must of course be limited in some way or other, and it is only as a means of effecting that limitation that value is introduced into the question.

The value of a commodity limits its quantity. Anything which can be obtained in a limited quantity, with a certain ascertainable amount of labour, and which is divisible, will serve the purposes of money. Furs have been employed in some countries as money, cattle in others—as in the *Iliad*, in the estimation of the respective values of the shields of Diomedes and Glaucus, the one being worth nine oxen, the other a hundred oxen—bricks of tea in Tartary, cowries in Africa, rock salt in Abyssinia. Other African tribes calculate in *macutes*, a money of the mind which has no substance corresponding to it, but the value contained in which has been sufficiently ingrained in their minds to answer the purposes of a measure of value. Bullion is chosen because it complies with these two conditions, difficulty of acquisition and divisibility, better than any known substance. Is it not strange that we should turn this servant into our master, and elevate that which is a mere medium for avoiding the inconveniences of barter into an indispensable necessary of life, hardly secondary to food and clothing? If by some convulsion of nature the precious metals gold and silver were utterly destroyed, the world would be impoverished by the loss of a commodity on the discovery and manufacture of which much labour and time had been expended, but the only result would be that we should have recourse to some other contrivance. The main business of life would go on as before, and the only difference would probably be that we should be obliged to have recourse to a paper currency, based on whatever might be found, after careful consideration, to be the most convenient or least inconvenient standard of value. The question would be, as it is now, a question of remedying the inconveniences of barter by providing some means of fixing prices. That would be all.

We are now in a position to examine with some confidence the claim of bimetalism to be regarded as a great and lasting improvement in our financial arrangements. The first question which it occurs to me to ask is, why we should limit ourselves to bimetalism. The advantages of monometalism can easily be stated, and are undeniable. Those advantages are, that by this means alone can we effect that which we have conclusively shown to be the object for which the contrivance of money was devised, the obviating the inconveniences of barter by creating a common measure of value, and thus regulating prices. Now it is perfectly obvious that this advantage, to obtain which in the first instance money was invented, so far from being promoted, will be destroyed by the introduction of bimetalism. Whenever you introduce two standards of different values, and make them both legal tender, you at once destroy the very object for which money was introduced. Whether you have two independent currencies, one of gold, the other of silver, and make each of them a legal tender, or declare that a certain portion of one shall always be equal to a certain portion of the other, the failure, as far as regards the establishment of a common measure, to obtain which money was originally invented, will be the same. You will have two prices. After the bargain has been concluded will come a second bargain, the nature of which may be expressed in the words, How will you have it? The value of money depends entirely on the cost of producing it. If, then, a second metal of equal value be introduced, nothing is gained, and the process is simply futile — confusion for confusion's sake. The only advantage which can be got out of the second metal is by a cheat — that is, by mixing an inferior with a superior article and palming them off on the customer as of equal worth, a practice well known to dishonest pedlars,

Lord Sherbrooke.

but, I venture to submit, scarcely fit to be adopted into the finance of an honest nation. The essence of bimetalism is not plurality, but inequality. Plurality is only the means to the end. Its whole end and object is to induce people to treat as equal that which has been purposely made unequal, and thus to deprive mankind of that power of measuring values which money was invented to bestow.

It must never be forgotten that however the currency of a country may be appreciated, it will always be able to perform what has been shown above to be its leading function, the regulation of prices. However much the volume of the currency may be diminished, the quality for which money was first invented, and which is its peculiar function, will remain unaltered. Ratios remain the same, whether they are counted in tens or in thousands. The proper definition of bimetalism would be a fraudulent contrivance by which the purpose for which money was invented is entirely set aside in order to enable a State to palm off an inferior metal as of equal value with a superior one. To such a device we are not, and I am happy to think, when it is once understood, are not likely to be, reduced.

It is thus perfectly clear that a double standard is not merely an inconvenience, but absolutely destroys the purpose for which money was invented, and, instead of performing the astounding feat of giving us two standards, leaves us instead nothing but a quarrel, which there are no legitimate means of deciding, and which may very probably end in adopting a third standard, by splitting the difference between the two. What makes the matter more absurd is that this bungling and unscientific contrivance is adopted to obtain an end which can be, and every day is, obtained by the simplest means. The advocates of bimetalism seem to treat the establishment of a gold currency in Germany as a great and irreparable calamity, as a sort of robbery of the treasure of England. But let them take comfort. The only condition on which Germany or any other country can hold any portion of gold is that that portion will command in that country as great a share of commodities as in any other. Instead of being an irretrievable loss, the absence of gold is of all things the most certain to correct itself. Every pound that is taken away increases the purchasing power of the gold that is left. The currency is a self-acting machine, which, like a balance, is always tending to an equilibrium. No doubt we must expect to see many and serious changes in the distribution of the precious metals. Old States are continually becoming more populous, and new States are continually springing into existence. These in the nature of things must demand a share of the universal medium of exchange, and the appreciation of gold can only be met by increased fertility in the mines. Should the mines not answer to the call, the result must be a gradual appreciation of the precious metals, such as existed in the Middle Ages. This it may not be in our power to prevent, but we may be quite certain that this distribution will take place in exact accordance with the rule which makes gold flow to those countries where it commands the highest price. The absolute value of gold may, and probably will, be appreciated, but its relative value will obey a single, an inevitable law. The history of gold has been a history of fluctuation, and will doubtless continue to be so. The fluctuations must be attended with loss to some and gain to others; and it is the business of the financier to see and provide against these inevitable vicissitudes. The bimetalist seems to conceive that we should be at present in a stable condition wêre it not for the wickedness of Germany. There can be no greater mistake; of all commodities money is the most easily attracted and repelled. We live in a boundless realm of unending change; and the gold which the bimetalist fancies he can enchain by his clumsy contrivance slips away from him in the very moment of his acquisition. He will fill the vessel of the Danaids only to see it empty by a power which he does not appreciate and cannot control.

SHERBROOKE.

WHAT IS A STANDARD?

From the *Nineteenth Century*, May, 1882.

One half of my economical friends take it as a personal grievance that I should advocate bimetallism, and the other half absolutely refuse to discuss the matter seriously at all. This arises partly from the extreme dislike which all Englishmen have for system of any kind, and partly from the almost mad enthusiasm with which they regard the very few systematic institutions they possess.

At this time of almost universal scepticism, when every one of our most cherished beliefs is being scattered to the winds, there is one thing, and one thing only, which most Englishmen concur in adoring, and that one thing is the English pound sterling. An English pound sterling unites in itself qualities to be found in scarcely any other coin. It has maintained its position unaltered for sixty-four years; it is the standard of value and measure of property throughout the length and breadth of Great Britain, and even in our unfortunate annexe of Ireland. It is the unit of accounts; it is the coin passing from hand to hand, at all events in England; and it is legal tender. It is, in fact, the golden image which Nebuchadnezzar the king has set up, and which, according to the serious portion of my economic friends, all Englishmen are bound to fall down and worship.

The present position of the question as it apparently presents itself to the Government may be shortly stated.

1st. The question does not concern England at all.

2nd. If it does concern England, it is not within the scope of present practical politics, but is only in the academic stage of discussion.

3rd. England, not having changed her standard since 1816, cannot be called upon to mix herself up with the discussions upon it until those countries which have been chopping and changing ever since 1868 have made up their mind what it is they want, and to what extent England can assist them in getting it.

4th. Supposing the object of these bimetallic discussions be to rehabilitate silver, England, by keeping open her Indian mints, has done more towards keeping up the price of that metal than all the other countries put together.

5th. England having accepted and put in practice that which is believed to be in accordance with economic law—namely, free-trade—and having in vain endeavoured to procure the adoption of it by other nations, including her own colonies, it is rather too much to ask her without a moment's hesitation to adopt another economic truth, supposing the possibility of bimetallism by agreement to be as capable of an academic demonstration as free-trade.

6th. But whether it be true or false, whether it be wise or foolish, the number of pressing questions and the party feelings in the House of Commons would render any attempt to solve the question in this present year absolutely hopeless.

I have endeavoured thus to state the present position of things and the views entertained by those who take it as a personal grievance that I should advocate bimetallism, and I now pass on to those who resolutely decline to treat the question seriously at all. The most conspicuous among

Mr. H. R. Grenfell.

these is Lord Sherbrooke, but I shall endeavour to deal with him later on. Besides his lordship, there are others who write week by week upon the subject, and find it a simple matter to crush bimetallism. To do so it is only necessary to take Lord Liverpool's book and Sir Robert Peel's speeches, to talk of Harris, Petty, and Locke, to bring out the most well-known passages in their writings, to ignore everything that has happened since 1868, and to speak of the impossibility of thwarting the eternal laws of production. Then, by mixing up in hopeless confusion standard, currency, legal tender, and unit of account, it is possible to produce a most able paper which must be quite satisfactory to the orthodox worshippers of the golden image which Nebuchadnezzar the king has set up.

In answer to an assertion of mine that the double standard existed in England up to and indeed after the suspension of cash payments, the *Economist* writes:—

> "It is difficult to understand how they—that is, Lord "Liverpool and Sir Robert Peel—could have represented to "themselves the mercantile money of the kingdom as anything "but gold. If they found the legal standard consisted of two "metals, but that in practice one only was used, what stronger "proof can be given of the impossibility experienced by us, as "by other nations, of keeping both metals in circulation at one "time?"

This extract is given to show the determination not to discuss the question in a serious manner; for how can we suppose that a writer in the *Economist* can be ignorant of the difference between currency and standard? nor do we know where he finds that the bimetallists desire that both metals should be kept in circulation at the same time.

The *Economist* is so far right in that it follows Lord Liverpool in using the expression "that the standard is the "principal measure of property—that is to say, the chief "coin in use"—and it would appear that this diction was followed by the Bullion Committee, which took "standard" and "chief coin in use" to be synonymous, and thereby held that gold was the English standard, anything in law to the contrary notwithstanding.

Now, what appears to me to be a correct meaning of the word "standard," as it is used at the recent monetary conferences, is that it shall be "the principal measure of property," but not necessarily "the chief coin in use."

A bank-note at this moment is legal tender in England, but not in Scotland. It is also current in England and not in Scotland. A Scotch bank-note is current in Scotland, but it is neither legal tender nor standard until it has been exchanged for gold.

In America it is very hard to say, with the perpetual changes taking place, what is standard and what is legal tender. In France, French bank-notes, pieces of five francs, and napoleons are legal tender at the ratio of 15½ to 1, but the coinage of silver having been suspended, the gold has not quitted the country, notwithstanding the fall of silver. It is, however, only kept therein by that and other somewhat forcible measures. Most of the economists declare that France has got what they call a gold basis, and this is true to a certain extent—namely, that while, if you take gold ingots to the Mint at Paris, you may get gold coin in exchange, of standard weight and fineness, if you take silver ingots you cannot get them coined. The double standard, therefore, exists still in France to the extent of coined silver, but no further. The double standard, according to law, is in that country less complete than it was in England previous to the suspension of cash payments, because during that time, notwithstanding that the free coinage of silver had been stopped, any one could pay his debts to the amount of £25 in garbled silver currency, and to an unlimited extent in silver by weight.

Mr. H. R. Grenfell.

Before continuing the subject of the standard, I will say a few words upon what I mean by money.

A friend of mine, of unequalled knowledge of commercial affairs, and of twenty years' experience in parliamentary life, was inclined last year to take an interest in bimetallism. He applied to Lord Sherbrooke for his opinion, and received for answer that only fools were to be found in favour of the double standard, and I have therefore naturally taken up his lordship's paper upon the nature of money with fear and trembling; the more so as I find that he considers bimetallism to be one of those "delusions," only worthy of being treated like the raging waves of the sea by letting them "foam out their own shame."

Having declared myself to be a bimetallist, I am astonished to find that I have been "deluded" into a question which "touches on the verge of the abstruse, "which the mass of mankind are content not to meddle "with." "The answer," according to Lord Sherbrooke, "appears to most minds"—that is, I presume, to most minds other than those of the mass of mankind—"so com- "plete and so crushing that it has been thought unnecessary "to give it at any length."

I do not pretend to understand *all* that has been written on the subject, for I do not know what Lord Sherbrooke means by the "discipline of bimetallism," but I have done that which he has not done, in reading most of the treatises which have been written on the question. His method of studying it has been, as Mr. Kinglake said of Lord Raglan at the battle of the Alma, to avoid clouding his brain with useless information or plans. The masses of pamphlets which lay upon his table,

> "Thick as autumnal leaves that strow the brooks
> "In Vallombrosa,"

have been put aside, and he has sought for information as to what he calls "the latest phase of the doctrine and "discipline of bimetallism" by looking exactly where he was sure not to find it. He goes to the printed report of a meeting summoned to agree upon the best mode of organising a society for the spread of the doctrine, and expects to find the whole theory explained in a speech made by the chairman to men almost all of whom had written or spoken upon it. He might as well have expected to find the Pons Asinorum or the first rules of syntax in it. In fact, to carry on his own quotation, in this he is like a "wandering "star to whom is reserved the blackness of darkness for "ever."

He tells us he is a disciple of Smith, Ricardo, and Mill, and I presume that the form in which that assertion presents itself to his mind is the following:—"I am a "disciple of Smith, Ricardo, and Mill; I disapprove of "bimetallism, therefore every one who approves of it is in "contradiction with Smith, Ricardo, and Mill."

My desire is to show that all that Mill says of the double standard is thoroughly understood by bimetallists; that what Adam Smith says of the standard refers to purity of coin more than anything else; and that the plan of Ricardo, for the paper circulation, is one which would bring out in a stronger light than any other the advantage, if not the absolute necessity, of bimetallism.

But here I am in the same unpleasant predicament of which Lord Sherbrooke complains: I am "jerked with "kicking at nothing." If he had read the papers before him, he would have known that the bimetallists have never relied, for their statement of the effect of the German demonetisation, on their own resources. They have derived their whole statistical information from the writings of Messrs. Giffen and Jevons. If these are exaggerated or erroneous, their mistakes can be corrected.

The effect of bimetallism to secure a diminution of the fluctuations in the prices of the precious metals is vouched for by Mr. Jevons in his work on money.

Mr. H. R. Grenfell,

The general principles of bimetallism are contained in a memorandum on an international bimetallic standard of value, dated Simla, June 2, 1880, which memorandum is to be found in the Blue Book containing the proceedings at the Paris Conference of 1881. Mr. Chapman, the author of it, was himself present at the meeting in November, and its contents are more or less adopted by all those who take an interest in this question.

Mr. Gibbs' pamphlet on the Double Standard, which contains the table of the relative prices of the precious metals during the whole period of the existence of the French mint prices, showing that their divergence dated from the exact moment when the double standard was destroyed, might have afforded a candid inquirer some food for reflection. But, as Lord Sherbrooke had omitted to read anything on the subject on which he lays down the law, so it was necessary for him to create a giant of some sort to destroy, and the one he has selected is a supposed assertion on our parts that we were "undergoing some "unheard-of plunder, some cruel and unjust humiliation," by the German demonetisation. I shall shortly show that our language upon that subject has been much less violent than his own.

What we have said is that Germany committed an error, now publicly acknowledged by her to have been so, in that she "reposed too much confidence in the doctrines inculcated "by the standard writers on political economy, and in the "success that had hitherto attended obedience to their "advice;" that she followed the counsels of doctrinaires who had no practical knowledge of the phenomena they undertook to explain, and that she thus altered her monetary system, confiding in "dark and dreary ambiguities," rather than in that which would bear the light of day from being based on practical experience and theoretic truth.

A subject "verging on the abstruse" is not exhausted by one quotation from Aristotle, and by paraphrases of Mill and Adam Smith's chapters concerning the nature of money, nor is it sufficient for an ex-Chancellor of the Exchequer to assert that, like the mother of Sisera, a question upon the subject would make answer to itself. The bimetallist theory, which Lord Sherbrooke has not examined, is believed by us to rest upon the definition to be found in his own quotation from the *Ethics*—namely, that the value of money, and the relative value of the precious metals, depend less on production than on the monopoly with which it is endowed by being money.

Aristotle tells us that money has the name "*νόμισμα* "because it is not so by nature but by law, and because it "is in our own power to render it useless;" thus, and thus only, was it in the power of the German Government to change its silver money and render it useless, and the consequences arising from that act are what we have to analyse and explain.

Lord Sherbrooke says that "the value of money "depends entirely on the cost of producing it."

McCulloch says the same thing, if possible, more explicitly; he says:—

> "A pound weight of gold is at present worth about fifteen "pounds of silver. The cause of the difference in the price of "the two metals consists entirely in the circumstance of its "costing about fifteen times as much to produce a pound of gold "as to produce a pound of silver."

In a correspondence between Lord Grey and myself last summer, he, while eagerly claiming for the precious metals the subservience to the general law of the cost of production, frankly admitted that qualification of the doctrine which all men, I believe, except McCulloch, in an unguarded moment, and Lord Sherbrooke, assent to.

Lord Grey says:—

> "It is true that variations in that cost do not cause rapid "fluctuations in the value of these metals, because they are so

"durable, and the total mass of them available in the world at "any one time is so large as compared with the produce of a "single year, that it is a good while before a reduction in the "cost of producing either metal, and an increase in the amount "produced, can cause any sensible variation in its value as "compared to the other, or to commodities at large."

This modification, if correct, shows that the truth of the value being governed by cost of production is a question of degree and not of principle. If the interval mentioned by Lord Grey between the change in the cost of production and the effect upon the market value be a very long one, say a century, it naturally becomes less important than the instantaneous effect upon the market by the arbitrary action of certain states. The discovery of the Californian and Australian gold fields, and that of the silver deposits in the centre of North America, had less effect on the values of the precious metals than the acts perpetrated by the German and Scandinavian Governments in their total or partial cessation of silver coinage. A comparison of these phenomena seems to me to be more pertinent to the question than allusions to Diomedes and Glaucus, bricks of tea, cowries, and rocksalt, or *macutes*, otherwise money of the mind, of which Lord Sherbrooke possesses so surprising a monopoly.

Mill's remarks on the double standard have not been neglected by the bimetallists; they are as follows:—

"It appears therefore that the value of money is liable to "more frequent fluctuations when both metals are a legal tender "at a fixed valuation, than when the exclusive standard of the "currency is either gold or silver. Instead of being only affected "by variations in the cost of production of one metal, it is subject "to derangement from those of two."

Lower down in the same page he says:—

"Some of the advocates of a double standard are influenced "by an exaggerated estimate of an advantage which to a certain "extent is real, that of being able to have recourse for replenishing "the circulation to the united stock of gold and silver in the "commercial world, instead of being confined to one of them, "which, from accidental absorption, may not be attainable with "sufficient rapidity."

These two assertions would be admitted by the bimetallists to have been fair enough at the time they were written; but the experience gained since the demonetisation of silver in Germany has proved that if the oscillations in the prices of the precious metals in respect to commodities would be somewhat more frequent, they would be also much less violent, with the double standard.

I now pass on to Adam Smith. In his days either of the two metals was legal tender at a fixed ratio. Lord Sherbrooke apparently fancies that some weak-kneed individuals were assembled at the India Office last November to hear the doctrine propounded for the first time. The following is what I find in Adam Smith on the subject:—

"In the English Mint the pound weight of gold is coined into "44½ guineas, which at 21*s.* the guinea is equal to £46 14*s.* 6*d.* "An ounce of such gold coin therefore is worth £3 17*s.* 10½*d.* in "silver."

Further on he says:—

"In the English Mint a pound weight of standard silver "bullion is coined into 62 shillings, containing in the same "manner a pound weight of standard silver; 5*s.* 2*d.* an ounce "therefore is said to be the mint price of silver in England, or "the quantity of silver coin which the mint gives in return for "standard silver bullion."

There is not a word in the famous chapter of Adam Smith indicating his belief in the necessity of a single standard; in fact, in his day the question of the standard was so

Mr. H. R. Grenfell.

mixed up with the necessity of standard weight and fineness in the coins forming the currency of the country, that no one that I am aware of was known to discuss the possibility of a standard of value, other than that depending on the standard weight and fineness of the coins of the realm, to which principally Lord Liverpool's famous treatise is devoted. Thus Adam Smith says:—

> "The money of any particular country is, at any particular "time or place, more or less an accurate measure of value, "according as the current coin is more or less exactly agreeable "to its standard, or contains more or less exactly the precise "quantity of fine gold or pure silver which it ought to contain."

I now come to Ricardo, whom it is the fashion at this day to decry. Lord Sherbrooke's devotion to him is derived, I believe, from one of the causes whence springs his contempt for the classics. That contempt is bred by familiarity with them, which, in the case of Ricardo, has produced admiration mixed with envy of that special knowledge to which his lordship can never attain.

Ricardo in his day, and Lord Overstone in ours, have enjoyed the peculiar advantage of what Mr. Squeers called "practical education:" that is, they can not only spell horse, but they have rubbed him down. Ricardo's scheme for a paper currency which has been publicly praised by Lord Sherbrooke, but the precise scope of which I fancy he scarcely understands, is exactly the example which appears to me to show the advantage of bimetallism.

Let us suppose, for the sake of argument, that Ricardo's scheme for a paper currency should be carried out to its fullest conclusion; that one-pound notes should be issued for England, as they are for Scotland and Ireland, and that there should be no such thing as coined sovereigns at all; that the security for the payment of these notes, either by a privileged bank or the State, should be the amount of securities declared to be sufficient, and the balance in bullion. It is manifest that with such a state of things there would be no necessity for a mint at all. The precious metals, whether one or two, would be kept in ingots of the standard weight and fineness in the vaults of the issue department. The volume of the paper circulation would fluctuate exactly to the same extent as if the whole circulation were metallic, and the raising and reducing of the rate of discount would be the regular expression of the existing value of money in the country—that is, a demand for circulation would cause the rate to rise, and a superabundance of it would cause it to fall. Bullion for the issue vaults would be attracted by high rates, and repelled by low rates.

Are the monometallists prepared to say that, with the circulation thus confined to paper, if the principal nations of the civilised world had agreed to treat both silver and gold as money at a fixed ratio, whether in coins or ingots, it would be to the advantage of England to restrict its operations to one metal only?

If they are not prepared to say this, they will no doubt answer that the fixed ratio is an idle dream and an impossibility, and that the reason why they wish for ingots of gold is that one metal alone can measure value. How then, if that be so, is it to be accounted for, that, during the whole period of the French mint prices being open to the world, the relative prices of gold and silver remained constant, notwithstanding the changes in the cost of production caused by the discoveries, first, of gold in Australia and California, and afterwards of silver in America? Instead of accounting for these phenomena, Lord Sherbrooke rejoices in such words as "confusion for confusion's sake," "fraudulent device," and "palming off by a practice known "to dishonest pedlars."

I have already shown that in the days of Adam Smith a standard meant the measure of weight and fineness of a coin or ingot, and I have also endeavoured to show that with Ricardo's scheme for a paper currency which Lord Sherbrooke publicly approves, there would be no need for coin at all, but bullion, and bullion only of standard weight and fineness in ingots, would be necessary to hold against bank-notes beyond the amount permitted to exist in securities. The standard weight and fineness being duly certified, the pounds sterling in such ingot would constitute the measure of value in the country, because each possessor of a sufficient number of bank-notes could at any time change them for an ingot, which might be sent anywhere. In such a case, the only use of the ingots would be to send abroad. Supposing the French mint prices to be restored anywhere, the holder of the ingot could procure currency with it in such places, but the monometallists would prevent the holding of silver against the notes, however "convenient "it might be to the merchant," lest it should be supposed that the bimetallic standard was that of the realm of England.

In America at this moment silver is legal tender, but nobody wheels about barrows full of silver dollars; but they have in their pocket-books silver certificates with which they can pay their debts or taxes. These silver certificates are, as near as possible, in accordance with Ricardo's proposition.

The most singular part of Lord Sherbrooke's omissions is his total oblivion of his own speeches. He thinks it a most dreadful presumption to attempt to alter the standard of the realm in England, forgetting that he has proposed to alter the standards used by two far more populous communities than ours. He first proposed to alter the European standard of value, and, secondly, that of our Indian Empire. In order that there may be no mistake whatever about his propositions, in making both of which I am bound to admit that his language about the double standard was fully as strong as it is now, I quote his words:—

"A gold and silver standard is not a double, but an alternate "standard. The two metals are always fluctuating in their "relations to one another. It is in the nature of things for the "cheaper metal for the time being to drive out the dearer. "Therefore, when the silver standard drives the gold out of "circulation, it leaves us nothing to compare our international "coin with except the silver standard to which it would have no "exact relation; and so I ventured to say in answer to the "question, that it would be impossible to hold out hopes of "assimilation [that is, of coinage with France] until France has "made up her mind to give up the silver standard and have "only a gold standard; and I am happy to say that France is "favourable to the abandonment of her silver standard. . . .

"But I wish here to point out that I believe it is possible for "England and France, if they can make up their minds to give "up a little of their prejudices for the sake of the great advantage "of having an international coinage, to obtain that object. I will "just show the House how that could be done. . . .

"It appears to me that the subject is not so difficult as might "be supposed, and that by a single measure we may secure to "ourselves the great benefit of saving all the expenses incurred "on our own gold coinage, without imposing those expenses on "any one else, and at the same time of striking a coin which "would have the advantage of an international circulation."

These extracts show that to change the standard of value all over Europe for the very small object of possessing a coin which would have the advantage of an international agreement, was in 1869 thought a very easy and simple operation by the then Chancellor of the Exchequer.

The next quotation is from his contribution as an Opposition leader to the Indian silver discussions. He was as strong as he is now, and as he was in the coinage

Mr. H. R. Grenfell.

controversy, against the double standard, and he placed his views before the House purely as suggestions, and without any assumption of authority. But, when looked at in the light afforded by the controversy about the standards, they showed that he exaggerated far more than any bimetallists do the evils to India arising from the demonetisation in Germany.

" We know from the accounts before us that India by this " means alone (that is, the depreciation of silver) actually loses and " is deprived of £3,000,000 yearly. This is a state of things which, " if it is to be regarded as permanent, and one not likely to be " speedily or immediately relieved, is one utterly intolerable to be " contemplated, if there be within our reach any means or power " of amendment. I think the case is made out, as clearly as can " be, that we should, if possible, avoid so terrible a calamity as that " with which India is visited through no fault of her own, which " springs from institutions which she has, which does not arise " from the nature of things, but comes from institutions made by " the will of man, and can be altered by the will of man."

What, then, was the remedy for the intolerable state of things brought about, as he correctly states, by the will of man and alterable by the will of man? He proposes a paper currency for India founded upon gold. After making his usual attack upon the double standard, which had been recommended by the previous speaker, Mr. Sidebotham, he adds :—

" The question is whether we cannot hit on some other " means. What appears to me to be wanted is a standard " identical with that of the country with which it is so intimately " bound up. . . .

" It would be perfectly easy, I think, to introduce notes into " India, and to make the regulations that Mr. Ricardo suggested, " that a person should receive gold for any notes he might bring " in. We know if there were any redundancy in the currency "that the process would go on until the redundancy ceased; but "it would go no further, and then we should be possessed of a "currency, not so showy, not so expensive, but for all practical "purposes just as good, as the currency of England and the silver "currency of India."

This crude proposition, at first believed to have been hastily advanced in the heat of debate, was afterwards enlarged upon in an article in the *Fortnightly* of July, 1879, under the title of "A Simple Way out of the Indian "Difficulty." It included a cessation of general coinage of silver in India, and the issue of notes convertible into gold.

The objections to it were—

1. That to procure the gold to pay the redundant notes would create so large a demand for that metal as would increase the divergence between the value of it and that of silver.

2. That the enormous amount of silver rupees in India would be crowded into the treasuries to exchange for the new notes convertible into gold.

3. That, notwithstanding the limit implied by the cessation of fresh coinage, the profit to the holders of rupees would be so enormous that it would have paid to set up mints in all directions.

This "simple way" showed the extreme simplicity of the author of it, who perhaps never suspected that it would be called "a fraudulent contrivance," tending to "confusion "for confusion's sake." However, this proposition very naturally was heard of no more.

The conclusions arrived at by Lord Grey in the correspondence to which I have already referred are as follows:—

"1. That the objections to bimetallism are insurmountable; "bimetallism being understood to mean a system under which "the character of money is given to both silver and gold coins, "and either at a fixed rate is made a legal tender in the payment "of debts.

"2. That the present standard of value in this country ought "to be strictly maintained, and that no departure from it or from "the principles of our existing monetary system ought to be "made.

"3. That if, in consequence of our determination to adhere "to our present monetary system, France, the United States, "Germany, and Italy, were to resolve that they also would "maintain gold currencies, and should make such changes in "their existing laws as to the use of silver as would be necessary "to keep the gold coins they might issue in circulation, the "demand for gold must be so increased as, for a time at least, "materially to raise its value, and thus occasion much commercial "embarrassment and very serious pressure on all branches of "productive industry in most nations.

"4. That authorising the Bank of England to use silver *at* "*the market price* together with gold as the basis of its issues "might avert this evil, by leading other nations to adopt similar "arrangements, and would, at any rate, mitigate the evils that "would arise from a great extension of the use of gold in the "circulation of those countries, by diminishing the amount of "gold required by England, and affording facilities for the "employment of silver as an instrument of exchange between "nations.

"5. That this measure would not involve the slightest depar- "ture from our present standard of value, or from the principles "of our monetary system."

It will be seen that Lord Grey accepts the fact of the evils which have followed the demonetisation of Germany.

Mr. Clarmont Daniell, an Indian writer, proposes that there should be but one standard and one legal tender of money for all the world—gold. To this he adds silver, to be equally legal tender to any amount, but upon condition that its value as existing in the bullion market shall be ascertained from time to time, and proclaimed by competent authority. Professor Bonamy Price supports this theory, and backs it up by the singular argument "that steadiness "of value is incomparably the highest quality which money "can possess." He therefore wishes to take away that quality from that which is the money of a very large portion of the human race, simply because he is unwilling to accept one fact which Professor Jevons has proved to be mathematically correct, and another which the French mint prices show to be historically true.

The objection which I feel both to Lord Grey's plan and to Mr. Daniell's is that they would have all the evils of a radical change without bringing us back to that state of the common measure of value which was lost when the French mint prices were given up.

The use of a standard is that, if the unit of account be a pound, a dollar, a mark, a rupee, or a franc, the persons having any number of these written in books against their names may know as exactly as possible what their debt is, and what quantity of what substance will suffice to free them from it. Now with a varying relative price between gold and silver, notwithstanding that both would be used as "instruments of exchange between nations," the above advantage would be lost.

The functions of a standard, as has been said before, are not necessarily limited to its connection with coins or other instruments of circulation within a state, more especially in a country where paper transfers of all sorts are so much in use as they are here. A standard may be, if I may use the term, the test of that "money of the mind" which is founded on the certainty of ultimately receiving that which will be as available in the international exchange as paper is within the state. It appears then to me that to recognise the standard of value in international exchange is more important than to regard it in its relation to interior currency, and that this consideration ought to induce the governments of those countries which have brought about the difficulty by their rash interference and ill-considered changes in their monetary arrangements, to think twice before they break up the present negotiations, even supposing that their continuance should involve an agreement with no other offer from England and the Indian Empire than that made last year.

I give this advice under the full conviction that the enormous international transactions of England will make her come into the agreement as soon as it shall be shown to be feasible, and giving due weight to the old objection which would of course arise on the part of other Powers, that they do not wish to pull the chestnuts out of the fire for us.

A great deal has happened since last year. The Italian Government has made a gold loan, 'but has not ventured upon a gold resumption. The American Government has shown its powerlessness to repeal the Silver Coinage Bill, notwithstanding the recommendation of the Treasurer and Director of the Mint. The silver material dollar may not have got into circulation; but the silver certificates which Lord Sherbrooke thinks better still are to be found in every railway station and custom-house, while the evils which were so intolerable in India have turned out to be only losses to the public budget of the State and the private budgets of the English officials.

Lord Sherbrooke has himself proposed an international agreement for coin which at once deprives him of the right to make the objection of its impossibility.

The French bimetallic standard was defended as far back as 1819 by Sismondi without anticipating either international agreement or free mintage, the two new elements brought in since that date. He says :—

" Si le gouvernement déclare que toute dette d'une once d'or
" pourra être légitimement payée avec quinze onces d'argent,

" ainsi que cela se pratique en France, la mesure commune du " commerce ne s'établira pas sur la quantité annuelle produite " par les mines d'or ou par celles d'argent, mais sur une moyenne " proportionelle entre les variations que subiront ces deux " quantités, et l'étalon désiré en acquerra plus de fixité."

Now the above is what we want answered; it will not answer itself. We are all agreed that the object in view is to have the greatest fixity which can be obtained from our common measure of value. We are all agreed that within a country where gold is the only measure of value, the fixity, though not absolute, is as great as can be had; but the question is how to obtain the greatest fixity in international transactions, and with reference to this point we believe that the effect of the demonetisation of silver has shown that "there are more things in heaven and earth" than were dreamt of in the philosophy of Lord Liverpool and M[c]Culloch.

Lord Sherbrooke has not refuted our arguments, but he approves of Aristotle's definition. He therefore believes that money is made by law and can be unmade by it; but he apparently disbelieves that the relative value between the two metals can be fixed by it; that is, he thinks that Aristotle's rule is good enough for either metal, but not for both. He is thus, in my opinion, landed in the dilemma suggested in Sheridan's famous paradox.

Sheridan was in the habit of walking with his aunt to the pump-room at Bath, but after a time that amusement palled upon him. One day he neglected to escort her, and on his visiting her next day she remonstrated with him.

" But," he answered, " it was raining all the morning." " Quite true," she said, " but it was fine all the afternoon, " and I heard of you on the public walks." To which he rejoined, " My dear aunt, it was fine enough for one, but " not for two,"

This argument, though in some respects defective, was meant to be, and no doubt was, good enough for an old woman. Lord Sherbrooke's limitation of the maxims of Aristotle appears to me to display a contempt for the understandings of his opponents similar to that which Sheridan felt for that of his aunt.

No doubt Lord Sherbrooke would have refuted all this if he had chosen to do so, but he has not read his brief. To use his own words in the paper mentioned above, "why "should he waste his time in thinking, when he is already "master of all that has been and all that can be said on "the subject? To try to impart to such a person a new "idea is a sort of insult, for it implies that there is some-"thing left for him to learn—which, as the mathematicians "say, is absurd."

H. R. GRENFELL.

BIMETALLISM.

At a meeting of the International Monetary Standard Association, held in the Egyptian Hall of the Mansion House, on the 8th March, 1882, under the presidency of the Lord Mayor, MR. H. R. GRENFELL, *Governor of the Bank of England, spoke as follows :—*

MY LORD MAYOR AND GENTLEMEN,—I must, in the first place, apologise for venturing, in the position which I occupy, to appear at a meeting of this kind at all. As one of the custodians of the currency of the country, it might be supposed that it would not be fitting for me to take any part in a movement of this kind. But as long as it is distinctly understood that I am only speaking as an individual, and in no degree whatever giving the opinions of my colleagues, I think there cannot be any reason why I should not attend a meeting of the citizens of London, after the somewhat lengthy study that I have given to this question. I think it right to say that I am a bullionist of the bullionists; that I have been brought up at the feet of a bullionist Gamaliel—if such an individual could be found in history—and therefore it is utterly impossible that I should swerve one single jot from that principle in which I believe, viz., that it is necessary above all things, that the currency and standard of this country should be founded upon wise and honest principles. Now, that being the case, I think it is not unfitting that I should move the resolution which I hold in my hands; but at the same time, as the resolution seems to be almost a truism, you might wish also that I should make a very short introduction to the general question, as well as speak to the resolution.

I presume it is known by all present that the standard of this country is a gold monometallic standard; that it was instituted by the great statesman, Sir Robert Peel; and that it was approved by the writings of another great statesman, viz., Lord Liverpool, who had given years to the study of the question. But it is not so generally known, and it is somewhat singular that it should have been so, that when Sir Robert Peel brought forward the measure for the resumption of cash payments and for the institution of a monometallic gold standard, he appealed to the House of Commons by every wish they had to act with good faith towards their creditors, that they should return to the ancient standard of the realm. I presume he meant that the ancient standard was a metallic standard; but the fact is, it was not a monometallic gold standard at all. The ancient standard to which Sir Robert Peel alluded was a bimetallic standard. Although there had been a monometallic standard in the country before, there had never been a gold one. There had been a silver standard up to the time of Sir Isaac Newton, and subsequently to that a bimetallic standard up to the suspension of cash payments. I, therefore, who have had to go through the labour of examining most of the points which Lord Liverpool wrote about, and which Sir Robert Peel spoke of, have no hesitation in saying that I believe if Sir Robert Peel and Lord Liverpool were alive at this moment, and were as keenly alive as they were in their own days to all the events passing around them, that they would have come to the conclusion that this question must be reconsidered. Now, why do I come to that conclusion? Just on this ground, that among the reasons which Lord Liverpool gave for thinking it absolutely necessary to have a single standard, and that a gold one, was that a statesman or state could only make men obey within the limits of his or its own dominion. From that I deduce the idea that there never came into his head the possibility of various states agreeing on a subject like this. Therefore, as the Lord Mayor has said, it is an entirely new matter to be considered. But that is not all, for in one of the best chapters of Lord Liverpool we find that he gave a description of what he calls "bank money," which existed in some of the great free ports in the last century in which receipts were given for the deposit of bullion, and which receipts passed amongst the great merchants of all classes of trade. This at once, though upon a smaller scale, shows that he contemplated that a good means of exchange might be found by an agreement among interested parties in the same place, though belonging to various nations. So much for Lord Liverpool; but my reason for believing that Sir Robert Peel might have been induced to reconsider this question is that, as a statesman, he knew, as all statesmen must, that it is not given to public men to sit down in their room, devise a strictly systematic plan, and carry it out; but he knew that statesmen are compelled to choose between two or three evils, and therefore he had the experience that it is impossible to neglect the consideration of events which are passing around them. What are these events which have occurred since the death of Sir Robert Peel, or since he quitted public affairs? They are practically a new set of events altogether. The beginning of them was apparently an accident; the first event was the calling together of a Conference at Paris in 1868, for the purpose of attempting to get a coinage of all nations; and scarcely had they met when they found it absolutely necessary to discuss the question of the standards. But that Conference came to the conclusion that the best of all possible standards was a monometallic gold standard, and, I believe, by a narrow majority passed a resolution to that effect. Shortly afterwards there came the Franco-German War, and when a large quantity of the French gold had passed into Germany, it was not very unnatural that with the result of the Conference of 1868 before them the German Government resolved to use the gold in order to inaugurate that which had been declared solemnly to be the best of all possible standards. Almost immediately the evils began to be shown arising from this great monetary revolution, and in 1878 another Conference was called to again discuss the question, and in the absence of any German delegate at that Conference, they passed a resolution unanimously that it would be a misfortune to the world if the functions of silver in the coinage of the world should pass away. The next matter was the Conference which is still, technically speaking, alive in Paris. The difference which existed between that and the previous one was that a German delegate appeared at that Conference, took part in it, and made certain offers with respect to it, which although they might not be all that was expected, were at the same time most important offers. There is one other great change since the days of Lord Liverpool. There are now numberless agreements between States upon all possible questions. We have postal and telegraph agreements, police agreements and agreements for lighting and signals, and other subjects in which the commercial world is deeply interested. Therefore, what would appear to the mind of Lord Liverpool to be impossible, might appear to us to be one of the easiest things in the world. These are the general arguments which I venture to submit to your notice with regard to this great and important question, and if you will permit me now I would say a few words with respect to some of the particular objections which are raised to what is called bimetallism. In the first place, it is said that do what you will it is utterly impossible to make a relative price between gold and silver, and that, however much you may fix it, the laws of Political Economy will be too much for you. They say that the law of cost of production is so certain that it is absolutely impossible to go against it. I will now give an instance, and if I am wrong there will no doubt be some here who know something about the question. The metal called platinum costs a great deal more to produce than gold, and yet you cannot get a pound of gold for a pound of platinum, and why? Simply because gold, being used for coinage, has a special monopoly and privilege that renders this cost-of-production law inoperative. We are told we are against science. I suppose everbody who has watched within the last few years any of the various discussions which have taken place knows exactly how that word "science" is used. We know when A differs from B and has proved his case, B says: "That is all "very well, but it is not scientific." But what we must look to when using such words as "science" is, what are the facts? and the fact is that during the time when the bimetallic law existed in France, the relative value of the two metals was kept as close as possible to the French legal price, notwithstanding the great fluctuations taking place in both metals in the cost of production. It is like the story of the old French Abbé who wrote an essay on the Swedish Constitution to show that it was eternal, and he had scarcely had the last proofs of it when they came and told him there had been a revolution and that the constitution was at an end. "They may destroy "the constitution," said he, "but they cannot destroy my "book;" and that is exactly the case with those gentlemen who are always throwing the cost of production in the face of those to whom I have alluded. But with regard to bimetallism being against nature, I think you will agree that that is a general proposition; for almost all things in heaven and earth are against nature. Everything in heaven is supernatural, and most things to be seen from the top of St. Paul's are interferences with nature, all that has been done by human beings since

> " Man walked with beast joint tenants of the shade,
> " The same his table, and the same his bed,"

may be said to be against nature. We need not then trouble too much about these general propositions. The great thing for those interested in this subject is to examine it as carefully as they can; and therefore having said these few words in introduction of the general subject for discussion I will pass to the resolution, which is to the following effect:—" That the contraction of the metallic " basis of the world's currency by the exclusion of silver " from its natural functions as domestic and international " money is to be deprecated as likely to render disturbances " in the buying power of gold more frequent and violent." I ask you all, have you calculated what the cost of the demonetisation in Germany was and the dislocation in the value of the precious metals? The amount that the German Government coined was £87,000,000 sterling of gold, and that is equal, according to the average production of the whole world for the last twenty years, to 3·3 years of that whole production. But that is not all, as affects the relative value of gold and silver, because besides buying that amount of gold, or, rather, annexing it, they sold £28,000,000 sterling of silver, which is equal to more than two years of the average production of the whole world of silver. That being the case, I ask you what you would think supposing the Latin nations, our Indian Empire, and the United States were to resort to some such measures as the German Empire did? That is the problem we have before us, and it is to this problem I invite your most serious and intelligent consideration.

Mr. H. R. Grenfell.

At the same meeting of the International Monetary Standard Association, MR. HENRY H. GIBBS, *President of the Association, said:—*

MY LORD MAYOR AND GENTLEMEN,—You have been good enough to ask me to say a few words upon this question, but there is no resolution before the meeting at this moment. The resolutions, happily, have all been carried, if not unanimously, yet very nearly unanimously. However, to put myself in order, as they say in another place, I will state that I intend to end with a motion. But first I should like to say a few words in answer to the gentleman who spoke in the body of the hall. It would be a great pity that his questions should not be answered, although I believe there is hardly anybody in this hall but knows the answers. He asks us, in the first place, why we are to assume 15½ as the proper ratio between gold and silver. I say we do not assume anything of the kind. There is no special virtue in 15½, but 15½ was once the fixed proportion in England as it is now in France, as it is in Germany, and as it is almost all over Europe. When that was the recognised ratio it was an approximate ratio. It was not one that was mathematically correct; no ratio ever was; because if those gentlemen who spoke of the cost of production were right, it must have varied every second. The ratio was 15½ in active practice all over Europe until Germany demonetised her silver. Instantly it was thrown down; but if Germany to-morrow were to remonetise silver, with the same rapidity it would come up again. (A voice—"Exactly.") Therefore if we in England should ever get so far in settling our minds about the double standard that the arrangement of the ratio came to be a question for consideration, and if that gentleman should be put upon a Royal Commission to settle what the ratio should be, he would find to his great surprise that before the Commission had sat at all the market price of silver would be at 15½ again, without his having had a word to say about it. Another question he put to us was, how are we to arrange between the various Governments, all of whom he seems to think have different standards; and he instanced the standard of gold in England, amongst other things, and the standard of gold in France. Well, the standard is different, no doubt; but we have not the least difficulty in making our international payments when they have to be made in gold, and we should not have the least difficulty in making them even if they had to be made in silver. But the remarks that our friend made upon the subject are really addressed not to an international standard, but to an international coinage, which is a perfectly different thing. We should, indeed, in that case have to make up our minds whether we were to give up our sovereign or whether France was to give up her napoleon. But to accommodate the standard of our country to the standard of another is only a matter of arithmetic, of the rule of three; and the parity of value between the different coinages of the world is thus easily settled. I have now touched on some small details of the subject, referred to by the gentleman who put these questions. I will now say a few words on the general subject. I have gathered from what has passed to-day and from what has been passing now for the last year or so, that we have all made up our minds by this time as to what we do not want and as to what we do want. Now, when a monometallist wants to say something disagreeable, wants to throw a stone at a bimetallist, and does not know where to look for it (I think it is a very difficult thing for him to find it), he says: " I see what you are about. You want cheap money: you " want abundance of money." Well, I have no objection to abundance of money, especially if it is in my own pocket, and as regards abundance of money, generally, abundance

Mr. H. H. Gibbs.

of the circulating medium as compared with scarcity of the circulating medium, I prefer abundance. Abundance brings mischief with it; but it brings some good. Scarcity brings mischief with it, and does not bring anything else. Therefore you may desire abundance so far, but abundance is not the point we are aiming at. What we do want is stability. What we do want is enough monetary circulation to serve for the wants of commerce, and progressively enough to serve for the progressive wants of commerce. If we mean by abundance something more than we want,—a little more than we can spend,—we do not desire anything of that kind. But stability we do want, and I do not need to convince you, nor to convince anybody else, I suppose, who has studied the subject, that stability is a consequence of having a double standard: that is to say, a greater measure of stability. For a testimony of this I appeal, as Sir George Campbell has already appealed, to one of the chief prophets of the monometallists, whose argument referred to by Sir George Campbell was a very ingenious argument. His way of putting it is this: He supposes you to have two vessels, one a yellow one and one a white one, both half full of water, and then, if, as Sir George says, there is a heavy drain upon one of them, say the yellow vessel, it is soon empty, or if more water were wanted and it were poured into the silver vessel, it would run over the sides of the vessel. But if you had a pipe connecting the two vessels at the bottom, so that the level of the water in them is the same, though you take as much as you please from one of them or add as much as you please to one of them the level at the top is still the same. Well, then, I have now said what we do not want and what we do want; I will now say a little about why we want it. I will not say that we want it because the present state of things is intolerable; but I will say, that it is far from satisfactory and threatens danger in the future, danger in the scramble for gold, and danger in the depreciation of silver, and I appeal again to another monometallist champion. According to him, and he is a very able man and statistician, very trustworthy when he does not speak against bimetallism—the existing state of affairs is an exceedingly dangerous one. I daresay it is, and therefore we want what will guard against that danger. Our opponents say "That is all very well, but the thing you desire is impossi-"ble. It is impossible to make any agreement with any-"body." I do not think that is the case. We have heard a great deal of late of the international concert. I do not see why we should not have an international concert in metals as well as in politics. I think the metallic concert would be the most harmonious and most lasting of the two. As to the matter of impossibility, I would repeat the words of a great man in regard to that: "If it is possible," he said, "it has been done already; if it is impossible, it shall be "done." I say that it is possible, and has been done already; and, when I say that I am only stating simple facts, because this impossible thing was done in France for seventy years, and "nobody seemed one penny the worse," but on the contrary appeared to be extremely well off. We have heard a good deal about the scientific part of the story from Mr. Grenfell. I want just to tell you one of the particular views of its scientific character. "It is all very well," a man said to me, "you may argue as much as you please, but you "will never turn me away from the great scientific principle "of one metal for the currency between people who trade "one with another." My answer to him was and is now—"There are two great scientific principles. There is the "principle of unity, and there is the principle of uniformity; "but the world has given up unity. They cannot have it, "and they won't have it. Uniformity we can have, and "sooner or later it appears to me we shall have it—that is a "uniform system of the two metals accepted by all as money." My next answer was—"As to your scientific principle, "which you won't be turned away from, you are turned away

Mr. H. H. Gibbs.

" from it every day. You give it up if there is the slightest " strain upon it. You tell me it is necessary for a man in " London dealing with a man in York to know exactly what " he is to receive. Well, then, I say it is necessary also " for a man in London dealing with a man in New York. " Your scientific principle is unseaworthy; no sooner does " it get on board ship than it goes to the bottom. It cannot " venture across from Dover to Calais, still less can it go to " New York." I have no more to say at this time upon the subject itself. But there is one thing I should like to say, and that is, that I perceive a great alteration since I went to the Conference in Paris in 1878 in the feeling of the people generally about this matter. I had not a word to say then in favour of bimetallism, because I had not opened my eyes sufficiently, but at that time if anyone in England did venture to suggest such a thing he was thought to be a lunatic. As has been said before, whatever we in this little island have been accustomed to do we think is absolutely right, and that whatever is done by the rest of the nations of the world is absolute lunacy. However, for that or other reasons any persons who thought of such a thing at that time were called lunatics. But now the tone which speakers adopt in reference to bimetallism is very different, and the way in which they look at the matter is very different also. They see that there is danger in the present state of things, and they think it right that the plans which are proposed to meet the danger should be considered seriously and not be put on one side as if the proposers were asserting the flatness of the world or making endeavours to square the circle. We are now listened to with patience; and, to come to the motion upon which I rose to speak, I think the Lord Mayor is an example of that patience. He has been listening to us for two hours with exemplary patience. I hope he has been in some degree rewarded for that patience by the interest he has taken in the conversation which has been going on. I think he not only showed his patience, but proved his kindness in giving us this hall to talk in. The motion I have to submit to you is—"That the best thanks of this meeting "be given to the Lord Mayor for his kindness and "hospitality in taking us in under his roof and giving us "this room in which to hold our Conference."

THE SCRAMBLE FOR GOLD.

From the *Bullionist*, March 18, 1882.

SOME of our contemporaries are never tired of pointing to the effect of the late action of the Bank of England in raising the rate of discount to 6 per cent., and assuring themselves and their readers that a complete and rapid success of that action in increasing the bullion in the Issue Department is a convincing proof that there can be no necessity for any reform in our present monetary system.

Nowhere is this assurance more clearly and more jubilantly expressed than in an otherwise well-written and thoughtful article in the *Saturday Review* of the 25th of last month, on the "Results of the Six per Cent. Rate."

We reproduce the last paragraph of the article in question, and propose to make for the benefit of our readers such remarks on it as may be necessary to expose the fallacies with which it is somewhat thickly sown:—

"The experience we have now had of the efficiency of the "6 per cent. Bank rate, in spite of all that is said of the scarcity of "gold and of the international struggle for gold, ought to convince "bimetallists that this country at least is not likely to suffer "seriously through gold becoming scarce. Rich countries can "always buy whatever they require of any commodity, and England "being the richest of countries can have as much gold as it pleases, "and when it pleases. In spite of the panic in Paris, of the "Italian preparations for resumption of specie payments, and all "the demands from so many quarters for gold, three short weeks "have seen the Bank of England replenish its stock of bullion and "raise its reserve more than two millions. And although under "other circumstances a 6 per cent. rate might not be equally effec- "tive, we have full assurance that some rate will be effective and "that England need never fear a scarcity of gold. Gold, in fact, "will flow to the market where its use is most profitable, and that "market is found in London. No doubt the United States and "France are also rich enough to obtain as much gold as they may "require, and they therefore, like England, are justified in main- "taining a gold standard. But poor countries like Italy, Germany, "and some others are not so justified. They suffer serious loss by "affecting to compete with countries so much more powerful in "resources than themselves. Italy at present is so little prepared "for a gold currency that, though she has a considerable amount "of gold for which she is paying a heavy interest, she does not "dare to put that gold in circulation, knowing that it would "instantly flow away to London."

The Reviewer appears to imagine that bimetallists are beset by an unreasoning dread that this country will have to stand helpless and with folded hands while it is either being absolutely denuded of gold, or seeing gold become so scarce that the circulation is dangerously and permanently contracted; and tells us triumphantly that England—and the United States and France too for that matter—are quite rich enough to buy as much gold as they please and as often as they please.

Now here are two patent mistakes. The fears of the bimetallists are misapprehended, and the remedy so confidently exhibited is itself one cause of the disease.

Gold leaves this country, and will always leave it from time to time; but it is only to redress the balance of trade that it does so—that is, to make up the difference when the imports have exceeded the exports—to pay cash, so to speak, when we have not goods wherewith to pay; and inasmuch as the balance of trade is necessarily variable, bullion will and must go, and no one need dread its going. No wise bimetallist will dread it, and no one who knows anything about the matter ever doubted that a timely rise in the rate of discount would bring bullion back again.

No doubt we can "buy" gold, not only as the *Saturday Review* is pleased to put it, as much as we please and as often as we please, but also as dear as we please.

It is that dearness that we dread, and not without reason, if not only France and the United States, as the Reviewer says, but Germany also and Italy (wisely or unwisely) are bidding for it in the same auction-room.

We are the richest, say the dwellers in a fool's paradise, and we can always buy it! Certainly we can; but at what a cost! But it is not only dearness that is to be dreaded. Dearness, moderate and steady dearness, is tolerable, and even advantageous; but excessive dearness, especially if it be fitful and oscillating, is highly prejudicial to trade. A constant rate of discount of 6 or even 5 per cent. is no pleasant subject for contemplation; but a rate frequently varying, but always high and sometimes at fever point, would be far worse than a rate of moderate height but reasonably constant.

So that that very power of buying (possessed by others as well as ourselves) which the Reviewer vaunts as our rock of safety, is the rock on which we split; and the so-called antidote which he holds to our lips is itself a poison.

The Reviewer hugs himself again in the fallacious reflection that England and one or two other nations are alone worthy to have a gold currency, and that inferior communities, such as Germany, Italy, and Austria, must be content with the inferior metal. In writing thus he seems to us to have misapprehended the nature and cost of a metallic currency.

Any metallic money, whether gold or silver, any medium

of exchange and measure of value which is made of a commodity possessing itself intrinsic value, is necessarily an expensive luxury, and must be bought and paid for. Every sovereign of the £120,000,000 supposed to be in circulation in England, whether in the coffers of the Bank or in the pockets of the lieges, has been purchased by an equal value of English goods. Every silver dollar in circulation in Italy has been paid for in silk or wine or oil, or other Italian produce; and so it must be in every nation in which gold or silver being in circulation as money are neither the produce of the land itself nor the spoils of war other than compensation for war expenses.

But if it be true that gold and silver purchase other commodities by dint of their own intrinsic value (whatever may be the co-efficients of that value), it must follow that it must cost a nation just as much to procure a silver coinage as a gold one. For every commodity exchangeable by means of money must be measured by a quantity of money exactly its equivalent in value; and just as "a "pound of lead is equal to a pound of feathers," so the cost of a quarter of wheat must be the same whether the Italian measures it in gold or silver.

A silver coinage then is suitable to a poor nation, not at all because its initial cost is cheaper than a gold one, but because the commerce of such a nation being made up of smaller transactions than that of her richer neighbours that coined metal is most convenient which is capable of the most minute subdivision of value.

Therefore, though Italy may possibly be unwise, even under the present uncertainty of the future value of silver, in choosing gold rather than silver for money, it is not because as a poor nation she is not "justified" in adopting it.

If, then, gold is naturally more suitable for great commercial transactions, it would seem that it is by natural and not by arbitrary selection that gold has hitherto formed sometimes a part and sometimes the whole of the standard money of countries whose commercial transactions are large, and silver alone the standard money of those countries whose commerce is less advanced.

But the cause of the present disturbance of the values of gold and silver is that some of these latter nations (and notably Germany) have thought proper to reject their ancient money and arbitrarily to select that which we suppose to be less well suited to their commerce.

Their action has been a resistance to natural tendencies, and we doubt not that if a remedy be found for the existing dislocation of the metals in the establishment of a convention between the principal commercial nations for the adoption of gold and silver jointly and at a fixed ratio for their standard money, the natural allocation to which we have above referred would again prevail; and though silver and gold would still be legal tender in all countries which would be parties to the convention, yet it seems certain that gold would prevail in England as heretofore, and silver in Germany and Italy when Italy has once resumed specie payments.

As to the late and present action of Italy in this respect, the "Reviewer" has failed to apprehend the true history of the matter.

He supposes that the Italian Government "does not "dare to put the gold into circulation, knowing that it "would instantly flow away to London;" but prefers to lose interest in vain, by keeping it locked up.

Italy loses no more interest on her gold than she will always lose so long as she has the luxury of a valuable currency. She never proposed to put her gold into circulation until she should have completed the full tale of £16,000,000 sterling prescribed by the law.

Were she to do so then or now without calling in an equivalent sum of her paper currency, the gold would of course flow out to London or elsewhere, because the circulation would be redundant, and the more valuable portion of it would be the first to depart.

But inasmuch as it is intended to call in an equal quantity of paper currency, thus leaving the volume of her circulation (presumably not now too much inflated) unaltered, we do not see what is to carry the gold away.

Two things only will do it, the shifting of the balance of trade, or the lowness of the rate of discount. If the balance of trade turn against the country, she will have to redress it, as England has been doing lately, by payments in specie; but that operation will last only so long as the rate of interest is lower in Italy (in proportion to the credit of the country) than in other countries with which she trades. When the rate of interest rises sufficiently the outflow of gold will cease.

Italy is now accumulating her gold, not by the natural law which regulates the outflow and inflow of the precious metals, but really by the way of purchase, intercepting that which would naturally come to this market. When she has got her gold and put it into circulation by the legitimate means of cancelling her notes, she will fight to retain it; and the weapon with which she will fight is our own weapon—the rate of discount.

That such a battle can be fought without serious and far-reaching commercial disturbance will hardly be contended.

Many will be the casualties recorded, and not to the weaker nations only, in the course of the struggle for gold.

HENRY H. GIBBS.

CONCERNING FAITH IN TREATIES.

From *The Bullionist*, April 15, 1882.

There is a well-known chapter in Horrebow's *History of Iceland*, entitled "Concerning Snakes in Iceland," and the chapter consists of but six words: "There are no snakes in Iceland." Our article might be as short, and might be confined to the words "There is no faith in Treaties," but that we wish to point out why there is no faith in them, and to finish, like a sermon, with an application.

The history of the world is the history of the making and the breaking of treaties. Treaties of peace are succeeded by declarations of war—allies become enemies, commercial treaties are succeeded by "Berlin decrees"—and that which was made for the good of two nations is overturned by the unwisdom of one to the detriment of both, and not unfrequently in greater measure to the harm of the nation at whose instance the treaty has been annulled.

Inter arma silent leges, war tears all treaties; but even without open war selfishness and supposed self-interest are too strong for the bands of any treaty, and whether the terms are imposed by a conqueror or settled by amicable agreement a change in the dispositions of the contracting parties will certainly bring the treaty to the ground. The conquered nation feels herself strong enough to tear the treaty imposed by her enemy—whether in the Black Sea or elsewhere—or if two nations have made a treaty—it may be concerning the Isthmus of Panama, or otherwise

—for their mutual protection or for the general good of commerce, one of them may think an advantage is to be gained by abrogating it, and will say candidly and cynically to the other, "Don't you see that it is in some parts disadvantageous to us? You can't expect us to be bound by it!"

Self-interest, real or imaginary, it is that in all cases dictates the breaking of any national engagement, and it is because the promptings of self-interest will never cease that we say there is no faith in treaties.

These very true but very trite sayings are amongst the weapons wherewith our opponents attack the advocates of the bimetallic standard. "Put not your trust in treaties," say they. "Who is to guarantee that if you make a treaty "or convention with Austria, Belgium, Chile, Denmark, and "the rest of the alphabet of foreign States down to Zanzibar, "some one or more of them, moved thereto by self-interest, "wantonness, or war, will not secede from your convention, "trample on the treaty, and overturn the whole fabric of "your bimetallic league?"

Doubtless it is impossible to guarantee that no one shall secede, but we think we shall prove that it is in the highest degree unlikely that there should be any such secession—first, because it would be to no one's interest to secede, and second because it would be an operation of extreme difficulty. Moreover, we shall show that if such secession were accomplished it would not break up the league, and would indeed be of very little moment.

How would a nation intending to secede from such a league set about it.

The changing from one metallic standard to another would be comparatively a very easy undertaking, though extremely costly to the Government which undertakes it. The discarded metal is called in, paid for in the adopted metal, and sold in other countries at a loss, yet Germany, even though aided by the enormous inpouring of gold from the French indemnity has lately found that however easy it may be to undertake such an operation it is exceedingly difficult to carry it through.

The changing from a paper currency to a metallic one is extremely easy, but very costly either to the Government which makes the change, and through them to the people who pay for it in taxes, or else directly to the debtor class. The former is the case of Italy, who is looking forward to the very desirable but very expensive luxury of a metallic circulation; the latter was the case of England at the resumption of cash payments in 1816.

But the changing from a bimetallic to a monometallic system is a very different matter, when the nation desiring to change is one of a group of States having a double standard of money, and we fail to see how such a nation can set about divesting itself of one metal and retaining only the other without passing through the stage of a paper currency. It may seem a simple thing to suspend the free mintage of one of the metals as France has done with silver; but if her neighbours had been bimetallic also France would never have been frightened into doing so, nor would any nation in that case have any temptation to follow her example, seeing that if she did she would not get rid of her silver, as that example shows. But some one may say, "Could she not send it to England as "Germany did? the cost of sending would be nothing." True, she would make no immediate loss in doing so, for England would by the hypothesis be bound to receive it and coin it into double florins; but what then? How would she obtain the gold in its place? It is the right of the debtor to choose which metal he will pay in, and she would have no remedy but to receive the English silver coin which would be tendered to her, and would have her labour for her pains. No, there is but one practicable way in which a nation once entering a bimetallic league can separate herself from her fellows without heavy and useless loss, and that is by discarding altogether her metallic money and resorting to a paper currency, after which if she chose she might do as England did in 1816, and adopt a single standard. But that any nation would suspend cash payments unless it were to provide for the cost of a war seems in the highest degree improbable.

War certainly would, as our opponents say, abrogate treaties between belligerents, but we fail to see that war would necessarily have, or, indeed, would have at all any effect upon this particular treaty, or could afford any inducement to a belligerent to break it. Our contemporary, the *Economist*, supposes indeed that it might probably be broken as an act of war, and to do damage to an enemy, but fails to show what hostile or hurtful effect it would have on the antagonist. We will presently show that it would have none.

In order to this we will first point out what the supposed convention would be, and secondly what it would not be.

Omitting minor details, it would be this:—That the contracting parties would engage to open their mints to the free coinage of both gold and silver, either metal at the option of the debtor being legal tender in the proportion of 1 to 15½.

It would not be the prohibition of any State to continue or to resort to the issue of paper money. England, for instance, who prides herself on the simplicity of her monometallic gold standard, would not be asked to give up her fifteen millions of paper circulation, which though payable in gold is not based, as the rest of the circulation is, upon a direct deposit of bullion.

A nation, then, resorting to an issue of paper money, whether complete or partial, would not *ipso facto* infringe the letter of the treaty; nor would the measure of itself have any hostile or damaging effect upon the adversary. It is true that a nation so acting would have denied itself

Mr. H. H. Gibbs.

the expensive luxury of metallic money in order the better to be able to levy war. She might conquer her enemy with the armaments which her discarded bullion would buy, but the fact of her discarding it, or of her secession from the convention, would not and could not be an act of hostility. The paper-using nation would be thereafter wholly outside the convention, and would exercise no influence upon it. She would in monetary matters be a neutral. She might even wholly discard metallic money and yet fulfil every article of the treaty to the letter, for she might safely adhere to her promise and coin every ounce of silver or gold brought to her mint for the purpose, inasmuch as it is abundantly obvious that not an ounce would be so brought; and this would be the case whether the secession, formal or virtual, were the offspring of war or of caprice. All the metallic circulation would have left the country (in accordance with the "Gresham Law"), and would have gone to augment the circulation of other commercial nations—silver and gold indifferently to the bimetallic nations, and if there were any outside the convention, then silver to the silver-using nations and gold to those whose money was gold.

Now what we desire to impress upon our readers is that this last result is precisely what would follow from the adoption of a paper currency by a nation under stress of war or otherwise at this present time, and could not therefore in any sense be traced to the adoption of a bimetallic standard. The immediate result of it would be exactly the same now in the absence of a bimetallic convention as it would be if such a convention existed; but the practical consequences to other nations would be somewhat more decided in the former case than in the latter.

Let us take Italy for example.

If after completing her resumption of cash payments and withdrawing £16,000,000 of paper currency she were unhappily to go to war, she would most probably think herself obliged to undo her work and re-issue paper. The £16,000,000 of gold would flow over, not into all other nations, but exclusively into those having a gold standard, and the effect, prejudicial or otherwise, would be so much the greater; for if she had entered with others into a bimetallic convention the £16,000,000 would, or might, be partly gold and partly silver, and the metal would pass into the currency of all nations having a bimetallic standard.

But let us suppose for the sake of argument that a nation bound by a bimetallic convention had succeeded in separating herself from her co-signatories, and adopting, let us say, a single gold standard. Beyond the confusion and mischief which the operation, whether successful or not, would have caused, no permanent alteration of prices would ensue. Her silver would have passed to her neighbours, and they would all have been laid under a contribution of an equal value in gold. They would but stand where France stood for seventy years, not however as France did, alone, but supporting one another, and not as France did, with all the world drawing from her one metal or the other, but with only one or one additional monometallic nation capable of doing any such thing.

Even if all the nations parties to the convention were to become monometallic but one, that one would stand exactly in the same position and under the same conditions as France did until 1873; and we take leave to think that the "sufferings" of France under those circumstances existed only in the imaginations of our own countrymen. Certainly the French failed to discover them.

We return to what we said at the beginning of this article. There is no faith in treaties where self-interest points to their destruction; but the conclusion to which the above considerations lead us is that that one incentive which is necessary to the breaking of treaties would be altogether lacking in the case of a treaty for the maintenance of a bimetallic standard in commercial nations. Not only can no ground of self-interest be discovered for destroying such a treaty, but self-interest would be strong enough in any nation in which both metals were by treaty with other nations in like case current as standard money, to cause her to cling to a system the destruction of which by herself alone could only be accomplished at the cost of confusion to her commerce and heavy loss to her exchequer.

HENRY H. GIBBS.

THE VALUE OF MONEY.

From *The Bullionist*, May 20, 1882.

Our contemporary, the *Economist*, sums up his leading article on "Bimetallism and the Bank Reserve," in the issue of the 8th of April, by saying that "whatever results "might follow from the adoption of a bimetallic standard "we may be certain . . . that cheaper money would not "follow from it, nor fewer fluctuations in the English "money market."

If the writer of the article supposed that bimetallists expected the adoption of a bimetallic standard to cause the rate of interest on loans to be permanently low, to bring about a new era of "cheap money," unvaried by any fluctuations, it would have been easy for him to have found arguments good enough to dispel such a hope. But no such expectation has ever been entertained, so far as has come to our knowledge, and we shall presently show that his arguments do not touch the real effect which the adoption of a bimetallic standard would produce.

Much of the error that seems inseparable from the subject of money arises, as most errors do, from a confusion of terms; and we propose to show in this article where the error lies, and what phrase it is that is so much abused in common parlance. The *Economist* perceives and strives to avoid the confusion, but it has not carried out what it has perceived to its legitimate conclusion, nor, indeed, would it have suited the course of its argument fully to do so.

It is the phrase at the head of our article—Value of Money—which is so frequently misused by being employed now in one sense now in another.

There is one simple and plain meaning of the phrase—the only philosophical one—which implies the comparison between money—between the gold, silver, or whatever substance is used as the common measure—and other commodities. What is the value of a quarter of wheat? So much of that common measure—so much money. What is the value of money? So much wheat, or other commodities that may be measured by it.

The value of money at large wanes or waxes in comparison with the mass of other commodities in the exact ratio to the quantity of money in the world and of commodities exchangeable for money.

It is to the value of money in this sense that Professor Jevons no doubt refers in his famous similitude of the two reservoirs of water liable to be differently lowered or raised in level by various accidents happening to one or the other, but which when connected by a pipe passing between them maintain the same level whatever happens.

When gold is money in one country and silver is money in another, a great increase in the quantity of gold, such as was caused by the discoveries in Australia and California, lowers the value of gold money in relation to silver and all other commodities, while the relation of silver money to all commodities but gold remains unchanged; a great increase in the quantity of silver, such as took place after the Spanish conquests in America, has exactly the converse effect.

The pipe of connection is, as Professor Jevons says, the law of the bimetallic standard. When that is applied, the increase of either metal is an increase, not of the gold or silver money respectively, but of the total money of the world, and, all other things being equal, a rise in the price or value of the mass of other commodities, and a fall in the value of money; the decrease of either metal, on the other hand, is a decrease in the total money of the world, a rise in its value, and a corresponding fall in the price or value of the mass of commodities measured by it.

So then the writer of the article in the *Economist* is manifestly in error where he says that "Professor Jevons' "observations on the point do not refer to the value of "money at all," and his saying so appears to us to be a striking instance of the confusion of thought and ambiguity of utterance on which we have remarked; for it is precisely to the value of money in the proper sense of the phrase—that is to say, to the value of metallic money as compared with commodities—that he does refer.

But it is not to that only that his illustration applies; and we propose to show that the equilibratory action of the bimetallic standard must affect the "value of money," taking that phrase in its most common and least accurate sense.

In the common acceptation of the term it is used—in City articles and the like—not at all for the value or purchasing power of metallic money, but for the rate of interest to be paid for the loan of capital, as, for instance, for the price to be paid for the immediate command of the sum drawn by a bill of exchange before the time when it would probably become due.

We may say in passing that in this sense the saying of the *Economist* that "the value of money is reckoned in "money itself" is indeed intelligible, but seems to us to be a very slipshod mode of speech, and not less so than the statement in the same paragraph that "money can "buy money." Money can buy commodities of all kinds, including gold and silver, when either of these are not money; but money it cannot buy. If it can, we would repeat the question which has been asked elsewhere in reply to the same statement—"How much of it can one "have for a sovereign?"

To return to Professor Jevons' equilibratory action, and to the belief in universal and continuous "cheapness "of money" which the *Economist* attributes to bimetallists. It would indeed be absurd to allege that the establishment of a bimetallic standard would do away with fluctuations in the market rate of interest. Those fluctuations are inevitable, and must take place from day to day according as the demand for loans and the supply of capital to be lent correspond or not with one another. But the *Economist*, in citing J. S. Mill as a witness, misleads its readers; for by his words, where he says that "the rate of interest "does not depend on the quantity of money in circulation," he certainly means "on the total quantity of money in "circulation in the world." It is hardly necessary to say that it may depend on the quantity of metallic money in circulation at any given moment in any particular country, and does depend in England, and that to a very considerable extent, on the amount of gold existing in the Bank.

The rate of interest depends then on the demand for and supply of capital available for loans, which demand, as the *Economist* truly says, includes in itself "every "demand arising from trade or commerce or from any other "source"; but the supply, under our laws, depends more particularly on the balance of trade and the necessity of paying the foreigner in cash that which at the moment we cannot pay in kind. Gold in that case leaves the vaults of the Bank of England for export, and by that means as by any other, such as for the needs of the Scottish circulation or for harvest purposes at home, the reserve of the Bank is diminished and there is less capital to lend, the supply falls short of the demand, and the cost of that supply, that is to say the rate of interest on loans is enhanced.

All these effects are inseparable from our commerce under the salutary provisions of the Act of 1844, and are wholly independent of the question whether two metals or only one should be used as money. The difference arises at a further stage, that is to say when the amount of capital available for loans is again being augmented by means of the rise of the rate of interest here and the consequent attraction of foreign capital to take the benefit of it.

Under a gold standard the metal which is to replenish our circulation comes practically, so far as it is attracted by a high rate of interest, from France or the United States or Australia only, and before enough can come it may be necessary that the rate shall be raised higher and higher and through a longer period of time. But if the void could be supplied by silver as well as gold, every country using a metallic standard would be a well from whence we could draw, and as a consequence of the multitude of sources of supply would come competition for supplying us, and therefore a lower rate of interest in this market would suffice to create an inducement to our neighbours to provide the supply.

The converse of this would of course be the case when the tide set the other way, so that when the demand was for the export of specie from this country there would be a greater number of markets drawing upon us for their supply. So then the fluctuations of capital to and fro would be more continual, and consequently the changes in the rate of interest might be more frequent; but both the sums passing and the rates charged would be for the reasons above stated less considerable in amount; and this is exactly what has been demonstrated by Professor Jevons.

We believe, then, that we have shown that while no sane person hopes to do away with the national fluctuations in the "value of money," that is to say in the rate of interest on loans, there is reason to believe that under a bimetallic law, to quote the words of the *Economist*, "the "replenishing of the reserve of the Bank of England "would be done more readily than before, and that a lower "rate of interest would be sufficient for this than has "hitherto been the case," or rather than would be the case under the continuance of a monometallic standard.

HENRY H. GIBBS.

THE RATIO OF VALUE BETWEEN GOLD AND SILVER.

From the *Bullionist*, May 20, 1882.

TO THE EDITOR.

SIR,—I beg leave to offer for the consideration of readers of the *Bullionist* a view of the bimetallic question which may perhaps not have been presented to them by any other of your correspondents. I am one of those who question the assertion that any bimetallic law does, or can, alter or do more than very slightly affect the natural and intrinsic ratio of value existing between gold and silver. The bimetallists distinctly assert that the force of law will avail to make gold and silver coins in currency exchange at the rate of 1 oz. of gold for 15½ ozs. of silver, irrespective of the fact that the same metals are exchanging in the market in quite another ratio, and expect that if the nations agree to employ gold and silver on those terms in their currencies the metals when not used for currency purposes will sell at a corresponding valuation, because no holder of silver will sell at any other price. It is for them to show that by law or otherwise the ratio of 1 to 15½ can be established as a permanent condition in the exchange of the precious metals. I have heard it asserted, but never seen it proved to be possible.

It is probable that the *sic volo sic jubeo* of the American and Continental Governments will give a value to silver which it does not naturally possess? Or is it likely that when the ratio of 1 to $15\frac{1}{2}$ is declared to rule the legal tender and exchange, the necessary result will be that no one will buy or sell gold and silver for other than currency purposes except at the mint rate? As regards the first case, the bimetallists must show that the force of law has at any time availed to make gold and silver exchange at any other than their natural value. M. Cernuschi asserts it, I venture to say, in the face of all history.

Up to the time of King James I. the English sovereigns were constantly engaged in regulating by law the relation of value between gold and silver. But between the commencement of the reign of King James I. and that of King Charles II. gold rose in value against silver 32 per cent. The variations were frequent and excessive. King James had altogether failed to modify them, and King Charles left the matter alone, wisely deciding to let gold, which was not then the legal standard of value, take its rate in the currency from silver at the market price of the day. In the course of time gold gained an acknowledged ascendency over silver, because the medium with which international commercial balances were settled, and was felt to be so convenient for domestic use that Lord Liverpool in 1816 converted the silver coin of the realm into a token currency, and made gold by law, as it had long been by custom, the standard of value.

The French nation have tried, as the English did up to the beginning of the eighteenth century (1707), the effect of law, and have found it fail. It is easy to assert that because it was law in France that gold and silver coins should exchange on the basis of 1 oz. of gold to $15\frac{1}{2}$ ozs. of silver, and because that result was actually attained, therefore it was law that fixed the price of the precious metals; but, if this were the case, how does the bimetallist account for the sudden collapse of the law and its failure to maintain the ratio? He does not perceive that the

Mr. C. Daniell.

municipal law only exercised any regulating power as long as it was in unison with the natural law of value prevailing between the two metals; when the former law ran counter to the natural order ruling the exchange, it ceased to operate.

As long as France and the rest of the Latin Union principally employed silver for their currencies, and the currency valuation of silver in exchange for gold continued to correspond with the natural value, or nearly so, silver exchanged with gold at the legal rate. Silver was in all those years, if anything, the dearer metal. As soon as silver became the cheaper metal, and very much the cheaper metal, it fell in the currencies of the Latin Union, and the bimetallic law could do nothing to arrest its fall. The Latin Union has given up the attempt to maintain by law a ratio of exchange between the two metals. But the vast amount of silver lying idle in Europe and the United States of America, by reason of its being excluded from its proper function—its use as money—has led its owners to agitate for an universal convention among nations to use the metal as coin on its former footing.

Bimetallists, however, trust not so much to the force of law to create an artificial rate of exchange as to the hope that if all nations will refuse to sell or buy gold and silver for currency purposes except at one valuation, all gold and silver bought and sold for any other purpose will exchange at the same rate.

But let us suppose that America and the Latin Union agree to sell 1 oz. of gold for 15½ ozs. of silver, in exchanging their coins they will still have a formidable difficulty to overcome.

It is this: Assuming the ratio of exchange for currency purposes to be fixed by all the associated nations at 1 oz. of gold for 15½ ozs. of silver, it is quite clear that unless the currencies of those nations absorb nearly all the silver which is available for coinage, there will be a considerable balance of silver in the world entirely unaffected by the metallic law, and that balance will be continually increased by fresh excavations of silver from below the earth. It may be argued that, following the example of their Governments, the people of the associated nations will sell no more than 15½ ozs. of silver for 1 oz. of gold. This argument is good *quoad* the currency; but the capacity of the currency to absorb the supply of silver is limited—very limited in comparison with the quantity of silver waiting for absorption. All the silver therefore offered for sale in excess of the quantity required for currency would clearly not sell at the high price of 15½ ozs. for 1 oz. of gold, but at any price at which it would pay the producer to sell it—16, 17, or 18 ozs. The result would be that silver would flow into the associated countries and be exchanged for gold at something between 15½ ozs. and 18 ozs. for 1 oz. of gold, and the gold thus obtained would be taken away from the associated countries, *i.e.*, from the western continents, and disappear in Asia.

In Asia there exists a continual and probably insatiable demand for gold, and at the same time a vast silver treasure which could be shipped to Europe, coined into the currencies of the associated nations without violation of the letter or spirit of the law of the bimetallic convention, and be used to buy up the gold coins; these on their arrival in the East would purchase in the silver current coins of Asia about 20 per cent. more silver than had been spent in the purchase of the gold coins themselves in Europe, and this operation would be repeated until gold had disappeared from the currencies of the associated nations. It must be evident that immediately the trader from Asia began to operate in this way, these nations must either withdraw gold altogether from their currencies, or, by limiting the quantity of silver employed in them, prevent the public from coining silver at its own discretion for the purchase of the gold coins in the same currencies. If either course

Mr. C. Daniell.

were taken, the "principle of bimetallism," the "bimetallic "law," and all the rest of it would vanish into air.

If the members of an International Monetary Union agreed to use gold and silver only on particular terms among themselves, their doing so would not affect the value in exchange of the two metals in countries outside the Union, unless it obtained a monopoly, or a quasi-monopoly, of the precious metals—an achievement which the following consideration shows is practically impossible.

India is the largest employer of silver, using about one-fifth of all the coined silver estimated to be circulating in the world. She alone absorbs from eight to ten millions sterling per annum in value of silver treasure; and the fact that no perceptible enhancement in the price of silver results from the demand made by India and other silver-using countries on the world's supply of surplus silver, proves that the stocks of metal are undergoing no sensible diminution, but that, on the other hand, they are being replenished by fresh excavations at a price which, although low, is profitable. What reasonable grounds, then, exist for the expectation that any possible stimulus to the use of silver, as currency, will cause the absorption of so large a portion of the metal already available for coin, as to fix the price of the remainder at the currency ratio of 1 to 15½? Whatever the quantity may be which can thus be absorbed, its place will be immediately taken by silver dug from the mines, and sold at a cost so low as to be fatal to the maintenance of the arbitrary ratio which the bimetallist convention seeks to establish. All the nations of Europe and America taken together cannot absorb all, or nearly all, the available silver above and below ground, unless gold be expelled from their currencies, when the *raison d'être* of their bimetallism would melt away; and until these nations do succeed in absorbing nearly the whole of these stocks of silver, they cannot maintain an artificial ratio of value in the exchange of the precious metals.

That the silver of Asia would be used to buy up the gold of Europe is a danger which the Conference that sat in Paris last year clearly foresaw, is proved by the suggestion of the German delegates, that the bimetallist countries should act alone in fixing the ratio of exchange—that other States should secure the States of the Monetary Union from an inundation of their silver; and that in any case England should give guarantees that the "International "Monetary Union should not by its gold flowing into India "be flooded with Indian silver."

Asia, then, is the rock on which such a bimetallic law as that which we are discussing will be wrecked; and it is clear that the natural ratio of value will always defeat any scheme to fix by law or agreement an arbitrary rate of exchange for the two metals.

People talk very glibly of the American and Continental mints coining silver to any amount, but this will not avail to raise its price unless there is a demand for it when it is coined—in other words it will not be coined in greater quantities than commerce requires; and what is that quantity? It will prove to be very small, because it is a well-established law of currency in its relation to commerce that the bulk of the coin in use can only be increased in correspondence with an increase in the value of the goods brought into the market to be exchanged into money. The coin now in circulation in the world is not less than is required—too much of it may be gold, perhaps, and too little of it silver—for general convenience, but the sum of the two metals used as coin is not so insufficient as to attract much more coin into the currencies of the world than is now in use. The owners of silver, therefore, can only gain their object—that is, get rid of their surplus silver by ousting gold from circulation to a value corresponding to that of the silver which they introduce into the currency. But how are they to do this? There is no such thing as forcing silver into a currency already sufficient for business

Mr. C. Daniell.

purposes. Some small quantity may be taken in fractional coinage, but no large quantity of silver can get a footing in any existing currency except it expel a corresponding value of gold. There is no possibility of extinguishing the ordinary laws of supply and demand, and when the surplus silver of the world is coined it will be just as much surplus silver as it was before.

Do the bimetallists really believe that they will be able to appropriate any large quantity of the coined gold of the world, or drive it out of circulation, substituting silver for it, and if not, how do they expect to float their silver without doing so? Assuming, for the sake of argument, that such a bimetallic law is thoroughly enforced, the first result would be that India would obtain such large quantities of gold in exchange for her silver that she would cry out for a gold standard and a gold currency from sheer lack of silver. She would be forced to coin her hoards of surplus gold probably exceeding £150,000,000 sterling in value. But this is not one of the objects of the bimetallists. They insist on England promising that India shall not change her standard. What would be India's condition then, depleted of her silver and not allowed to coin her gold? The interest of money would rise enormously, and the necessaries of life fall in price in correspondence with the diminution of the coin in currency.

The order of nature and the laws of supply and demand equally forbid the hope that the currency value of the two metals will be other than their intrinsic value as long as Asia is found a field for the employment of silver as coin in free commerce, unfettered by any artificial bimetallic law. The nation which undertakes to use both gold and silver in its currency, and at the same time places no limit on the quantity of either kind of coin in circulation, but such as the needs of commerce and the volition of the people provide, can only make each kind of coin exchange for the other without loss to the holders of either, by fixing the rate of exchange in strict correspondence with the ratio of intrinsic value which from time to time prevails in the market between the two metals. Every other plan for working a bimetallic currency, without limitation in the supply of coin, experience and reason show to be impracticable.

CLARMONT DANIELL.

INDIA, *April,* 1882.

"WHITHER WOULD THE DEARER METAL GO?"

From *The Bullionist*, June 24, 1882.

THIS important and vital question is asked by Mr. Gibbs in the 53rd page of his pamphlet, *The Double Standard.* Mr. Clarmont Daniell, in a letter published in the *Bullionist* of the 20th May, has endeavoured to answer it.

His letter is *apparently* merely a contribution to the discussion upon the ratio of value between gold and silver, and as such a most excellent answer appeared from the pen of Mr. B. Kisch in the columns of the same paper on the 11th inst.

But no notice was taken of the bold handling by Mr. Daniell of the crucial question, "Whither will the dearer metal go?"

Concurring in Mr. Kisch's answer to the remainder of the letter, we desire to say a few words on the point which to a certain sense Mr. Daniell has made his own.

He published in 1879 a pamphlet on *Gold in the East.*

The remedy proposed therein for the evils existing from loss by exchange was—To coin gold in India: to make the coinage of that country a gold one: to recognise the fact that gold is and must be the "universal measure of value."

For this proposition there is a great deal to be said, and if the debtor world are ready to face the expense of it

s 2

to them, or if the creditor world are ready to enter into some compromise tending to diminish their interest in the operation, it might be a good thing.

We should in such a case have to supplement the question of Mr. Gibbs by an enquiry, "Whither would the "cheaper metal go?"

We mention this fact with regard to Mr. Daniell's past writings in order to account for the bold answer to be found in his letter now under consideration.

His statement is that there exists in India an unlimited treasure of silver and an insatiable demand for gold, and that no sooner was a bimetallic union declared between the Great Powers of the world, than the Indian people would at once dispose of all their silver at 15½ to 1, or even more, in order to procure that gold.

In order that there may be no mistake about Mr. Daniell's proposition, we quote the paragraphs to which we allude in full:—

"All the silver therefore offered for sale in excess of the "quantity required for currency would clearly not sell at the "high price of 15½ ozs. for 1 oz. of gold, but at any price at "which it would pay the producer to sell it—16, 17, or 18 ozs. "The result would be that silver would flow into the associated "countries and be exchanged for gold at something between "15½ ozs. and 18 ozs. for 1 oz. of gold, and the gold thus obtained "would be taken away from the associated countries, *i.e.*, from "the western continents, and disappear in Asia.

"In Asia there exists a continual and probably insatiable "demand for gold, and at the same time a vast silver treasure "which could be shipped to Europe, coined into the currencies of "the associated nations without violation of the letter or spirit "of the law of the bimetallic convention, and be used to buy "up the gold coins; these on their arrival in the East would "purchase in the silver current coins of Asia about 20 per cent. "more silver than had been spent in the purchase of the gold

Mr. H. R. Grenfell.

"coins themselves in Europe, and this operation would be "repeated until gold had disappeared from the currencies of the "associated nations. It must be evident that immediately the "trader from Asia began to operate in this way these nations "must either withdraw gold altogether from their currencies, or, by "limiting the quantity of silver employed in them, prevent the "public from coining silver at its own discretion for the purchase "of the gold coins in the same currencies. If either course were "taken the principle of 'bimetallism,' the 'bimetallic law,' and "all the rest of it would vanish into air.

"If the members of an International Monetary Union agreed "to use gold and silver only on particular terms among them-"selves, their doing so would not affect the value in exchange of "the two metals in countries outside the Union, unless it obtained "a monopoly or a quasi-monopoly of the precious metals—an "achievement which the following consideration shows is "practically impossible :—

"India is the largest employer of silver, using about one-fifth "of all the coined silver estimated to be circulating in the world. "She alone absorbs from eight to ten millions sterling per annum "in value of silver treasure; and the fact that no perceptible "enhancement in the price of silver results from the demand "made by India and other silver-using countries on the world's "supply of surplus silver, proves that the stocks of metal are "undergoing no sensible diminution, but that, on the other hand, "they are being replenished by fresh excavations at a price "which, although low, is profitable. What reasonable grounds, "then, exist for the expectation that any possible stimulus to the "use of silver as currency will cause the absorption of so large a "portion of the metal already available for coin as to fix the price "of the remainder at the currency ratio of 1 to 15½? Whatever "the quantity may be which can thus be absorbed, its place will "be immediately taken by silver dug from the mines, and sold at "a cost so low as to be fatal to the maintenance of the arbitrary "ratio which the bimetallist convention seeks to establish. All "the nations of Europe and America taken together cannot "absorb all, or nearly all, the available silver above and below "ground, unless gold be expelled from their currencies, when the "*raison d'être* of their bimetallism would melt away; and until "these nations do succeed in absorbing nearly the whole of these "stocks of silver, they cannot maintain an artificial ratio of value "in the exchange of the precious metals."

The difficulty of understanding Mr. Daniell's proposition is that he does not state clearly what position he attributes to India with regard to the supposed bimetallic league.

We must therefore do for him what he has not done for us.

I. We will suppose that the whole British Empire including India should be part of the bimetallic league.

If such were the case, on what ground does he suppose that a mere insatiable desire for gold, alleged by him to exist, would enable India to use all her silver treasure and all her silver coin to purchase and take away all the gold from her sister bimetallic nations.

The statement, if it means anything, amounts to an assertion that an Indian having silver coin in his possession and owing rent, and having to pay wages and other debts which the bimetallic law permits to be paid in silver, will at once insist on paying the carriage of that coin to a seaport in order to get gold back, which will only when it arrives pay the debts he owes precisely as the silver would have done.

But supposing the transactions within the country are, as monometallists assure us, on so small a scale that no gold coin would be small enough to carry them on, how is this insatiable desire for gold to make up to the people for the loss of their fractional currency?

Let us now turn to the great merchants and cosmopolitan traders of Bombay, Kurrachee, Calcutta, and Madras.

Mr. H. R. Grenfell.

Are we to believe that they, having dealt in silver rupees all their lives and having been accustomed to a silver currency, will at once with the stroke of the pen, at the moment when agreements have been made to rehabilitate silver, declare their preference for gold and insist upon paying a premium for the metal the superiority of which beyond the ratio has just been destroyed; and that having exchanged all the silver which the country wants for fractional currency against gold which cannot be used for it, they will create a paper fractional currency, founded on their stores of gold?

But should they do so, the Indian public being accustomed to a metallic currency, would most probably refuse to take it since it is notorious that the present issues, even though guaranteed by the statutes of the Bank of Calcutta, Bombay, and Madras, are not easily circulated.

The proposition then that India would, notwithstanding her membership of the bimetallic convention, absorb all the gold from the other countries from mere insatiable desire, cannot be taken seriously.

II. Let us then take Mr. Daniell's next suggestion as found in another paragraph.

" That the silver of Asia would be used to buy up the gold
" of Europe is a danger which the Conference that sat in Paris
" last year clearly foresaw, is proved by the suggestion of the
" German delegates, that the bimetallist countries should act
" alone in fixing the ratio of exchange—that other States should
" secure the States of the Monetary Union from an inundation of
" their silver; and that in any case England should give guaran-
" tees that the 'International Monetary Union should not by its
" 'gold flowing into India be flooded with Indian silver.' "

By this we presume that he contemplates India being left out of the Bimetallic Union as proposed in last year's Conference, at which, with a view of getting the other countries to adopt bimetallism, the Indian Government proposed a covenant not to alter the silver standard for ten years. If such an arrangement had been brought about, how is it possible to suppose that men in India from mere love of gold, which they could not get coined or with which they could not pay their debts, would part with all their silver which would serve for both purposes?

Both or either of these propositions, if sifted, amount to this: that Indians will give some sum varying between 15½ and 18, in order to procure a metal which in one case has no more value than that shown by the fixed ratio, and in the other has less.

Such suggestions as these are, however, most valuable contributions to the controversy. They are in fact features in it which have to be considered.

And in considering them before setting them aside we are bound to enquire wherein the fallacy in them is to be found.

Mr. Daniell's proposition is evidently founded on the idea that a nation will not absorb more currency than it really has need for, and that when all the metals necessary for coinage have been absorbed by the bimetallic nations there will still remain a large balance, which he thinks will be of silver, for which there is no demand. In this he makes a statement which is in part accurate, but founds on it a most unreasonable conclusion, because he forgets that there exists between the money in circulation and the raw precious metal a store of money for future use.

If the silver in the world is redundant, and if by the bimetallic law all possessors of silver have a right to have it coined at 15½ to 1, instead of the owners of silver selling it at 18 to 1, they will send it to the bimetallic mints to be coined, and the silver so coined will be added to the stock of money existing. The existence of such a stock will cause the value of money to fall and that of commodities to rise, precisely in the same way as when a large new discovery of gold takes place or a large issue of paper currency.

The principal delusion under which Mr. Daniell labours is that Indians will ship silver to Europe solely to obtain gold for it. It is quite true that if he is correct in saying that the desire for the latter is insatiable, they might have even with the bimetallic practice to pay more than 15½ to 1 for it, because the debtor would have the right to pay in whichever metal he chose. But for any other purpose than to satisfy the insatiable desire, silver would be at the fixed ratio and no other. To buy cotton goods, copper, iron, coals, steam-engines or any other ordinary articles the price of which is written in pounds sterling, silver would be as good as gold, and gold as silver at the statutory price.

In conclusion, we congratulate Mr. Daniell on an earnest endeavour to answer Mr. Gibbs' question, and on the serious and suggestive manner in which he has handled it.

H. R. GRENFELL.

"BIMETALLIC ENGLAND."*

From *The Bullionist*, June 24, 1882.

THE heading of our article is the title of a remarkable pamphlet by N. Ottomar Haupt, and we propose to give a succinct account of the work, and to supplement it by some remarks of our own.

M. Haupt is a German resident in Paris, and has been for many years an enthusiastic advocate of bimetallism—how good an advocate is shown by the arguments of the pamphlet before us, and how courageous an advocate by the language in which it is written. It is very seldom that a man, however good a linguist, will venture to write a treatise on a difficult subject in a language not his own, and we must congratulate M. Haupt on the success of his present effort. An occasional failure in idiomatic accuracy causes us the more to appreciate his mastery of the language; for such slips show us that he had no English reviser, and that the credit therefore is all his own.

The object of the pamphlet is to prove that England could and ought to join a general bimetallic league; that her doing so would be convenient and advantageous not only to commerce in general, but to English commerce in particular. The author begins by enumerating—in answer to Lord Sherbrooke's arrogant denunciation of the folly of

* Published by Effingham Wilson, Royal Exchange.

bimetallists, and in confutation of the scornful innuendoes by which he strives to make his readers believe all eminent students of political economy to be of his mind—the goodly array of writers, French, English, and German, all foremost in the ranks of political economy, who have either advocated bimetallism or allowed its practical possibility.

He adds, as a counter-assertion to Lord Sherbrooke's, that—

> "Those who are not convinced of the fact that bimetallism "can stand on its own legs, and that the action of a double "standard adopted by all the leading European nations and by "the United States of America is fully in harmony with the "existing economical laws, and must lead to satisfactory results, "simply wish to shut their eyes on purpose."

M. Haupt then gives a table of the numbers of francs, marks, florins per kilo. fine, and of dollars and shillings per ounce fine, which would be coined under a bimetallic league at the several mints of the Latin Union, Berlin, Amsterdam, Vienna, New York, and London, and of the several sums which would be delivered per kilo. or ounce at the several national banks after deductions for commission, interest, and brassage.

Further he presents a tabular view of what he calls the mint-pars of France, Germany, Holland, and America with England, and the "gold point," or exact point in the exchange at which gold can be profitably exported into or imported from those countries, showing that were silver accepted by them all as well as by England the same figures would apply to silver.

He then contemplates a time when "the English four-"shilling piece shall have been created—a handsome brand-"new coin, struck on the basis of 1 gold to 15½ silver, that "is to say a piece weighing 378·7 grains of the usual British "standard ·925 fine, at par with the similar coins of the

Mr. H. H. Gibbs,

"Latin Union, of Germany, of the United States, etc., and "convertible without any loss whatever any day into their "monies, based as they are on the same metals at the same "ratio between gold and silver, and kept in circulation "on the same footing. In other words," he says, "it is "excellent money at home—international coin in the "fullest acceptation of the term."

He complains of the present condition of silver, circulating, where it is standard money, at a nominal value of 15 per cent., and where it is fractional currency, at a nominal value of 22 to 24 per cent., above the value to which arbitrary legislation has temporarily degraded it, and foresees the instant cure of this disorder in the repeal of this arbitrary legislation and the return to the ancient law of England and France consolidated by agreement with other countries.

In the remainder of the pamphlet M. Haupt points out the dangers of allowing the question to sleep, gives a sketch of what has been already done to awaken Germany, France and Belgium to the urgent necessities of the situation, and referring to the good work of Arendt, de Laveleye and others in this direction, he concludes with—

> "And against this overwhelming majority of the best "authorities of the day, against the countless manifestations of "all classes of society, against this compact front of public "opinion, it is thought that old-fashioned prejudice, ignorance, "custom, and all the other futile pretexts which are employed "to hinder the development of bimetallism can hold their own "in England! Away with the idea! It may be that years will "elapse before the full necessity of a change in the monetary "policy is realised in the leading circles of the country; the "movement itself is there and cannot any more be arrested."

In presenting this book to our readers and urging their perusal of it, we do not endorse every word of its argument, although we consider it a remarkable production and a valuable contribution to the literature of the subject. Its author has treated of bimetallism in England as he hopes and as we believe that it would be ; but we must add a few words by way of showing what it would *not* be ; for such words are necessary as a corrective to the fruits of the vivid imaginations of writers like Lord Sherbrooke and Mr. Crump, which have been lately offered to and (notwithstanding their being so much out of season) swallowed by an unsuspecting public. For the public—too many of them—do swallow, though they make no attempt to digest these fruits of imagination. Of Mr. Crump it must be said that he committed suicide, as far as the bimetallic discussion is concerned, when in an evil hour he was tempted to appear in his own person, instead of as the occult authority of Printing House Square, which still exercises sway over a few minds, if only by its audacity in saying on Monday the direct opposite of what it said on Saturday. But of Lord Sherbrooke people ask, was he not Chancellor of the Exchequer, and must it not be supposed that a Chancellor of the Exchequer knows all that can be known about money matters? Now in that supposition they are at direct variance with his Lordship, who says frankly that he does not know anything at all about bimetallism—cannot indeed make out what it is. But that is not in the least a reason why he should not write about it. He is not the first and will not be the last man of transcendent ability who has talked, and talked well, of what he does not understand. We have before expressed our enjoyment of his article, which is very pretty reading, written in the choicest English, and lacking nothing but a knowledge of the subject. We should be the first to admit that our monometallic friends have retained a most brilliant advocate for the defence. We picture him in wig and gown, with brief unread, catching at the whispers of his junior behind him, and then pouring forth an impassioned diatribe, which may satisfy and convince a jury to whom Standard and Currency, the Gresham Law, and all the other terms employed are so much heathen Greek, but who think "the learned counsel must be right, he speaks so well!" and who cannot fail to be convinced by his metaphor of "the waves foaming out their own shame." "Why, he "has Scripture on his side, hasn't he?" In a previous article we have noticed Lord Sherbrooke's remedy for the lack of gold, namely a fall in prices, or in other words heavy loss to the selling class—and now we come to another instance of the superficial character of his Lordship's thoughts, which presents itself in connection with our present subject. He tells us that the necessary consequences of having two independent currencies, of having a bimetallic standard, in short, is that there will be to every transaction two bargains, one as to the price to be paid, and a second as to the metal in which it is to be paid; and the reason in his mind is, that the varying cost of production will necessarily alter the relative value of the metals from day to day, and that it will be more to the advantage of the buyer to pay in one and more to the advantage of the seller to be paid in the other.

But if any fact in political economy be established, it is this, that the influence of the cost of production on the vast stock of the precious metals produced that they may be stored, is wholly different from that of the cost of production on those commodities which as money those metals purchase, commodities ephemeral in their nature, perishable, and produced in order that they may be consumed and perish. There can be no temptation to the English seller to stipulate for one metal rather than another, when he can by law not only pay his own debts to his English creditor in one as well as in the other, but his Italian, French, German, and practically every other creditor also. We deny, therefore, the possibility of two bargains, and have yet to meet with any well-considered statement which should show how such bargains could find a place in the market of "Bimetallic England."

We may be excused devoting much space to Mr. Crump's waggon-load of silver which he dreads he may have to drive home to pay his housekeeping bills. If a waggon will be needed for silver in the future, surely a wheelbarrow must be needed for gold now; yet we do not find that mode of transport required when every transfer of £100,000 Consols is paid for. Mr. Crump should know, and perhaps really does know a great deal better than this, but he must have forgotten for the moment that he was writing in London, the city of banks and cheques and clearing houses, where every conceivable banking expedient is in daily use, and where the British sovereign is confined either to its praiseworthy use of tipping school-boys, or at most to its office of discharging debts under five pounds. It is no doubt conceivable that this last operation might be performed on very rare occasions with an equivalent number of double florins as the instrument; but there is no manner of fear that the establishment of a bimetallic standard would be the signal for the sudden flight of every British sovereign from this country, nor for the coming of a time when either, as in Spain, porters shall be seen carrying bags of dollars on their shoulders to pay their patron's tailor's bills, or as in the imagination of Mr. Crump, waggoners shall be seen passing between all parts of London with their jingling loads of silver.

The specie in the vaults of the Bank of England, whether gold or silver, would serve as it now does to discharge the international indebtedness of England, and the hundred millions of sovereigns said to be in the pockets of Englishmen throughout the country would circulate among them as heretofore, until at least the time should arrive when our opponents, zealous for the purity of the standard and detesting above all things the depreciation of the national money, should issue or cause to be issued a flood of one-pound notes, at which time our sovereigns will indeed make themselves wings and fly, and we shall be reduced, so far as the issue of notes is fiduciary, to a currency of pure and unalloyed paper.

We are not bigots in the cause of bimetallism; we keep our minds free and our ears open, and are most willing to hear arguments which shall show that our present belief is wrong; but hitherto the advocates of the bimetallic standard have rarely been met with any attempt at serious argument; the usual weapons of their adversaries have been tirades like Lord Sherbrooke's, rich in vituperation, but barren in argument. This last week a writer in the *Saturday Review*, discussing "Question-time" in the House of Commons, speaks of "the paradox of bimetallism" much as the late Dr. Dionysius Lardner once spoke, in the hearing of the present writer, of the "paradox" of proposing to send steam-vessels across the Atlantic; or as if some Lardner of the present day should maintain that though France and England had sent steam-vessels thither for forty years it would be a paradox to assert that other nations could do it. It cannot be too often repeated that that which the *Saturday Review* calls a paradox was the law of England till 1816, and the law of France till 1873; that it did not "break down" in the latter country, as Mr. Clarmont Daniell supposes, but maintained intact the equality of silver and gold in the proportions fixed by the law till the very moment when an unwise timidity induced the French Government to relax and then to suspend the law.

There is indeed a paradox in the money doctrines of the present day, and that is this, that while monometallists assert that it is indispensable for safe and just commerce between man and man that we should have one uniform medium of exchange, and while they deem it impossible that either gold or silver alone should be that medium, they are satisfied that England should use gold as her standard money, while India uses silver, and other nations either gold or silver or gold and silver.

The folly of *this* paradox must before long become evident to all who think on the subject, and the only thing now wanting to the establishment of a uniform though compound medium of exchange throughout the commercial world is the concurrence and co-operation of "Bimetallic England."

HENRY H. GIBBS.

PAPER OR METALLIC INFLATION.

From the *Bullionist*, June 24, 1882.

THE pleas of the monometallists are substantially the same as the proverbial pleas of the man who was accused of borrowing a kettle entire and of sending it back to its owner with a hole in it. The pleas were that he borrowed it with a hole in it; that he sent it back entire; that he never borrowed it at all.

So with the monometallists.

They urge that the proper cure for the evil existing is paper currency.

That bimetallism is an improper cure.

That there is no evil at all.

Evidence has been produced as to the borrowing of the kettle or the existence of the evil.

The evil has been admitted by Lord Grey, Mr. Jevons, and Mr. Giffen. Prices have fallen to an unwonted extent. Their fall cannot be attributed to ordinary trade oscillations or to the usual alterations of undue caution and extravagant confidence. The fact that all producers, both agricultural and manufacturing, have been working to a loss cannot be disputed. It can also not be seriously disputed that things in time will accommodate themselves without any empirical remedies. But it is equally manifest that the present state of things cannot remain, and that unless some remedy be applied the monetary revolution of Germany will be repeated by other States, augmenting the evil according to the monometallist calculation fourfold.

What then are the remedies proposed?

One is to increase the fiduciary issue of paper; the other to resort to the bimetallic agreement.

Great fault has been found with the Governor of the Bank for venturing to assert that it is probable that Lord Liverpool or Sir Robert Peel, with the new facts before them presented by the German monetary revolution, would, according to the principles on which their writings and speeches were founded, have looked with favour on an international agreement for bimetallism.

Lord Liverpool said that "Every branch of the circu- "lating medium should be founded on solid, wise, and honest "principles." He also told us what he meant by a currency founded on feeble, unwise, and dishonest principles—namely, an unlimited issue of paper money. He thought a paper currency to be good so far and no further as the issue was limited to the amount of the "gold and silver" of which it supplied the place. What he considered unwise was to admit the contention of certain "speculative writers" that paper currency "may be made to represent even "immovable property." He says, "It seems to have been "discovered of late years in this country that by a new sort "of alchēmy coins of gold and silver may be converted into "paper, and that the precious metals had better be exported "to serve as capital to foreign countries where no such "discovery has yet been made."

Ricardo proposed that the benefits of a paper currency and a metallic basis should be secured to its fullest extent by keeping all the circulation in paper, but maintaining a sufficient amount of bullion to meet every note issued.

The Act of 1844 was a compromise between the extreme views of the alchemists and Ricardo, the intention of its author being to entice the English country bank issues to

Mr. H. R. Grenfell.

die out gradually, and the Scotch to live on as long as the then existing banks had any life in them.

The proposal of those who admit the evils now resulting from the dislocation in the prices of the precious metals by the German demonetisation, is to supplement the diminished volume of the circulation by a return to unrepresented paper currency.

Mr. Fowler's proposition in the House of Commons was an abstract resolution in the sense of "forthwith" devising a scheme with that view, and to enlarge the basis of the fiduciary issue in the direction of an emission of one-pound notes otherwise than on the deposit of bullion.

Many most eminent writers have been in favour of some such alteration, but the most distinguished of them have been or are interested in deposit banking combined with what we call private coining.

We bullionists believe that coining is an attribute of the State. The monopoly or privilege still left to the Bank of England in its issue department we deem to be a part of its Government business rather than of its private adventure. Our opponents are apt to suggest that all bimetallists are either interested in silver mines or in trade with silver-using countries. It might be said on the other hand that all monometallists are either issuing or would-be issuing bankers.

Such accusations on either side are beside the question. All men are apt to feel partially towards the laws which engender profits to themselves, and all wise men admit the fact and make just such allowance for it as marksmen do for currents of air.

The opponents of bimetallism are continually accusing us of wishing to increase the volume of the circulation, and of thereby diminishing the purchasing power of the pound sterling. They have asked us over and over again to define our objects, and if they are not as they have stated them to be, to say what they are. They have also requested us to adjudicate in the matter of contracts already entered into, and to express ourselves clearly, if possible, as to what would happen if silver were once more raised to what we call its normal value, and what they call its artificial value.

With regard to contracts a reply has been given over and over again. It is no more a hardship to carry measures tending to alter the terms of a contract in one sense than in another. In 1816 all contracts were altered by the erection of the gold standard to the detriment of the debtor, and in 1872 by the demonetisation of Germany the same thing took place. If then the effect of the enactment of the double standard were to have a contrary effect, why should creditors complain?

With regard to the diminution of the purchasing power of the pound sterling, or, in other words, the raising of prices, we are not alone in our contention.

Many of our monometallic friends are in favour of measures which would entail the same consequences.

What would be the effect of increasing the fiduciary issue of paper? Let us suppose that the Act of 1844 should be repealed or modified, and that the Bank of England or some other authorised body should issue more notes other than against a deposit of the precious metals, would that not be diminishing the purchasing power of the sovereign? If Lord Liverpool or Sir R. Peel were now alive they would most probably deprecate the course of curing an acknowledged evil by creating a greater one. They would most assuredly object to leaving the safe basis of a metallic currency for the unsafe one of paper founded upon nothing.

Ricardo considered the test of the safety of a paper currency to be the having every penny of it secured by a deposit of the precious metals. Lord Liverpool and Sir Robert Peel said that the expansion and contraction of it being the same as that which it would be if wholly metallic, made it safe.

Mr. H. R. Grenfell.

But their disciples propose to fly away altogether from the principles of those statesmen in the matter of paper, in order to defend their doctrines in reference to the monometallic standard.

The dangers attending the undue expansion of a paper currency are ten times as great as they were in the early part of the century. The temptation to over-trading, commercial extravagance, and the consequent fluctuations in commercial enterprise, are daily increasing. But the evils of unlimited issue were those with which Lord Liverpool and Sir R. Peel had to deal. Those arising from a change of standard as we now regard it were unknown to them. Those connected with the competition of issuing bankers are now so far from us that we have almost forgotten them, and men are very apt not only to forget the circumstances, but the reason why bank notes issued recklessly form so peculiarly a dangerous form of credit. When a deposit bank stops payment it is a debtor only to those who have voluntarily trusted it; but when an issuing bank stops payment in a district where the notes are current, hundreds of people may lose their money who have never knowingly entered into any transactions with the bank at all.

In 1793, 100 out of 400 issuing banks suspended payment. After Lord Liverpool's time the same thing recurred again and again. In 1810, one-quarter of them stopped. Many in 1812. In 1814-15-16, 360 went down; in 1825, 70 succumbed in six weeks. But these would-be new issuers of paper think that the world has grown wiser since those days.

When Sir R. Peel brought in his Act of 1844 he laid on the table a return of the banks which had stopped payment during the five years previous to that year, and in that return we find that 82 banks had stopped, of which 42 paid no dividend at all. Since the passing of that Act we have had three panics in which it had to be suspended for a short time, and each of these were banking panics bringing down great joint-stock banking establishments with large and lucrative business.

Mr. Fowler and his friends doubtless contemplate some other system than the old unlimited and uncontrolled issue; some plan for an issue founded on deposit of stock. But this would require lengthened inquiry and all that labour and attention which has been in vain invited for the discussion of bimetallism. The Chancellor of the Exchequer, and the financial, official and ex-official authorities, must have some occupation other than the degrading solution of Irish problems if such questions as these are to be brought forward. Till that happy day arrives we must be content to remain in an academic stage. But our work will if possible clear the way of some of the irrelevant matter which obstructs the course of close discussion.

The difference between diminishing the purchasing power of the sovereign by bimetallism and doing the same thing by an emission of one-pound notes is, that in the one case we damage *pro tanto* the convertibility of the note; in the other we make a currency which is equally known in China, India, Chili, and the United States, and which no panic can depreciate, no commercial crisis render less valid.

To those monometallists who are strict bullionists in the sense that Sir R. Peel was one our remarks may not apply; but with those who, on the one hand, cry out against watering the currency with a precious metal and, on the other, loudly demand a fresh issue of paper, we can have no common ground, and to them we can give no quarter.

H. R. GRENFELL.

THE RATIO BETWEEN GOLD AND SILVER.

On 30th September, 1882, the "Economist," in commenting on the address of Professor Bonamy Price at Nottingham, made the following observations:—

Two propositions are put forward which it will be needful for those who advocate the concurrent coinage of gold and silver as legal tender to meet before the subject can be approached at all closely. The first is the difference in present value between gold and silver at the ratio of 15½ to 1, which it has been very generally agreed by bimetallists to adopt. The second is the necessity of bringing not only all civilised countries but the whole world into the international union which it is proposed to establish. Unless this is done, silver will undoubtedly move from those centres where it is worth less, to those where it is worth more. Though there is a vast demand for silver in the East, there is also a very large demand for gold there as well; and if silver would exchange for more gold in Europe than in Asia, we may be quite certain it will find its way to the best market. The essence of money is, as Professor Bonamy Price stated, to give equal for equal; value for value. To start with a ratio of 15½ to 1 when the real market price is now 18 to 1, and may be something else to-morrow, fails in the first condition which money, as a measure of value, should fulfil.

The foregoing gave rise to the following correspondence:—

SIR,—In your paper of last Saturday, you say that there are two propositions which the bimetallists must meet before the subject can be approached at all closely.

I. The question why $15\frac{1}{2}$ is to be the ratio between gold and silver when 18 to 1 is the existing market price of silver.

II. The necessity of bringing all nations, and not only the commercial ones, into a bimetallic union.

To these two points I propose, with your leave, to address myself.

I. The first has been cleverly dealt with by Mr. Grenfell in his letter to the *Times*, of the 27th September; but I will try to supplement his answer with some explanatory words.

I admit that 18 to 1 is the existing market value. We do not propose to adopt it as the ratio, because if we did, then so soon as silver was restored to its ancient function in the monetary world, it would be gold which would be the over-valued metal.

The essence of the question is not what is the market value of one metal as measured in the other, for that may have been, and has been, affected by temporary circumstances, but what is the true comparative value of the two metals existing and likely to exist, supposing both to be in full work at all the occupations for which mankind has adopted them?

Now, I fail to see the existence of any *natural* cause which can have altered the relative value which attached to the two precious metals 12 years ago. The outpourings of silver from the Nevada mines has been as nothing in comparison to the discoveries of gold in Australia and

Mr. H. H. Gibbs.

California; yet it is in evidence that these last produced no effect worth speaking of on the price of one metal measured in the other; and I conclude, therefore, that the *artificial* cause once removed by the restoration of the demand for silver as money, the true ratio—necessarily an approximate one—will be found to be just what it was, and there cannot, therefore, be any reason whatever for the adoption of 16, or any other compromise. Let me add that I consider perfect exactness of ratio a matter of very little moment. If you adopt 18 to 1 you over-value gold; but the only practical result, except at the instant of change, is that you contract the circulation of the world. If you adopt 15½ to 1, then, even on the supposition, which I do not admit, that by this ratio you under-value gold, the only practical result is that you re-expand the circulation of the world to the point at which it stood in 1873.

There are two reasons which make me think 15½ the ratio most likely and most proper to be adopted, irrespective of its nearness to the truth.

1. Great mischief was done in 1873 by an arbitrary act which disturbed the ratio, and however arbitrary the act of restoring it, such a course would but be precisely the undoing of the mischief then done.

2. 15½ is the ratio which actually exists in the Latin Union and in Germany, and which would be accepted by the United States. It is, therefore, the ratio which is practically possible, as provoking the least amount of resistance.

In another article you speak of 18 as the true ratio, and ask what is to hinder the real ratio from being, say, a year hence, 21 or 22 to 1?

I reply, What is to cause it so to be? If the Latin Union should demonetise silver, there is every probability of the market value (a very different thing, as I have explained above, from the ratio) being 21 or even 25 to 1.

Must you not admit, that the necessary effect of this will be a further and sudden appreciation of gold? that whereas a sovereign was to be had for so much wheat, suddenly, and by the stroke of a pen, the buyer of a sovereign will have been forced to give so much more wheat for it? The permanence and immovability of your standard, on which you lay such stress, will have gone to the winds.

I propose with your leave to deal with the second point in another letter.

Yours faithfully,

HENRY H. GIBBS.

October 7, 1882.

SIR,—I return to your article of the 30th September, in which you assert the necessity of bringing all nations, and not only the commercial ones, into a bimetallic union, otherwise "silver will undoubtedly move from those centres "where it is worth less, to those where it is worth more."

I did not think it would have been necessary to argue this point in the pages of the *Economist*, or anywhere where merchants do most congregate. You say, "Silver "would exchange for more gold in Europe than in Asia, "and we may be quite certain it will find its way to the best "market." I agree with you. But for how long would silver exchange for more gold in Europe than in Asia? For how long would Europe be the best market? Some years ago the answer would have been,—during a course of post; the answer must now be,—for the time occupied in getting a telegram!

Mr. H. H. Gibbs.

The operation which Professor Price imagines (following, I think, Mr. Clarmont Daniell*) would be possible only on the supposition that one single person had the monopoly of commerce and communication between Europe and the East, and that he had, under a bimetallic system, the power to demand gold for his 15½ oz. of silver thus cheaply bought in India. As it is, he would receive silver for his silver, and have his labour for his pains.

Even were it otherwise, so long as commerce was free and the telegraph working, what would tie the hands or dull the brains of other merchants while this creature of imagination was making his gain of 2½ oz. silver on each ounce of gold? Is it not obvious that competition will instantly level the prices in the two countries, except so far as the daily variations of exchange affect them?

In my opinion, the apprehension of "two prices" of either metal under a bimetallic union of the chief commercial nations is a mere dream, dreamed by Lord Sherbrooke in his study, and by Professor Price, dormant for once in his professor's chair.

I wait for some merchant or cambist—someone engaged in active business—to explain how such two prices can coexist. It is not enough that someone, however experienced, should assert that they can. I want an instance. I ask to see the operation.

Let us suppose Guatemala to be outside the union; and I beg that it may be demonstrated to me what will induce the Guatemala miner (who knows that every 15½ oz. of his silver is equal, in all civilised countries, to 1 oz. of gold) to give 18 oz. for that quantity of gold. What are the grounds upon which any reasonable man can assume such a course of conduct possible? A knowledge of the

* Mr. Daniell's proposal is to retain Gold as the Sole Monetary Standard, but to supplement it with Silver as unlimited legal tender, at a fixed Ratio to be named from time to time by competent authorities.

price obtainable in Europe must necessarily equalise the price in Guatemala, always saving the fraction involved in exchange, and I can only regard a miner who could be guilty of the ignorance and stupidity ascribed to him as another creation of the imagination. If he really existed, he would not long survive the competition of his neighbours.

If the miner should raise an unusual abundance of silver, so much the better for him. The Australian who got gold for the picking up received his 77*s.* 10½*d.* an ounce for it so soon as he and his buyer knew that it *was* gold. He was not so obliging as to give it to his neighbour for 40*s.* an ounce. Why should he? Those who think the matter out will avoid confounding, as people are apt to do, the profit of the miner with the market value of the metal.

The only real result of a cheap, that is, an abundant, find of either of the precious metals under a bimetallic system would be that the circulation of the world would be *pro tanto* expanded, and that prices of commodities would rise. And in the same way, if the production of either metal fell off, prices would fall in proportion.

My denial of "two prices" does not, of course, go so far as to deny a possible agio on either metal, though the wider the union the less the probability of an agio. When the debtor has the choice of metals in which to pay, I do not deny the possibility of a creditor who may desire one hundred sovereigns for the convenience of a foreign tour, having in very exceptional circumstances to pay a trifle if he insists on taking gold instead of silver; but such an instance, and others similar which may be adduced, are as slight bubbles on the stream of commerce, which in no way affect its volume or its course.

HENRY H. GIBBS.

October 14, 1882.

To these letters the *Economist* replied on 21st October:—

Mr. Gibbs, in writing to us on the subject of the ratio between gold and silver, in his letter published in the *Economist* of October 7th, says:—"The essence of the "question is, what is the true comparative value of the "two metals existing and likely to exist, supposing both "to be in full work at all the occupations for which man- "kind has adopted them?" This is entirely intelligible; but when Mr. Gibbs goes on to say, as he does, "Let me "add, that I consider exactness of ratio a matter of very "small moment," we lose at once any common ground on which to discuss the matter with him. If "the essence of "the question" is to discover "the true comparative "value," we fail to see how "exactness of ratio" can be "a matter of very small moment," as it seems to us that on the ratio adopted, as Mr. Gibbs himself says a few lines further on, the whole point, whether "the circulation "of the world" is "expanded" or "contracted," would depend. We cannot see how a standard the purchasing power of which is subject in this manner to artificial fluctuations can be in any true sense a real arbiter of value. Expansion seems to be the aim desired in the proposed change. Mr. Gibbs says in his second letter:—"The only "real results of a cheap, that is, an abundant, find of "either of the precious metals under a bimetallic system "would be that the circulation of the world would be "*pro tanto* expanded, and that prices of commodities "would rise. And in the same way, if the production "of either metal fell off, prices would fall in proportion." But the production of the metal which was obtainable with the least labour would be continually stimulated by the artificial enhancement of its price. Hence the continuation of this production might be looked upon as certain. The whole history of the course of exchange of the two metals shows, that during the last three centuries it has from time to time been needful, whenever the relative value of the two metals has been tested in an open market, to give more silver in proportion for the same weight of gold. There seems no reason to doubt that the same course will continue, with a corresponding effect on the standard based on it. With respect to the value of either metal, Mr. Gibbs considers that "the price obtainable in "Europe must necessarily equalise the price" elsewhere. If he looks back to the early history of the Australian gold discoveries, he will find that it was some time before the mint price in England regulated the market price in Australia. Yet there was free and unlimited coinage of gold all the while in England. Thus Mr. Newmarch states that in 1851 gold bullion was sold in South Australia at 45*s.* per oz. while the price was 60*s.* in Victoria. We cannot doubt that what has taken place before would take place again. The object of bimetallism is to make the cheaper metal as valuable as the dearer one, which can only be done, according to their argument, by lowering the value of the dearer metal. The nearer this ultimate end is to attainment, it follows that the greater the relative depreciation of the standard of value must be.

The discussion was concluded by the following letter:—

SIR,—I have read your remarks in last Saturday's paper on my letters in your issues of the 7th and 14th, and I should be glad to be allowed to correct some misapprehensions of my meaning into which you have fallen.

I gave you two reasons why I thought 15½ to 1 the ratio most likely and "most proper to be adopted, irrespective of "its greater nearness to the truth."

Mr. H. H. Gibbs.

You attribute to me another reason, which I not only never gave, but which I wholly repudiate, viz., a desire for expansion of the circulation.

I must protest that neither in my letter on which you comment, nor in anything I have ever written or said, is there the slightest ground for attributing to me such a desire. I referred to the incontestable fact, that a ratio of 15½ would cause a return to the volume of circulation as it existed in 1873, while the adoption of 18 would prohibit such return, and perpetuate the existing contraction, but I said nothing to suggest a preference for either ratio on these grounds. Neither expansion nor contraction of the circulation is in itself advantageous to trade; what is advantageous is steadiness, and an absence of the fluctuations which you and I alike deprecate.

My contention is, that these fluctuations in the relation of money to the commodities measured by it, are more likely to happen among a monometallist than a bimetallist nation, inasmuch as they can be caused by the adoption or rejection, on the part of other countries, of the single metal which the monometallist nation employs as money.

One question in your issue of September 30th was, "Why choose 15½ rather than 18?"

I repeat my answer in plainer terms, if possible. Market price shows the present value of the precious metals as measured in each other: but it fails altogether to show the true comparative value of the whole mass of each, as it would be, were the full demand for one of them restored. That 18 to 1 would be widely distant from the true value is proved by the continuous price which prevailed while that full demand existed. My point is, that 15½ to 1 is as near as we can get, or, at any rate, is sufficiently near to the true comparative value.

A fixed ratio has always been, and must necessarily be, approximate and not exact, and therefore it is that I deem perfect exactness not only unattainable, but also unimportant. Let that be as it may, it is impossible that the ratio, when once fixed, can be changed by law, without producing at each change a change also in the quantum of the circulation, and a prejudicial, because sudden, change in the relation of money to commodities.

To suppose that the fixing of 15½ or any other ratio could produce future fluctuations shows, so I venture to think, misconception of all the conditions of the problem.

For in proportion as the fixed ratio departs from the market price, the circulation is doubtless expanded or contracted at the moment of fixing it; but once fixed the relation of the aggregate of the two metals used as money to the commodities measured by it (leaving out of the account any circumstances affecting those commodities) depends and must depend on the total excess or defect of production of the precious metals over the consumption of them by wear and tear, taking also into account the increased or diminished use of metallic money in the world.

Your reference to the relative value of the two metals in the last three centuries*—you do well to omit the first 70 years of the present one—is surely not germane to the question, for in those centuries no properly organised bimetallic system was in existence. Had it been in operation, the effect of the changes to which you refer would have been *nil*, if the falling off in gold production had balanced the increase of silver; or there would have been an

* It is suggested to me that the *Economist* means the last 300 years, and not the 16th, 17th and 18th centuries: but if so, his statement, which I had thought correct, is inaccurate, for during the first 70 years of the present century there have been no variations of any consequence in the relative prices of gold and silver, although there have been more sudden and more important variations in the relative production of those metals than in any of the preceding time.

H. H. G.

Mr. H. H. Gibbs.

advance in the prices of commodities if both silver and gold increased in volume, or one increased while the other remained stationary.

You close your remarks by saying "the object of bi-"metallists is to make the cheaper metal equal to the dearer." Pray accept the assurance that this is a total misconception of their object. The result at which you suppose them to aim (which I take to be not the equalising the metals—which no one in his senses could propose—but the restoring them to their old relations of price) would be accomplished approximately, without the aid of a bimetallic agreement, on the remonetisation of silver in Germany and elsewhere, and restored accurately, if France restored her bimetallic standard. The object of bimetallists is to secure perfect stability in the relations of the two money-metals, and increased stability in their joint relation to the commodities measured by them.

A few words as to your remarks on what I wrote as to the Australian Discoveries.

I have a full and personal recollection of their early history, and they exactly bear out my statement, some important words in which you have overlooked. I repeat that the Australian received standard price for his gold "so soon as he and his buyer knew that it *was* gold."

Mr. Newmarch was, I think, far too accurate a man to have said what you think he said, or at least to have implied what you suggest that he implied. I am sure he can neither have said nor thought that gold bullion was knowingly sold at 45*s*. and 50*s*. per oz. standard. What really happened was this. No one knew for certain what was the quality of the gold found, nor how much of it was gold at all. It was said, and believed, that it contained inferior metal—platinum, to wit. There was no assaying instruments within reach of the finders, and no available means of smelting, or even completely separating the metal from the quartz. Every sale was a speculative one; but from the moment that account sales from England showed the metal to be real gold, like any other, all difficulties were swept away, and the prices were levelled, saving the difference of exchange.*

What possible analogy exists between this transitional state of things and ordinary increase of production?

If the miner mines cheaply, so much the better for the miner and his men. If he doubts for a moment, or his buyer cajoles him into believing that his gold is dross, it is the buyer who makes a profit and not he; but neither the price he gives, nor the profit which either of them makes, has anything whatever to do with the relation of gold to the commodities it measures.

You will agree, I am sure, that it is above all things desirable that the arguments on both sides of this question should be made clear and intelligible to those who study them. On this ground I trust you will find room for this letter.

I am, SIR, yours truly,

HENRY HUCKS GIBBS.

London, October 24.

* It is scarcely necessary to say that the difference of exchange consists primarily in the freight, insurance, interest, and other charges of transit, and that the land charges, when the quality was known and robberies frequent, would make the value at the diggings—whether to the digger or his buyer—much less than the value at the port.

BIMETALLISM AGAIN.

Extracts from Professor BONAMY PRICE's *Address at the Social Science Congress at Nottingham, September* 25, 1882.

[As reported in *The Times*, September 26, 1882.]

" The amount of the money given is determined by the " cost of producing the metal, precisely as the price of a " coat or of a loaf of bread is determined by what they cost " to produce."

" The cost of production of gold or silver is the amount " of goods of all kinds which the miner must have to induce " him to get the metal out of the mine."

" Steadiness of value is the highest virtue which money " can possess. Its importance is supreme."

* * * * * *

" But now there is a question which ought to be put " categorically to every bimetallist, and which he is speci- " fically bound to answer. He seeks to make England a " bimetallic country, to make both metals legal tenders in " her currency, to place silver on the same level with gold. " In organizing this change at the present hour, why does " he not take the two metals, at their true, their actual " market values? Why does he not make the start with a " ratio of gold to silver of 1 to 18? Why does he not " demand that in the coinage 18 ounces of silver shall be " the value of one ounce of gold?"

The following letter appeared in *The Times*, Wednesday, Sept. 27, 1882.

TO THE EDITOR.

SIR,—I venture to send the following answer to the direct question to be found in your report of Professor Price's speech at the Social Science Congress—"Why "does not the bimetallist take the two metals at their true, "their actual market value at 18 to 1?"

To understand this question it is necessary for him to define what he means by "truth," and when "actuality" is to be asserted. The truth of a comparative value, according to ordinary economical writers, depends either on the cost of production of the commodities to be compared, or else on the demand for them.

If you give an artificial demand in 1872 to one commodity and deprive the other of the same artificial demand, that which was true and actual value in 1872 becomes untrue and unactual in 1873. This is the contention of the bimetallists.

The comparative value of kelp and pounds sterling was changed by a stroke of the pen. The comparative value of gold and silver was changed by the demonetization of Germany in like manner.

If Professor Price's question is stated in the usual terms, it means that the relative value of gold and silver must eternally depend on the cost of production and on no other cause. According to him, artificial value given to either metal by the conferring of the privilege of money has nothing to do with it. We bimetallists assert that it has everything to do with it.

M'Culloch in one place states that the reason why gold and silver are at the ratio of 15½ to 1 is, that it costs exactly 15½ times the amount of labour to produce an ounce of gold as it does to produce the same weight of silver. In other parts of his treatise he so qualifies and pares down the assertion as to leave nothing of it.

Bimetallists assert that during a period of 70 years in which the comparative cost of production of the two metals varied several times the relative value scarcely changed at all; that this period of 70 years tallies precisely with the period during which French bimetallism, or rather free coinage of both metals, existed; and that this constancy in the price of silver told in gold, or *vice versâ*, ceased exactly at the time when the artificial value of silver was taken from it in Germany. They also assert that if this artificial value or privilege was as suddenly taken away from gold and conferred on platinum the same effect would be produced upon gold. They, therefore, deny that the terms "true and actual market value" have any ascertainable meaning.

I remain, SIR, your obedient servant,

H. R. GRENFELL.

BANK OF ENGLAND.

Extract from the City Article of *The Times* of Wednesday, September 27, 1882.

The admirable address of Professor Bonamy Price at the Social Science Congress, Nottingham, yesterday on Economy and Trade touches upon a point which deserves attention. In treating of bimetallism, and once more exposing some of the fallacies into which the advocates of that system of currency have fallen, Professor Price himself goes astray and, singularly enough, upon the most vital point, the non-perception of which has probably involved several able men in the espousing of a cause which they never would have associated their names with had they clearly perceived the fallacy to which we refer at the outset. Professor Price says, " The amount of the money given is determined by the " cost of producing the metal, precisely as the price of a " coat or of a loaf of bread is determined by what they cost " to produce." The leading advocates of the bimetallic theory themselves admit, we believe, that the whole gist of the question is involved in that of value in exchange. Their fundamental error from the beginning has consisted in their not having understood the technical meaning of that phrase " value in exchange," and, with all his clearness otherwise, Professor Price has fallen into the same mistake. That he has done so is easily proved. The fallacy lies in the assumption that the value in exchange of the metal is determined alone by the cost of production. Why has silver fallen in exchangeable value with gold from 15½ to 1 to, say, 18 to 1 of gold? No one who really understands the point admits that it was the diminished cost of production that alone caused that depreciation. The main cause of the fall was its diminished utility. This requires no further demonstration than to say that the fall in the price of silver in the market began with the demonetization of the metal by Germany. It is allowed on all hands that the value of a thing is what it will fetch. In other words, it is determined by the demand in relation to the supply. If the utility of a thing diminishes, as it has in the case of silver, the demand obviously becomes less, whether the cost of production increases or diminishes. A thing which people do not want is said to be dear at any price. At a large meeting of bimetallists some months ago, in London, this very point of cost of production was raised with reference to platinum. It was sought then to be proved that the axiom was a fallacy which set forth that the cost of production determined the value of a thing, the cost of production of platinum, as compared with that of gold, being cited in support of the argument. No such axiom exists, or is acknowledged by sound political economists, unaccompanied with the condition that utility is an essential element in value. It was said, and rightly, at the meeting referred to, that platinum cost much more to produce than gold, and yet it was relatively cheaper; the essential element of utility being lost sight of, in the absence of which it was, of course, useless to attempt to account for the apparent anomaly.

From *The Times*, Friday, September 29, 1882.

The subjoined letter replies to the remarks on Professor Bonamy Price's address to the Social Science Congress at Nottingham, in Wednesday's article, and we are glad to be able to state that in referring to the important point to which we drew attention, Professor Price was guilty of nothing worse than a *lapsus calami*:—

September 28.

SIR,—I beg leave to thank you for your kind notice in *The Times* of Wednesday of my address to the Social Science Congress at Nottingham. But you will allow me,

I trust, to show that I have not fallen into the "mistake" imputed to me of not having understood the meaning of the phrase "value in exchange," with reference to the exchange of commodities for money. I do not, and never have imbibed "the fallacy that the value in exchange of the "metal is determined by the cost of production alone." On the contrary, I have distinctly held that "if silver has fallen "from 15½ to 1 to, say, 18 to 1, the diminished cost of "production did not alone cause that depreciation."

Here is my proof. In an article in the *Contemporary Review* of last February, on "How Money does its Work," I said, page 252,—

"Thus we are brought to the conclusion that, while cost of "production is always ultimately the essence of the value of "money—of metallic money—as of all commodities save those "whose prices are governed by feeling and fancy, the fluctuations "which fall upon that value through the universal law of supply "and demand are more frequent and last longer than those which "befall most commodities."

Again, page 258,—

"It cannot be doubted that M. de Laveleye is correct in "attributing the fall in no slight degree to Germany selling her "silver, combined with the prohibitions against its free coinage in "most civilized countries. What is this but the action of supply "and demand? A large quantity remained in stock; a fall of value "became inevitable, whatever was the cost of production."

These passages show, I submit, that instead of holding "the fallacy," I entirely agree in the view taken by the City Article of *The Times.*

I come now to the letter of the Governor of the Bank of England, Mr. H. R. Grenfell. I pressed all bimetallists to answer distinctly the question, "Why does not the "bimetallist take the two metals at their true, their actual "market value, at 18 to 1?" He replies by calling on me to define what I mean by true, by actual value. I answer, the value of the two metals in the metal market, without any reference whatever to coinage: what a man who buys them to make ornaments must give for them. To this meaning Mr. Grenfell opposes what he calls an artificial value, as I understand him—the privilege of being legal tender, which increases the value of the metal when coined. Take away the privilege, as Germany did when it demonetized silver, and the value of silver falls to 18 instead of 15½, being now worth an ounce of gold. This being so, to make a metal legal tender is to give it an additional, an artificial value. I need say no more. I call that an untrue, a false value. Artificial money is the last thing to be called good money.

I am, &c.,

BONAMY PRICE.

From *The Times*, October 3, 1882.

The following letter refers to Professor B. Price's comments in last Saturday's article on the letter of Mr. H. R. Grenfell, which appeared on the previous Wednesday:—

BANK OF ENGLAND,
October 2.

SIR,—In your Money Article of Saturday Professor Bonamy Price has answered my enquiry as to what he means by "truth" and "actuality" in the relative value of the precious metals, by saying that he means "The value "of the two metals in the metal market, without any "reference whatever to coinage: what a man who buys "them to make ornaments must give for them."

Again I ask him by what criterion he tests the value of gold if stripped of that which we are agreed in saying is an artificial value conferred upon it by the privilege of the Mint. Does he mean to say that the relative value of gold and silver, if gold were demonetized, would be 18 to 1?

And, if so, on what ground does he make the assertion?

I remain, your obedient servant,

H. R. GRENFELL.

FROM PROFESSOR B. PRICE TO MR. H. R. GRENFELL.

WELTON, BROUGH, YORKSHIRE,
October 5, 1882.

MY DEAR GRENFELL,—

I am no bimetallist. I have never held nor admitted that the *mere fact* that "an artificial value is conferred "upon gold by the privilege of the Mint," in the sense—that the fact that gold is made legal tender—gives it increased power of exchange for other commodities. An artificial ratio of value between two metals in the coinage is perfectly possible, and may easily be, and is, involved in the present bimetallist proposal; but the power of purchasing commodities lies quite in another region, namely, in the worth of the coined metals as commodities.

I have no fear: the actual proposition of bimetallism is irrational.

Yours,

B. PRICE.

P.S.—I do not use the expression labour as the basis of value, but cost of production. That, with the incidents of the universal law of supply and demand, is the essence of the value of true money.

FROM MR. H. R. GRENFELL TO PROFESSOR B. PRICE.

BANK OF ENGLAND,
October 6, 1882.

MY DEAR PRICE,—

I neither assert in this letter, nor do I deny, that the privilege of the Mint gives an artificial value to gold and silver.

All I say is, that if it gives it to one, it gives it to the other, and that when you try to pin me to the value in exchange of the one, I have a right to pin you to the value in exchange of the other as tested by your own standard, viz., what it would fetch for ornaments irrespective of its artificial Mint value.

What I say is, that your figure of 18 to 1 is no more the real proportionate value than 40 to 1, or 3 to 1, or any other imaginary figure.

If the "Bland Bill" and the legal tender of silver dollars were repealed, and if a gold standard were enacted in India, it might be 40 to 1.

But the main question you have never answered, nor has any monometallist: How the constancy of the relative value all over the world during the existence of French bimetallism is to be accounted for?

The usual slip-slop leading article way is to state that bimetallism was tried and failed in Germany and in France, and therefore the former resorted to the gold standard, and the Latin Union to the cessation of minting silver.

But of this failure not a jot of proof is adduced.

So much for what I say. Now for what you say. "An "artificial ratio of value between two metals in the coinage "is perfectly possible, and may easily be, and is, involved "in the present bimetallist proposal; but the power of "purchasing commodities lies quite in another region: viz. "in the worth of the coined metals as commodities."

Now, here we are all agreed. This is an accurate definition of that for which we are contending. And taking your definition to be correct, we bimetallists assert that the advantage of a standard at all is to get the greatest possible amount of fixity of value of the standard metals told in commodities.

We do not assert that they will not vary, or that it is possible to fix it completely. But what we say is, that the fixity of value is greater when the mass of the standard consists of two metals than if it consists of one.

A caviller may rejoin: Why not three? To this we reply: Because the mass of coins actually now in use throughout the world consists of the two metals of which we are speaking, and that what may happen if others are added is outside the question at issue.

When brought alongside we are much nearer each other than you are aware of.

Yours,

H. R. GRENFELL.

FROM PROFESSOR B. PRICE TO MR. H. R. GRENFELL.

WELTON, BROUGH,
October 7, 1882.

MY DEAR GRENFELL,—

Your letter, received this morning, divides itself into two parts. I will first speak of the second part.

It gives me great pleasure. You say very truly that we are nearer to each other than was supposed. I have no objection of principle whatever to bring against it. We agree that "the power of purchasing commodities lies in " the worth of the coined metals as commodities." This is the essence of the manner in which good money performs its work. It gives me most lively satisfaction to hear you say, "Here we are all agreed."

Further, we are unanimous that to "get the greatest "possible amount of fixity of value of the standard metals "told in commodities" is "the great advantage of a "standard."

Further, you have a perfect right to say that "the "fixity of value is greater when the mass of the standard "consists of two metals than if it consists of one." This is a proposition perfectly fair to assert. There is nothing whatever in it against the principle of the best money. Whether it is true, as a fact, is another question; it may be asserted or disputed; but in both cases no breach against the right conception of money can be alleged.

I am inclined to hold that two metals will yield less fixity of value than one only; but I freely admit that I may be mistaken here. It is a very hard question to come to a confident decision on.

On the first part of your letter I fear that our agreement is not so well assured. I agree—"When I try to pin "you to the value in exchange of the one metal, you "(H. R. G.) have a right to pin me to the value of the other "by my own standard—namely, what it would fetch for "ornaments." But I cannot add "irrespectively of its "artificial Mint value," for I deny that there is any such artificial Mint value.

However, you come to the pinch of the matter. You say "that my figure of 18 to 1 is no more the real pro- "portional value than 40 to 1, or 3 to 1, or any other "imaginary figure." I answer, first, that 18 to 1 is the actual proportion in the bullion market to-day: it is the existing fact, and, so far, is real. That is a quality of immense importance in dealing with it.

Certainly, with alterations in the currency of many countries, gold might be so wanted as to bring out the ratio of 40 to 1. That is conceivable—probable, I cannot believe it to be.

I freely concede that the *actual* values of gold and silver as commodities are difficult to explain at any time. As I said in the *Contemporary* of February, it is a question dependent on the cost of production of the metal won from the dearest mines, coupled with the incidents arising from the action of the law of demand and supply which falls on all commodities. This is a very difficult matter to trace out. Thus it is not easy to say, why the relative value was constant all over the world during the existence of French bimetallism. But is it not an admitted fact that the French ceased to coin silver because the ratio had become false, and gold was leaving the country?

Then again as to Germany: is it or is it not the fact, that she demonetized silver because the supply of cheaper silver from the mines had broken out in America?

One remark I would make to which I beg to call your attention. On bimetallism, I admit that if one metal went up or down, the other might do the same and keep up the ratio: or they might do the reverse, one going up as the other goes down, making the ratio more false than ever. For my part, I cannot bring myself to believe that gold and silver would keep company in their costs of production and variations of value.

Why don't you take into consideration Clarmont Daniell's scheme of occasional adjustments of the ratio in coinage to the ratio of the bullion market, especially as it was done in England for more than 400 years by proclamation from the Crown?

Yours,

B. PRICE.

From Mr. H. R. GRENFELL to Professor B. PRICE.

Bank of England,
October 9, 1882.

My dear Price,—

We are getting much closer to each other than you fancy.

1. My authority for saying "that the fixity of value is "greater when the mass of the standard consists of two "metals than if it consists of one," is to be found in Jevons' work upon Money, page 137. I have never heard of any one who had read up to that point in the controversy having disputed his decision.

2. Your expression, or rather your use of the expression, "cost of production," is, I submit, not the correct one.

Cost of production means the labour required to produce a commodity.

When the economists laid down the law that cost of production ultimately ruled the value of a commodity, they meant that after all stocks were exhausted, and the various incidents terminated, the new start would be governed by the cost of labour to produce a commodity.

The "incidents arising from the laws of demand" may govern or influence for a certain time, but, ultimately, the labour to produce governs the value.

3. The relative value all over the world during French bimetallism is strictly in accordance with the laws of supply and demand. If in France, at all times, whatever the cost of production, men could dispose of either gold told in silver or silver told in gold at the ratio of 15½ to 1, there could be no other price anywhere, because whichever, according to the

laws of the cost of production, was the cheapest could find in France an artificial demand at that rate. This is our explanation. Yours is, "that it is not so easy to say."

4. Referring to what you say about Germany and France, I reply that the proof of the change in prices being posterior and not anterior to the demonetization, and therefore that the German change could not have been caused by the fall in prices consequent on the silver discoveries in America, is to be found in Gibbs' pamphlet, page 27, quoted from Seyd. Germany demonetized silver in accordance with a deliberate decision in favour of monometallism, arrived at at the first International Conference. The tribute from France enabled Germany to carry out the measure, which has proved a most costly and ruinous operation to Germany.

The Latin Union was forced by this monetary revolution to follow suit. The evils arising from these changes cannot be disputed by you, because you have already admitted them in your writings.

5. You ask me why we won't take into consideration Clarmont Daniell's scheme. I have been in long correspondence at times with him, and was under the impression that I had thoroughly shown the impracticability of it. But my simple answer to you is, that I am not considering vaccination, or the quadrature of the circle, or the procession of The Holy Ghost.

His plan for the solution of the question of the "standards" is to create something that is not a standard at all, and it does not therefore necessarily come into a discussion of whether a single or double standard is best.

Yours,

H. R. GRENFELL.

B. Price, Esq.

From Professor B. Price to Mr. H. R. Grenfell.

The Rectory, Kimbolton, St. Neot's,
October 13, 1882.

My dear Grenfell,—

I am very glad to get your letter.

1. As to Clarmont Daniell's proposition, you have missed altogether the main point on which I ask on all sides for a discussion. It is this. Daniell proposes that the ratio of the silver coins to the gold ones in a currency, as in England, avowedly monometallic, should be adjusted by an official authority from time to time according to their relative values in the *bullion market.* This was done by proclamation for more than 400 years long in England up to James I. There was nothing arbitrary in it: the metal market was to govern the ratio.

I do not say that the plan is feasible, but I am perfectly sure that it is quite sound in principle. The bimetallists never deign to speak of it,—their reason why is quite plain to me. They want to put up the value of silver: Danieli's plan would leave it to the market value.

My "Jevons" is at Oxford, and I forget what he said; but I know of no answer to the argument that gold might grow scarcer from the mine, silver much more abundant at the same time, and then the divergence of the value and bigness of the ratio might increase at a gallop.

2. My expression, "cost of production," comes from Mill. Labour is not the word for it. Labour was a favourite word with Adam Smith, but few economists use it now in this connection. Cost of production means the price which must be paid for an article, or else it will not be produced at all. It is composed of several factors besides labour.

But, as I fully explained in the *Contemporary* of February, cost of production falls under the incidents of temporary supply and demand—all commodities do: but as you say—(labour)—cost of production "ultimately governs "the value."

3. Yes, *if at all times*, whatever the cost of production, the ratio of 15½ prevailed in France, there could be no other price anywhere. But, will it at ALL times? Unbelievable!

4. You do not give the reason why Germany demonetized silver.

But, as you say, Seyd's tables show that the demonetization was not the consequence of a fall in price through silver discoveries in America.

Yours,

B. PRICE.

FROM MR. H. R. GRENFELL TO PROFESSOR B. PRICE.

BANK OF ENGLAND,
October 14, 1882.

MY DEAR PRICE,—

1. When proclamations were made during the 400 years you speak of, they had solely reference to the state of things within the realm, and the object was, not to be done by your neighbours. The example is of no moment whatever, when we are discussing the possibility or practicability of coming to a general arrangement with our neighbours. Again I repeat, Daniell's proposition is one which is to call something a standard which is not a standard at all.

These are my reasons for not considering it as part of the question I am arguing. You have no right to attribute to me a desire to raise the value of silver. It is a dangerous method. Please read the other article I sent you, written by me. Many of the monometallic writers in England are interested in raising the value of "paper."

2. I think, if you get to close reasoning, you had better at once admit that you made a mistake in your definition of cost of production. Your present definition is correct down to "labour." After that, you seem to fall into your error again. Then you attribute to me the expression cost of production "ultimately governs the value." This was not my doctrine; it was a statement of what I understood to be the economist's definition of cost of production.

3. My assertion is, that whatever the cost of production is with open mints at $15\frac{1}{2}$ to 1, that will be the relative price all over the world. My example is the 70 years of the French open mints.

4. The reason why Germany demonetized has been given so often by me, that I took it for granted you must have read it. But I will give it you again. The first Monetary Conference at Paris, in 1868, came to a decision in favour of gold monometallism. It was summoned, not for the purpose of discussing the standards, but, to discuss an International Coinage. The necessity of discussing the standard arose at once, and it was in accordance with the most recent decision, and with the gold gained by the conquest of France, that Germany demonetized. All this is in my article, "What is a Pound?" *Nineteenth Century*, 1881.

The very next meeting of a Paris Conference reversed the previous decision, and said it would be an incalculable disaster for silver to be demonetized.

Yours,

H. R. GRENFELL.

FROM PROFESSOR B. PRICE TO MR. H. R. GRENFELL.

KIMBOLTON RECTORY,
October 17, 1882.

MY DEAR GRENFELL,—

The proclamations of the changes in the ratio were facts: the immediate motives for them are utterly unimportant. Nor is "the coming to a general arrange-"ment with our neighbours" of any weight whatever in regard to the action of those proclamations economically. The question is, solely and simply, Are such alterations of the ratio between gold and silver, founded entirely on the ratios existing in the bullion market, sound economical acts —the right thing to be done when two metals are used as legal tenders? I care not a straw what other nations may or may not choose to do, in a discussion which deals with principles. Negotiations with nations come later,—after principles have been settled.

So Daniell's proposition remains unexamined, though warranted by the proclamation precedent.

I do not know what you mean when you say that "the "monometallist writers are interested in raising the value "of paper." What paper?

I am quite at a loss for anything like a proof that "if "either gold or silver increased ever so much the standard "would not alter, or the relative value, as long as the "bimetallic nations, or one of them, opened their or its "mint to both metals." It would be very funny indeed, if silver increased so much as to be worth only 30*d.* an ounce, and its relative value to gold—(hypothetically unchanged) —remained unchanged, because France, say, kept her mint open to both metals. That passes my understanding.

I made no mistake about the expression, cost of production. Labour, as I said, was Adam Smith's word—it is practically given up now. Mill's phrase—cost of production—has taken its place. Labour is appropriated to wages generally. The cost of a commodity involves interest, profit of capitalist and employer, freight and many other factors of price, besides labour. You gain nothing by taking your stand on labour.

What I said was that you agreed—in terms—that "*the* "*power of purchasing commodities is the worth of the coined* "*metals as commodities.*" You called this "an accurate "definition," and then argued upon it as such. This is not "a statement of what you understand to be the economist's "definition of cost of production," but *your own* doctrine of what the value of the metals in buying consisted of.

That being so, you cannot, without contradicting yourself, assert that "whatever the cost of production, with open "mints at 15½ to 1, that will be the price all over the world." The worth here is NOT "that of the coined metals as "commodities," but of an arbitrary ratio between the metals, chosen without any reference to them as commodities.

Yours,

B. PRICE.

FROM MR. H. R. GRENFELL TO PROFESSOR B. PRICE.

BANK OF ENGLAND,
October 19, 1882.

DEAR PRICE,—

1. You ask the question, "Are such alterations "of the ratio between gold and silver, founded entirely "on the ratios existing in the bullion market, sound "economical doctrine?"

My answer is, as usual, another question. On what are the ratios existing in the bullion market founded? and you answer, "I cannot say,"—at least, you have answered so when I asked you how you accounted for certain phenomena in the past.

2. You say you don't know what I mean when I say the monometallist writers are interested in raising the value of paper. I answer that many of them are, or were, connected with the paper-issuing banks. They all are, or were, anxious to see the issue of paper extended rather than bimetallism. It is a most worthless argument, I admit; but it is quite good enough for those who are always accusing bimetallists of being interested in silver and its price.

3. I must ask you to read your "Jevons on Money" if you want proof of the diminution of oscillation in the bimetallic doctrine, and to read Gibbs in last week's *Economist* as to the impossibility of silver being at 30*s*. per ounce if mints are opened to it at 15½.

4. In my opinion, you originally made a mistake about cost of production. You now try to shift it on me by distinguishing between labour (wages) and general cost of production. Suffice it to say that I concur in your definition of cost of production, meaning the whole cost of bringing a commodity to market.

5. My own doctrine, as you say, is that the power of purchasing commodities is ultimately the worth of the coined metals as commodities. And whether gold and silver run up and down at different times, according to their separate values as commodities, or whether a system shall have been invented by which the value of each shall tell upon the value of the mass of the two, is of no consequence to the theory. Thus, if discoveries of silver are quadrupled, the only effect would be to raise the general price of commodities whether told in gold or silver. The same with gold.

The only difference would be that in the former case you would read in the money articles "Silver was shipped yesterday to Egypt, River Plate, New York,"—or, in the latter, Gold was.

Yours,

H. R. GRENFELL.

B. PRICE, Esq.

FROM PROFESSOR B. PRICE TO MR. H. R. GRENFELL.

2, NORHAM GARDENS, OXFORD,
October 22, 1882.

MY DEAR GRENFELL,—

I am sorry that you quit the question, Is it practicable, as in the past, to alter the ratio of silver coins to gold according to the state of the bullion market? I have never said that Daniell's scheme was practicable, but I have said that it is founded on a right conception of what money is. If bimetallism goes on, the question, I am sure, will have to be faced.

I have not made a mistake about cost of production, nor altered a single element of my view respecting it. The question still remains unanswered, Why, in the new system, give a value to silver of 15½ to 1, when it is worth as a metal only 18 to 1. And yet you write now, "My own "doctrine is, that the power of purchasing commodities is "ultimately the worth of the coined metals as commodities." Silver as a commodity is worth only 18 to 1, yet you claim to make it worth 15½ to 1. How to put these two things together!

Yours,

B. PRICE.

FROM MR. H. R. GRENFELL TO PROFESSOR B. PRICE.

BANK OF ENGLAND,
October 23, 1882.

MY DEAR PRICE,—

Very well!

You mean the general proposition that the relative price of gold and silver should be from time to time rearranged by proclamation, as being the thing which ought to be examined, not Clarmont Daniell.

Let us examine it:

We assert that there could be no other price with an international agreement as to terms of open mint than that laid down by such agreement.

Why?

Because, one nation having held its mints open for seventy years the price did not vary, it stands to reason that if two did it, or four, or eight, no other price of bullion could exist anywhere.

To suppose otherwise is to suppose that some fool is to be found willing to sell for 52 that which at an open mint he can get 60 for.

Let us then suppose such agreement made, and a manifest disinclination to take silver was shown, owing to its extra bulk, and, consequently, that an agio was paid for gold, then we admit that there is no reason why a reconsideration of the relative price should not take place by agreement.

But although we admit that, we believe the thing would be improbable, not to say impossible.

The question, however, which you say is still unanswered is, why give a value of 15½ to 1 to silver, when it is worth as metal 18 to 1. I thought everybody acknowledged I had fully answered that question.

However, I will try again.

To begin with—the statement of the question is wrong in every particular. Silver is not worth 18 to 1 in the bullion market (according to your own criterion) for ornaments.

Silver is worth 18 to 1 for ornaments and coinage.

If gold were demonetized and reduced to its value for ornaments, neither I nor you know what it would fetch in reference to commodities. Therefore your figure of 18 to 1 is merely an accidental ratio consequent on certain changes in the coinage laws of certain nations.

My next answer is that neither 18 to 1, nor 15 to 1, nor 20 to 1, nor any other ratio, affect in the smallest degree the truth or fallacy of our abstract proposition, which is, that whichever ratio the law lays down will regulate the price of gold told in silver and silver told in gold.

If you will grant us that proposition, then we are ready to show cause why on the whole we think it would be most politic to go back to the French mint prices.

It is not, however, in any way of the essence of the question.

Yours,

H. R. GRENFELL.

B. Price, Esq.

From Professor B. PRICE to Mr. H. R. GRENFELL.

2, Norham Gardens, Oxford,
October 24, 1882.

My dear Grenfell,—

I am very glad to get your letter.

You state the proposition to be examined rightly; but it is the same as Daniell originated for India in principle. It is that principle for which I claimed investigation. In detail there is a very serious difference between one country and a combination of many nations.

I think your objection, derived from this source, is very hard to answer. Remember—I *never*, anywhere, asserted that the plan was practicable: I asked only (as the principle, in my opinion, was right) that it should be considered. As you say, the positions of the several nations acting together may be radically different, consequently some might refuse a proposal to fix the ratio, and their opposition might be insurmountable. So far, at present, I see no answer to this your objection. But it raises another grave question. Is it desirable to have a bimetallic alliance, if it subjects particular nations to a false ratio, and, consequently, to a false money? That desirableness is not evident to me.

I hold that you have not answered the question,—Why not adopt the bullion ratio of 18 to 1? It is no answer to say, that 18 to 1 is one thing for ornaments, and another for ornaments *plus* coinage. The naked fact is solely and simply this: In a bullion shop next door to the Bank, will the prices asked of me, a buyer of both silver and gold, be in the proportion of 18 to 1, the dealer asking no question whatever as to what use I am going to put the metals to? That is decisive, so far as the state of the market to-day.

But you may say: Let the nations adopt bimetallism, and that ratio will at once be altered. I answer: That is to meet a fact with a theory—a theory open to very great uncertainties. The very day the new ratio is adopted, a new *cheaper* mine of either metal may be discovered, and the 15½ to 1 will become false, whatever may have been the fine conjectures that coinage will work the miracle of turning an 18 into a 15. So the question always remains unanswered, Why not adopt the bullion prices of the day of legislation? Till it is answered, how can you be surprised if Dr. Bamberger goes on with the notice he has affixed to the room of the Conference—"This is the room where cheap "silver is made dear."

Yours,

B. PRICE.

FROM MR. H. R. GRENFELL TO PROFESSOR B. PRICE.

BANK OF ENGLAND,
October 25, 1882.

DEAR PRICE,—

Your question is: Why not adopt the bullion prices of the day of legislation?

I believe I have answered this over and over again.

But, as usual, with another question: What do you mean by "day of legislation?"

If you mean that, a bimetallic union being determined on with a double standard, the ratio to remain fixed, then I answer there is no reason at all. We have always admitted that 18 to 1, or 15, or 20, or 25, could equally be fixed. All we say is that, on balancing the advantages and disadvantages, it appears to us that to return to 15½ to 1 offers fewer disadvantages.

But we again remind you that it is not the bullion price according to your criterion. To arrive at that you must demonetize gold and then see what would happen.

But if you do not mean by legislation an International Union with a fixed ratio, but mean something else, such as C. Daniell means, a gold standard everywhere, with fluctuating ratios according as the demand for silver tokens arose, then I answer, as I have answered over and over again, it is not a standard at all as far as silver is concerned, and it would be much better to do what your allies want,—go to PAPER tokens.

But the main point we were or are arguing about is, whether the demand produced by coining affects the value. How it can be otherwise you do not say, except by calling it "false ratio and false money." It may be false. So, in fact, is all demand for silver false, except the silver pokers and jugs and basons at Dunham Massey. But they are false in the sense that pottery-ware and iron would have done as well.

Yours,

H. R. GRENFELL.

FROM PROFESSOR B. PRICE TO MR. H. R. GRENFELL.

2, NORHAM GARDENS, OXFORD,
November 2, 1882.

MY DEAR GRENFELL,—

The law of supply and demand, with its effects, was not an alternative to cost of production, but an addition to it. What I meant was that, in such cases as wheat and the precious metals, the variations for a time were often very large, and, consequently, that the cost of production and its repayment by price must be calculated on an average of years. In all cases, cost of production, in the long run, rightly calculated, governs the value of metallic money. That is what I have said, in substance, all along.

All I can say, in reply to the reasons given on behalf of 15½ to 1, as you put them, is that they are theoretical. They are untrue to the actual relation at starting in the bullion market. They speculate as to what is likely to happen. Such speculations seem to me very hazardous and very unsafe. I cannot help feeling that the favour shown to 15½ is derived from the fact that it was the ratio adopted by France, &c., &c.; and equally cannot help suspecting, as many others do, that there is a wish in many minds to give an undue value to silver. At the same time I am quite willing to admit that it is possible that 18 to 1 would not prove the true ratio in the bullion market after bimetallism was set up.

On Daniell's plan the silver coins would not be "tokens": they would contain silver of the true value in exchange for gold. That is the very essence of what he seeks,—real equal bullion values of the two sets of coins in their legal relation to one another. Both coins would be standards if their relative values were identical with those in the bullion-dealer's shop.

Concerning my treatment of the law of supply and demand in my Nottingham address, one of the very ablest men in England, a distinguished economist, and one of the most powerful writers in the press, writes to me that:—

> "As to the objections made to what you said, they seem to "me utterly puerile. That a man should be told that, because "he has said the price of cotton depends in the long run on the "cost of production, he is blundering to forget that at a particular "moment a good deal may depend on the quantity in the market "and the demand for it, is like telling a man he blunders who "says that the velocity of a railway depends on the steam-power, "because he does not add anything as to the friction or the "application of the brakes."

I do not deny, and have never denied, that "a demand "produced by coining may affect value": all I have said is, that the market ratio to-day is 18 to 1, and I simply asked why it was thrust aside and 15½ to 1 chosen instead at starting. The word "false" I used strictly as meaning a ratio not in conformity with the ratio between the prices of the metals in their own and true metal market.

Yours,

B. PRICE.

From Mr. H. R. GRENFELL to Professor B. PRICE.

Bank of England,
3rd November, 1882.

My dear Price,—

I have your letter of the 2nd. Your correspondent may be right in his view of *The Times*' criticisms on your original statements.

All I can say is, if you were right, then platinum must be dearer than gold. But it is not—even in a bullion-dealer's shop.

If *The Times*' criticism was puerile you ought not to have retracted your original statement; but, having retracted it, you should not have re-asserted it.

You now, in your letter to me, continue to put wheat and precious metals in the same category as regards the effects of cost of production, whereas they are generally reckoned as the two extremes.

With regard to Daniell: It is not sufficient for him to say a thing is a standard; he must show that his scheme will bring about in the two metals that which other people call a "standard." If the two metals are to vary in relative price according to cost of production it is not possible that they should both be standards; because "standard" means that a given weight and fineness of one metal or either metal should have the *vis liberatrix*.

This is what Sir Robert Peel understood, when he said that you might have a gold standard, or a silver standard, or a double standard with a fixed ratio between the two metals, without departing from the principle of a metallic standard.

Yours,

H. R. GRENFELL.

FROM PROFESSOR B. PRICE TO MR. H. R. GRENFELL.

2, NORHAM GARDENS, OXFORD,
November 4, 1882.

MY DEAR GRENFELL,—

I do not in the least understand your allusion to platinum.

I do put wheat and metals in the same category; first, as to cost of production; secondly, as to the effect upon them of supply and demand. The degree of the effect is not the point; that it exists is the important thing. I fancy that you and I do not quite estimate, to the same degree, the varying yields of the mines for precious metals.

Of course, Daniell's plan does not give two standards, but only one—gold: the ratio of silver, on the basis of the metal market, being adjusted to gold from time to time. Both metals will be legal tenders: but the assumption will be that gold will be left unaltered, silver being altered in value to it from time to time.

Mind, I have never said that Daniell's plan was practicable: I have only asserted that it was founded on a right principle and deserved examination. If it could be made to work, it would give two metals to the coined legal tender money of a country—but only one standard, the untouched, unchanged gold. There would be no contradiction here of what Sir Robert Peel said: "the principle "of a metallic standard would not be departed from."

Yours,

B. PRICE.

From Mr. H. R. GRENFELL to Professor B. PRICE.

Bank of England,
November 6, 1882.

My dear Price,—

In my opinion the question put to bimetallists in your Nottingham address means that cost of production alone settles the value of the precious metals, while your letter to *The Times*, of the 28th September, would leave it to be implied that you were ready to admit that which we wished to have admitted, namely, that demand influences it also.

And now I ask you to follow me into the discussion as to the degree in which demand so affects the value of the precious metals as to neutralize the absolute doctrine of cost of production.

Our proof is not in our own writings, but in the list of prices during the whole time the French mint was open, ceasing at the exact moment when the mint was practically closed. This argument you seem to be afraid to face.

You are not in business as a profit-seeker; but you are in business as a truth-seeker, and are a master of words.

If we are wrong you must have a far greater capacity for showing us where than we can have.

My allusion to platinum is mentioned in *The Times* article on your address, therefore I naturally supposed you to be familiar with it.

If cost of production be the test of the value of the precious metals, and of all commodities, how do you account for the fact that an ounce of platinum costs more to produce than an ounce of gold, but it is cheaper in the market? We account for it by saying that there is an artificial demand for gold, which gives it what you are pleased to call, when applied to silver, "a false value"; and that if platinum were monetized and gold demonetized, platinum would be far dearer than gold. If we are wrong in this, tell us WHERE.

I don't think much of your "eminent friend," and his steam-power and brakes.

If you have a load to pull, and find your horse cannot do it, you may put a donkey on to help you, and your load may get up the hill. In like manner, if your first-class engine will not pull your train, a second-class engine may be put on; and the aggregate of steam-power thus procured may take the train smoothly along at a given speed, not, as your friend would suppose, at jerky paces dependent on the separate steam-power of each.

Yours,

H. R. GRENFELL.

FROM PROFESSOR B. PRICE TO MR. H. R. GRENFELL.

2, NORHAM GARDENS, OXFORD,
November 12, 1882.

MY DEAR GRENFELL,—

I did say, and do say, that the value of money is determined by the cost of production of the metal, like the value of a loaf of bread is determined by what it costs to produce.*

And I say further, that, at particular times, the state of supply and demand will alter the value of the metal in exchanging, precisely as the character of the seasons may largely affect the price of wheat in a particular year.

* By saying that, on an average of years, cost of production must be met, and is met, by value in the market, the truth that cost of production governs price is fully retained.

By cost of production I meant the cost of production on an average of years. A farmer may, under the influence of the season, get more or get less than the cost of production of his wheat; but, as a rule, and upon the average, he sells his wheat for its cost of production, profit included, or else he will cease producing wheat.

There is, in this, no affirming and denying at the same moment that cost of production governs price. There is merely a statement that the state of supply and demand at particular moments will make value vary from cost of production. *All* markets alike are subject to these incidents.

You then ask me to enter upon a "discussion as to the "degree in which demand so affects the value of the "precious metals as to neutralize the absolute doctrine of "cost of production." I am very sorry to have to say that I do not understand the question. I do not know what you mean by "as to neutralize," &c. I dare say I am very stupid: if so, pray forgive me.

Yours,

B. PRICE.

FROM MR. H. R. GRENFELL TO PROFESSOR B. PRICE.

BANK OF ENGLAND,
November 13, 1882.

MY DEAR PRICE,—

You say you don't understand me when I ask you to discuss the extent to which the demand has neutralized the cost of production theory. I will once more try to explain.

The point to which we have brought the discussion is, that cost of production governs ultimately the value, although the demand influences it. Your analogy with wheat is the very worst you could have adduced,—but let that pass.

What we want you to take in is, that the artificial (fictitious, false, if you will) demand created by law, by erecting the precious metals into a standard of value for all other commodities, gives them an exceptional position, and that one of the incidents of that exceptional position is that it has been decreed that the thing written as £1 sterling can be paid at all times at the rate of 123·274 grains troy; that the £1 sterling is that amount of gold utterly irrespective of cost of production; that the cost of production has varied and is varying, and yet that amount of gold is the £1 sterling. This, I presume, you will not deny.

From that point we get to silver, and we find that whoever has got 180 grains troy of that metal can pay his rent of one rupee in India.

The cost of production of silver has changed over and over again. Still, 180 grains troy pays a rupee debt of any kind.

Then we go a little further, and find that the French mint fixed the ratio between the two, and said that whatever the cost of production, they were willing to give for 99·561 grains troy gold twenty francs, capable of paying any debt in France written in that coinage, and for 385·808 silver five francs.

We find that whatever the cost of production, and whatever the "DEMAND FOR ORNAMENTS," the relative value of gold and silver by this artificial arrangement, which we contend is not more artificial in principle in respect to commodities than our gold standard, remained substantially the same during the whole period in which this law demand existed.

Can you alter these facts?

Are they the truth?

Are they pertinent to the consideration of the new events which have occurred since 1868?

Supposing that the cost of production of wheat influences the value and price in five years, and that the cost of production influences the value and price of the precious metals in the long run—say 200 years,—is it worth while making preparations for that which may occur 200 years hence?

But I have stuck absolutely to M[c]Culloch in his distinction between the effect of the cost of production on perishable articles and that on those not perishable.

Where is my fallacy?

Yours,

H. R. GRENFELL.

FROM PROFESSOR B. PRICE TO MR. H. R. GRENFELL.

2, NORHAM GARDENS, OXFORD,
November 16, 1882.

MY DEAR GRENFELL,—

I have heard from "my eminent friend,"—and he is one of the very ablest men I know. He laughs. "I have "known," says he, "a coat or a loaf of bread much more "seriously altered from that of the cost of its production "by the stringency of the demand and the smallness of the "supply, than I have ever known the cost of gold altered "from the same cause."

The case I will state once, for the last time. The cost of production determines the value of a metal; and that cost—that price—must be procured, as a rule, in the market, or that metal will not be produced. But, on a given day, the buyers in the market may be few and poor, by accidental causes; or, the supply offered for sale may have fallen off, when buyers were eager; in either case, the selling price will differ from the cost of production. These are accidents which befall every commodity put up for sale. The two forces—the cost, and the state of the market—are perfectly different things, and they affect every commodity under the sun.

It was the word "doctrine" which misled and puzzled me. I do not see how demand—special demand, I presume—could neutralize the doctrine: it might and does neutralise, or at least weaken or strengthen, the fact of the cost of production. There was no want of will to understand the question.

And now, a fresh sea to navigate! The coining of a metal, and making it legal tender, in no way determines its value. Legal tender merely informs a creditor what *weight* of metal he will get paid for his goods if he gives credit: that is all. Legal tender does not say a syllable about the worth of the metals.

But to adopt a metal as the legal tender coin of the country of course creates a demand for it, precisely as using gold to make watches with.

Of course, the prescribed weight of gold is the £ sterling. I always define a sovereign, or a £, as so many carats of stamped gold; a shilling, as only the $\frac{1}{20}$th of a sovereign.

In India, silver is the standard; and, of course, a rupee is so many grains of silver. Really, you pour out truisms. Of course, whatever the *value* of the silver, a debt specified in rupees is so many times 180 grains of silver.

Of course, again, the French fixed the weight of their gold and silver coins, and made them both legal tenders. Who in the world disputes these facts, which any intelligent boy can easily master; but value—power in exchanging for other commodities—does not enter into these statements one bit.

Then you make a very remarkable assertion. You say, that "whilst the law demand existed," this law ratio was not more artificial in principle than our gold standard remained during all that period. In *principle,* it was far more artificial: for the proper ratio in paying debts depended on two metals instead of one; each having its own way of varying in value. What the monometallists say is, that it is far better to take the chances of variation of one metal than of two. It is possible, no doubt, that the variations of the one may correct those of the other; but they may also make them infinitely worse. The Latin Union could not go on coining silver.

I prefer the variations of one metal only; and Gibbs tells you and me that England has—for herself—a perfect currency.

No doubt perishable articles may be terribly influenced by the variations of supply and demand. An excessive supply of fruit or eggs, that won't keep, may make them almost worthless: that is right enough: and that is *one* very good reason for not making them money, but good hard metals.

You ask for your fallacy. First, in making an ounce of gold, in coin, worth only 15½ of silver, instead of the true value, 18; and, secondly, of exposing England (unless you adopt a check, on Clarmont Daniell's principle, by the process called the Gresham law) to lose all her gold, to be filled with silver only, to the grave injury of every creditor and the profit of every debtor.

Yours,

B. PRICE.

FROM MR. H. R. GRENFELL TO PROFESSOR B. PRICE.

BANK OF ENGLAND,
November 17, 1882.

DEAR PRICE,—

I think less of your "eminent friend" than I did. Or rather he must think less of me if he believes that it is *ad rem* to say that he has "known a coat or a loaf of bread "much more seriously altered from the cost of production "by the stringency of demand and the smallness of supply "than he has seen the cost of gold altered from the same "cause."

I have neither time nor inclination to get at the reasons why an old woman at market charges, or does not charge, an extra profit on a handful of apples. Your friend, eminent though he be, had better read J. S. Mill's *Political Economy*, vol. 1, pp. 537, 538.

I now come to the serious part of your letter. I knew you would say that though the law fixes the written figure in the creditor's books, it does not "say a syllable about "the worth of the metals." Very good! I have nothing to say against that dictum.

What *does* say anything about the "worth of the "metals"?—our old friends, cost of production and demand.

I have nothing further to say against all your letter up to the point where you very unwillingly, for the first time, come to the crucial point, and say

"In principle, it (that is, bimetallism) was far more "artificial; for the *proper ratio* in paying debts depended "on two metals instead of one, each having its own way "of varying in value."

"Now the monometallists say that it is far better to "take the chance of variation of one metal than of two."

Do they?

The first of monometallists, Jevons, may say that it is better as a matter of policy, but as a matter of securing the greatest possible fixity of value which, according to Professor Price, is the one thing needful, he says exactly the contrary, for he endorses the calculations of the bimetallist writers as to the compensatory action of the double standard.

Then you say "the variations of the one may correct "those of the other; but they may make them infinitely "worse. The Latin Union could not go on coining silver."

Why?

Because of the demonetization in Germany. Because of the sudden and ill-considered change from bimetallism. It is that phenomenon we are examining. If France had gone on coining while Germany and America were taking to gold, of course the whole of their coinage and circulation would have become silver.

Why?

Because of the (according to Professor Price) fictitious, false, artificial demand set up for gold in those countries. You then say you prefer the variations of one metal, notwithstanding that your own champion tells you the oscillations are greater, and less likely to produce that which you say is the greatest merit money can have, namely, fixity of value.

I asked you to tell me where is my fallacy. You answer me, in making 15½ the relative value when it is 18.

So we must begin all over again.

Why 18?

Because a false, fictitious, artificial demand has been taken away from silver and given to gold.

But I accept 18, if you like it. I think 15½ would have been better last year. But next year, if the Bland Bill is repealed, and Germany and Holland sell their silver, it will be more likely 30,—to the profit of every creditor, and the grave injury of every debtor.

Every creditor has already profited to the extent of the fall from 15 to 18, and you wish them to be favoured still more.

Yours,

H. R. GRENFELL.

FROM PROFESSOR B. PRICE TO MR. H. R. GRENFELL.

2, NORHAM GARDENS, OXFORD,
November 21, 1882.

MY DEAR GRENFELL,—

"You accept 18, if I like it." I do. This is an immense fact: a foundation of great strength for, I hope, a good superstructure.

We are almost agreed: certainly not far off now.

1. We have Gibbs' proclamation, that the currency of England is perfect, and that, were it not for other nations, he thinks it ought not to be changed.

2. I have all along held the opinion that it was desirable to bring silver into the currency, if it can be introduced in a manner that shall violate no sound principle of currency, nor injure the one which England possesses.

3. If silver is to be introduced, I have all along insisted that it should be on the basis of its value in the metal-market. 1 : 18 gives me what I ask for here.

I believe that we agree so far: there remains only one problem more to solve—namely—In what way shall silver be made legal tender in England by the side of gold, with free coinage of all silver presented?

Here I conceive that we have a precedent, which, most probably, can solve the problem. For 400 years, we are told, the ratio in which the silver coins should be related to the gold ones was regulated by proclamation from the Government. Why not examine this precedent closely, and see whether it will not bear repetition?

It is Daniell's proposal in substance; and I have from the first markedly claimed that it should be closely considered by the bimetallists. I have never said that a scheme of practical working has yet been found for it: but I have maintained that Daniell's went on a right principle, and that some sound method of working might probably be discovered.

If successful, the adaptation from time to time of the ratio in the coins to the ratio of the values of the metals or metal would give an excellent bimetallist currency—and I have always declared myself as the advocate of such money. If a right scheme can be devised, the two metals would be related to each other in the national money on their true metallic values; and, I submit, you and I ought to be agreed.

Yours,

B. PRICE.

From Mr. H. R. GRENFELL to Professor B. PRICE.

Bank of England,
November 21, 1882.

Dear Price,—

My acceptation of 18 to 1 is simply because neither 18, nor 15, nor 20, is of the essence of our argument. What we contend is, that any of them could be the fixed ratio.

If you agree on this proposition, we do not fear that we could show you that 15½ would be better than 18. Gibbs' proclamation is merely admitting as a historical fact that the currency within England is perfect as far as being understood and known by all the lieges.

But he has never said, nor do we admit, that as an instrument or tool of exchange between nations it is perfect.

You have, as you say, admitted all along and in several writings the necessity of using silver, but you want to have a varying standard instead of a sound one, notwithstanding your assertion that fixity of value was the highest quality of money.

1 in 18 may be the price to-day. 1 in 15½ was 12 years ago. 1 in 100 may be in a year or two, if the monometallists have their way.

My final answer to the rest of your letter is to repeat that your proposition, like that of Daniell, is not a standard at all.

Yours,

H. R. GRENFELL.

CORRESPONDENCE.

FROM MR. T. H. FARRER TO MR. H. H. GIBBS.

ABINGER HALL, DORKING,
March 25, 1883.

MY DEAR GIBBS,—

A friend, who takes interest in bimetallism, puts to me the following problem:

"It is admitted by bimetallists that in a sound currency the "value of the standard coin is determined by supply and demand, "and not by any action of the Government: that this is effected "by enabling all persons to get any quantity of the standard "metal turned into coin; and that the relation of value between "the standard coin and all other commodities is in consequence "the result of the ordinary action of the market, and is not the "creation of direct law.

"Assuming this to be the case, how is it that bimetallists "justify the direct determination by law of the relative values "of two particular commodities, viz. gold and silver?

"And how is it that they satisfy themselves that direct "Government prescription will operate with certainty and success "in determining this particular relation of value, when they admit "that it would do in respect of no other relation?"

I think I know what the answer would be: but as that answer seems TO ME open to a reply, I should be much obliged if you could direct my friend to any writing where the answer to this question is distinctly given in terms which bimetallists would accept.

Sincerely yours,

T. H. FARRER.

H. H. GIBBS, Esq.

FROM MR. H. H. GIBBS TO MR. T. H. FARRER.

ST. DUNSTANS, REGENT'S PARK,
March 30, 1883.

MY DEAR FARRER,—

I don't think your first sentence would be "admitted by bimetallists."

I have written certain theses which show what I think they do admit and assert; you will see that the 1st, to which I believe you will assent, differs from yours.

1. In a sound currency the value of the standard coin compared with the commodities which it measures is determined by supply and demand.

2. The Government, *i.e.* Law, affects supply: it provides for its even flow by keeping an open Mint.

3. Law can fatally affect demand: for by demonetising the standard coin in any country, it *pro tanto* diminishes the demand for the metal of which the coin is composed.

4. If the Law restricts the Mint as to the amount which it may coin, it raises the purchasing power, *i.e.* the comparative value, of the coin of the country.

5. If the Law demonetises the metal, it lowers the purchasing power, *i.e.* the comparative value, of the coin of other countries whose money that metal is.

6. It is impossible, under good government, that Law should prescribe the quantity of standard coin which shall or shall not be given for a purchasable commodity.

7. But that in no way affects the power of Law to determine what the standard coin shall be, nor, if composed of two metals, what proportion they shall bear to one another.

8. It is an abuse of terms to include either gold money or silver money—both being money in the same country—among purchasable commodities.

9. But, if gold and silver money *are* to be considered as purchasable commodities, the measure of their value is the mass of other commodities, and in that measure no Law does or can *determine* their price.

I will see if I can refer you to any printed writings in which the answer is distinctly given. The distinctness of an answer must depend in some degree upon the question having been distinctly before the writer. So you may, perhaps, find none yet in print that clearly answers your letter.

I touched on the point in pp. 36-7 of the "Double Standard"; and again, indirectly, in an article which I suppose will appear in the *National Review* of May next.

Yours, &c.,

H. H. GIBBS.

FROM LORD BRAMWELL TO MR. H. H. GIBBS.

FOUR ELMS, EDEN BRIDGE, KENT,
September 1, 1883.

DEAR MR. GIBBS,—

At length I understand the good of bimetallism: It is to relieve taxpayers and debtors generally. It is not necessary for currency purposes. I agree with all you say, except in the propriety of doing the good you propose; as to that I have a doubt. Would it be honest? Of course you think so or you would not propose it. But is it right to alter the currency for the purpose of benefiting debtors at the expense of creditors? Would it be right to alter it to benefit creditors at the expense of debtors? I speak as a pensioner. Would it be right to lighten the sovereign, or add to its alloy and diminish its gold, for this purpose? But what is the difference between that and what you propose? And this from a Bank Director and Member of the Political Economy Club! Alas! Political Economy is sent to Jupiter and Saturn, and—but I will not proceed.

Very truly yours,

BRAMWELL.

FROM MR. H. H. GIBBS TO LORD BRAMWELL.

ALDENHAM HOUSE, NEAR ELSTREE, HERTS,
September 30, 1883.

DEAR LORD BRAMWELL,—

On my return from Scotland I found your note of the 1st inst., and now write to thank you for it, and to say a few words in reply.

If, as you suppose, bimetallists considered that the relief of taxpayers generally, and of debtors at the expense of creditors, was a "good" end, and one for which they should strive, I should think their object was *not* honest, and it would find no support from me. I have no love for "remedial legislation" when its aim is to gratify Paul by giving him some of Peter's goods.

Neither would it be right to benefit creditors at the expense of debtors, though such a course might be, from our circumstances, more satisfactory to you and me, than the other.

Yet both these things have been done, not without bitter remonstrance on the part of those injured, but with the approval of the majority of the nation, and of posterity. When cash-payments were suspended in 1797, all creditors were injured. When cash-payments were resumed in 1816, all debtors were injured in their turn. Those of the creditors and debtors who thought of the matter grumbled on their several occasions at the injuries they suffered; but none of them, so far as I know, imagined that the Government had adopted those two measures *for the purpose of* giving a bonus to debtors by the first, or to creditors by the second. They knew well enough that the injury to the one, and the benefit to the other, were only accidents of measures necessary or just in the main, and they submitted to necessity.

In like manner, creditors have been benefited, not indeed by the action of our own Government, but by the action of Germany and France, and now the benefit which debtors or taxpayers would in their turn receive from the arresting of that appreciation of the measure of value which I suppose to be taking place, and which must now be giving, as it has hitherto given, a benefit to creditors, would be but an unavoidable accident of a measure having no such thing for its main object, but only the giving of greater steadiness to the relations between the measure of value and the commodities measured, and thus diminishing the amount of injury that may be done now to debtors and now to creditors by changes in those relations.

I don't think there is anything opposed to Political Economy in the adoption of two metals in a certain relative proportion as our measure of value, nor that if it be true that their adoption would produce a great and permanent benefit to commerce, we wait till that science is banished to a distant planet before adopting that good, even though it should be accompanied by a small and temporary evil.

Yours, &c.

H. H. GIBBS.

From Lord BRAMWELL to Mr. H. H. GIBBS.

Four Elms, Eden Bridge, Kent,
October 3, 1883.

Dear Mr. Gibbs,—

I write to you thus in answer to your letter of the 30th September.

I say that for currency purposes—on currency considerations—in order to improve it, you may change the currency though you raise or lower the exchangeable value of any coin or circulating medium. I say that you ought not in fairness to alter the currency only for the purpose of benefiting creditors at the expense of debtors, or debtors at the expense of creditors. This last is what I understand you to propose. I say to you as a Bank Director, *proh pudor!*

Now, what are your arguments? You admit, I am glad to find, that what I say is wrong, would be wrong. But you say it has been done with the approval of the majority of the nation, and you prophesy that of posterity. As an instance, you cite the suspension of cash payments in 1797. Prodigious! Do you really approve of that on any other ground than that it could not be helped, or rather, that it was supposed it could not be helped? As to resumption of cash payments; do you not approve of it because it was the right thing to do, and could not be done otherwise? And is it not true that all holders of depreciated currency put a value on it because in time it would rise to par; and so of stocks and debts? As to appreciation of gold owing to the action of France and Germany, I say so much the better for creditors. If they alter and revert to a silver currency, or bimetallism, so much the worse for them; or would you alter the currency for their benefit? But I say unless bimetallism is good for its own sake, it is not justifiable to counteract the action of other countries—*i.e.* to lower the exchangeable value of gold. And this, I repeat, is what I understood you to say. Justify your bimetallism on other grounds, and I agree you entirely justify it. I do not think Political Economy is opposed to it. I still have faith in that, and envy the inhabitants of Jupiter and Saturn. I think bimetallism possible. Did you ever see a letter in *The Times* on the subject, signed "B."? I abide by that.

I am glad that we agree in our principles. If one-pound notes would improve the currency, let us have them. So of silver. Pray did you ever think of this: at present no one pays £1 unless in gold. Would it be different under bimetallism? If not, what good would that do? If yes, are we to carry about fifty or more crown pieces?

Ever yours jointly and severally,

BRAMWELL.

FROM MR. H. H. GIBBS TO LORD BRAMWELL.

ALDENHAM HOUSE, NEAR ELSTREE, HERTS,
October 6, 1883.

DEAR LORD BRAMWELL,—

Mr. Grenfell has forwarded to me your answering shot at him and me. I plead not guilty to the charge.

I never said (or, if my words seemed to bear that sense, I never meant) that it could be good to do any act for the purpose of benefiting the debtor at the expense of the creditor. Moreover, I disclaimed, or meant to disclaim, any such opinion, or any such desire, in my last shot at you.

Consequently I entirely agree with you, as I do with Grenfell, where you denounce it, and I should deserve your "*proh pudor*" if I did not.

Nor did I at all mean to suggest that the Act of 1797 was passed with that object, nor the Act of 1816 with the converse object. Those Acts were passed with no such evil intent, but—the first because it was, or was supposed to be, a necessity of the time; the second, because it was just; and the fact that they both of them involved more or less injustice to creditor or debtor did not deter the statesmen of that day from doing what they believed, on grounds totally distinct, to be necessary and just.

I agree with Grenfell that the wisdom, if not the justice, would have been greater if they had returned to the ancient standard of England—gold and silver.

It was the good (or supposed good) which was done by those Acts, and not the involved injustice, which I suppose posterity approved; but I am far from prophesying, as you think I do, that posterity will approve bimetallism: first, because "I don't know;" and, secondly, because our grandfathers' posterity have done so many foolish things in this generation that I have lost all confidence in posterity. I fear our own may be no wiser, and don't, accordingly, attach much value to their judgment.

I entirely agree with you that "unless bimetallism is "good for its own sake, it is not justifiable." Also, I envy with you the inhabitants of Saturn. They are better governed, apparently. *Redeant Saturnia Regna.*

H. H. GIBBS.

I read and remember "B.'s" article, and very good I thought it.

FROM LORD BRAMWELL TO MR. H. H. GIBBS.

FOUR ELMS, EDEN BRIDGE, KENT,
October 18, 1883.

DEAR MR. GIBBS,—

I hate a controversy. But that is no reason why I should not write to you, for we do not differ. I wrote my first note because somewhere you said, as I thought, that among the reasons for bimetallism was this, that it would relieve debtors and taxpayers. I think this is not a reason for, but against it; for, unless for good reason, it is wrong to alter the value of debts. I believe you both think so, too; therefore, there is no difference between us. If, indeed, an alteration in the currency is a good thing in itself, and it cannot be accomplished except by altering the value of debts, &c., then it may be that that must be borne.

I am not going to discuss bimetallism with you; that might involve a controversy. It might have been well if "the ancient standard" had been reverted to by Peel. I do not know. I agree that the variations in the value of the £1 would have been less, though more frequent. I said so in my letter signed "B.," and was delighted to find that Jevons had said the same thing—which I did not know. Whether it would be an improvement *now*, I doubt. You say nobody carries 50 sovereigns. No; nobody wants as many—cheques are used; but people do carry 5*s*. × 50 = £12 : 10*s*. I ask again, would more silver be used? If not, how would it rise in value?

Ever yours,

BRAMWELL.

FROM LORD BRAMWELL TO MR. H. H. GIBBS.

FOUR ELMS, EDEN BRIDGE, KENT,
October 22, 1883.

DEAR MR. GIBBS,—

One word more,—not from a wish to have the last. I believe more silver would be used in England. I think our friends the Germans and Yankees would favour us with some of theirs in exchange for our gold ; and that when we had it, perforce we must use it somehow. But I agree more might be used by the world, though we did not use more. Then, 1st, Why can't they do without us? 2nd, Why should we help them at a loss and inconvenience to ourselves? I prefer patriotism to cosmopolitanism.

Ever yours truly,

BRAMWELL.

THE GOLD QUESTION AND THE FALL OF PRICES.

From the *National Review*, July, 1883.

I PROPOSE in the following paper to discuss the present condition of what has been called the Silver question, but which at this time and in this country, as directly affecting the English medium of exchange, should rather be called the Gold question.

I propose also to show that many evils have flowed and are flowing from the demonetization of silver by Germany, and that a remedy for them might be sought in the return to our ancient system of gold and silver money, if the prejudices of the present day did not so strongly militate against it.

Yet, deeply-seated as that prejudice still is, it is certain that there is a great difference between the present position of the question and the position it occupied in 1878, the date of the second Monetary Conference in Paris; and greater still, if we compare it with the ground taken by the first Monetary Conference of 1867 and by the Royal Commission of 1868. At that time, the conclusion at which the members arrived was, that the universal adoption of a Gold Standard was desirable. The Conference of 1878, on the contrary, having before them the fall in the price of silver, and the consequent inconveniences which had arisen, unanimously urged the necessity of silver taking its full part in the monetary service of the world. The fall of prices which had begun in 1874 and had continued till 1881, the date of the third Monetary Conference, led its members to consider more closely the effects both of the fall in the purchasing power of silver, and of the correlative rise in the purchasing power of gold; and the result was a further advance of opinion, and a wider spread feeling amongst its members, of the wisdom of reverting to the use of a Bimetallic Standard. France and the United States and Holland were anxious to return to it; and Germany, unwilling to send representatives to the Conference of 1878, appeared now to be willing, on conditions, to join a Bimetallic Union; and England, though as much opposed as before to a return to a Bimetallic Standard of value, was willing to admit that its adoption by other nations would be a great advantage to herself, and to discuss the possibility of making some changes, unimportant in themselves to her own interest, but likely to conduce to such an end.

The same change, the same progress of opinion, has been everywhere visible in the pages of that part of the Public Press which pays any attention to the subject.

The bimetallists themselves have learnt much of the working of their system, and of the mischief existing, and likely to increase, from the contraction of our monometallic currency. Their opponents, also, have begun to perceive that there are more things in heaven and earth than were dreamt of in their philosophy, and that, as Prince Bismarck said, when ten men try to lie under a blanket which has barely covered five, inconvenience must result.

The Press in England was till lately wont to treat the matter as a crotchet of a few theorists, having no real bearing on the fortunes of commerce; as an academic question at best, not worthy of serious consideration by economists and still less by statesmen, in whose eyes it was held to be "outside the range of practical politics." The financial portion of the Press, and those masters in Political Economy, who had learnt their own lesson once for all and long ago, could not at once be induced to believe that with changed premisses new conclusions might be possible, and permitted themselves, therefore, to class our contentions with pretended demonstrations of the flatness of the earth, and of the squaring of the circle. It was very natural. These our instructors (and very useful instructors they are on subjects which they have thoroughly studied) were too much inclined to think that they were born to teach the world, and too little inclined to accept instruction from men or matters.

Now all this—or nearly all—has been changed. Statesmen, indeed, do not give the subject much consideration; but statesmen, in England at least, are very loath to examine any question for themselves. They wait till Public Opinion is too strong for them, and then they suddenly find that they, in common with all wise men, have always believed in the urgent necessity of this or that measure of reform. So will it be with the reform of the Standard of Value. Public opinion, though not yet converted, and not yet taking a real interest in the matter, is on the right road towards conversion. The question is now no longer contemptuously passed by in the Public Press (except where a simulated contempt is sometimes used as a cloak for ignorance), but is seriously discussed from time to time both in the financial newspapers and among students of Political Economy. The money columns of the newspapers contain serious and elaborate articles for and against the Bimetallic Standard: the opponents of it professing to demonstrate our fallacies, but unfortunately omitting the demonstration, and combating in most cases not the assertions and arguments of the bimetallist, but some other assertions and arguments which they are pleased to father upon him.

Sometimes an ex-statesman, rejoicing in his freedom from parliamentary strife, rushes into our arena; and using for his weapons much wit and little logic, much prejudice and little knowledge, tells us of the manifold disadvantages which must flow from the two prices in one market, which, as he thinks, will be the inevitable consequence of two metals of differing value being employed to do service as money; but he, in common with all those who use this argument, wholly omits to show us how such two prices will come about, or indeed, under a law of free mintage, could be possible.

Sometimes a learned and able Professor takes up his parable, and finds himself unwillingly and unwittingly playing the part of Balaam the son of Beor: he comes to curse, but blesses us altogether. He allows the necessity of admitting silver to bear its part in the world as money; he virtually admits the soundness of our theory, but he, also, trips over the imaginary stumbling-block of the two prices, and proposes to make chronic that temporary disorder in the relation between debtors and creditors which the fixing of a ratio between two money-metals must in some greater or less degree produce, and would make such fixing and such disorder recur again and again at indeterminate periods, at the discretion of some central "authority."

On the other hand, Mr. Goschen's speech in Parliament on the 19th of February last, not indeed touching on the remedy advocated in this paper, but fully discussing the causes and incidence of the evil which it is intended to cure, shows that one statesman, at least, perceives the importance of the subject, and that one a man better fitted than others, by his early training, to gauge the necessities and difficulties of trade.

The *Spectator* comments on this speech in its issue of the 24th of February; and recognizing the magnitude of the evil, and the weight with which it presses on English

Mr. H. H. Gibbs.

industries, and especially on agriculture, asks if the time has not arrived for the appointment of a Royal Commission to inquire into the whole subject.

Again, a writer in the *Statist* of the 24th of the same month, commenting upon Mr. Goschen's speech, takes much the same line as Mr. Giffen did in his interesting paper read before the Statistical Society, as long ago as January, 1879, and fully acknowledges the effect on prices which the scarcity of gold must produce. He does not admit the efficacy of bimetallism as a remedy (and on his arguments on this point I shall comment in the course of this paper), but he, and all those who really think upon the matter, are now fully aware what are the true objects of the advocates of the Bimetallic Standard. We need no longer take pains to explain those objects, nor to protest that we do not consider the adoption of that system a panacea for all the ills that Trade is heir to, but only a remedy for one particular ill.

I may assume that it has been demonstrated—

1. That the fixing by law of the proportion in which silver and gold, jointly adopted as money, as the measure of value and medium of exchange, shall be received in payment of debts, bears no analogy to a vicious fixing by law of the price of a commodity as measured in money.

2. That that proportion once fixed, and the mints opened for coinage of legal tender money in that proportion, it is impossible that there can be a market price of silver measured in gold, or of gold measured in silver, which shall differ from the mint price or legal ratio; and that, therefore, under an international agreement, it is impossible that there could be a dearer and a cheaper metal, of which the former would "leave the country."

3. That such an international agreement would be easily brought about if England would join it, or would cordially

promote its establishment in other nations, and that once established on a broad basis such an agreement must practically be maintained.

4. That it is no part of the creed of bimetallists that Commerce is, in the long run, benefited by inflation of the currency; and that what they really desire, and what they believe will result from the adoption of a Bimetallic Standard of value, is a greater steadiness than can be attained under a Monometallic System.

These matters have been treated pretty fully by many writers of late years—in the United States by Dana Horton, in Belgium by Laveleye, in Germany by Arendt, in France by Wolowski; and in this country by Mr. Grenfell, in two papers in the *Nineteenth Century*, by myself, in a pamphlet on the Double Standard in 1881, and by many others.

Besides this, the establishment of the International Monetary Standard Association in this country, and the foundation of sister Associations in Germany and Belgium, insure that public attention will be continually called to the importance of the subject, and, by their frequent publications and unrefuted arguments, prepare men's minds for a return to the sound and practical system, the benefits of which were extended (until the suspension in 1873 of the French law of free mintage) even to those countries which nominally had but one metal—gold or silver—for their measure of value.

Silver was not, indeed, while free mintage lasted in France, true money in England, nor was gold true money in Germany; but remittances of silver to England, and of gold to Germany, were practically remittances of cash; because the fluctuations of value between the two metals, notwithstanding the enormous fluctuations in the relative amounts annually produced of each, were almost imperceptible, and were measured only by the natural operation of the Exchanges.

Mr. H. H. Gibbs.

This condition of things would evidently be restored by the return of France to her former practice; but it is believed that France will not move in this direction, unless Germany and the United States will join with her and the rest of the Latin Union in adopting a bimetallic standard with a fixed ratio, and free mintage of both metals.

It remains to be seen what steps England will take to render this action more easy to Germany and the other nations concerned.

In the year 1881, some steps were taken in this direction, and there would have been, I believe, no difficulty on the part of England in guaranteeing, for a certain time, the maintenance of free mintage of silver in India, in authorising the Bank to carry out the provisions of the Act of 1844 as regards that metal, and perhaps in extending the amount of silver receivable as legal tender; but the negotiations on the subject came, for that time, to no practical end; a failure very much to be regretted, inasmuch as the part to be performed by England was in no way onerous to her, and, the condition of its performance being the return of the Continental nations and the United States to a Bimetallic Standard, it would have been of the greatest advantage to her, both in the interests of commerce, and as solving the monetary question as regards India.

But, while a better understanding of the subject is increasing, the march of events is unfortunately in the opposite direction.

Italy has announced that in this present month she will put into circulation the sixteen millions of gold which she has withdrawn from the circulation of the other gold-using states. The result will be, indeed, that that gold will be obtainable by those states, if they choose to pay for it. The gold will leave Italy if she is indebted to her neighbours, *i.e.*, whenever the Exchanges are and remain against her; and she will have to contend with them for the retention of the metal, and the weapon which both parties to the contest must use will be the rate of discount, a weapon which wounds both the striker and the stricken.

In Holland, a Bill is before the Chambers authorising the Government to sell their silver so as to substitute gold in its place; and if that Bill passes there will be yet another combatant in the same contest.

In the United States there has been already a very large absorption of gold. The return of the 12th of March shows £34,000,000 in the Treasury, £11,000,000 in the Banks, and £70,000,000 in circulation in the country—£115,000,000 in all; and the tendency, even irrespective of the question of repealing the Bland Bill, seems to be to increase the amount.

The Session of Congress being over, there is no imminent danger of the repeal of the Bill, and of the consequent cessation of the coinage of silver, but though it is difficult to believe that the United States, a silver-producing country, can really desire to further the demonetization of silver, or can be blind to the evils likely to accrue to themselves as well as to Europe by the contraction of the circulation, if they also should adopt a single gold standard, still it would be unwise to leave such a contingency out of the calculation. The causes of the agitation for the repeal of the Bill appear to be two. First, the desire of a large number of politicians to adopt the gold standard, as being, so they think, one source of the prosperity of England; and, second, the action of others whose aims are directly opposite, and who would deem the permanent adoption of a gold standard a great misfortune for their country, but who hope, "by declaring "war against silver," to make the position intolerable to England, and induce her to retrace her steps.

Certainly the position would be intolerable, as will be readily seen, if we look at the amount of silver in the States which would be thrown on the market by such a policy.

Mr. H. H. Gibbs.

The dollars coined under the provisions of the Bland Bill up to the 1st of February last have been $135,405,080, and of these about $38,000,000 were in circulation in specie in possession of the people, and $72,745,470 more in circulation also, but under the form of certificates, which pass readily from hand to hand, and which may be considered as State notes or vouchers for dollars and bullion stored in the vaults of the Treasury, of which sum $4,306,650 were held by the Treasury itself.

Now if all this silver is demonetized, and thrown on the market together with what existed in the country before the passing of the Bland Bill, and with the monthly produce of the mines, what will be the loss suffered by the Indian Government, and by all who receive fixed sums payable in silver, or who trade with silver-using countries, and what will be the effect on prices of the absorption by the United States of the further quantity of gold which must take its place!

I do not think such a catastrophe is likely; but it is impossible to foretell what the exigencies of party or the needs of private interest, real or imaginary, may bring about under a system of popular government.

As a further illustration of what I have said as to the improved tone of the Public Press in their treatment of this subject, I cannot but refer to an article on Trade and Finance which appeared in the *Daily News* of the 20th of March. It is a perfectly fair and well-reasoned statement of the case, as regards the influence of the growing scarcity on prices, and the influence of decreasing prices on the commerce of the country. The writer of that article admits the disease, but, like the writer in the *Statist,* rejects the remedy. He says, "Let the suffering cure "itself; commerce, it is true, is on infirm ground and feels "herself sinking; let her not fear, she will come to firm "ground at last!" But how if the quagmire be deep, and she be suffocated before she reach the bottom?

A remedy is proposed, a reasonable remedy, which shall give all nations composing the world of commerce a uniform standard of value. But we are content to wrap ourselves up in our prejudices, and trust to an unseen future to cure our admitted ills, and we reject the remedy that will cure them. So also a remedy was proposed to cure the inconvenience of a diversity of money in the states of which Germany was composed. Every state had its own coinage, to the manifest inconvenience of Germans and those that had commerce with them. No doubt there was the same cry, "Let well alone," even though well was ill; but a better wisdom prevailed there, and will some day prevail here.

That England should make some such concessions as those which were proposed in 1881, is, in my opinion, very much to be desired, both for the sake of her commerce, and for the sake of the general well-being of Englishmen, for whom the prosperity of English commerce is a vital question.

We have been told, year by year, that "next year" was infallibly to bring with it improvement of trade; and that England's Commercial Prosperity, which had been so long under a cloud, was to shine forth again with double brightness so soon as commercial activity should revive in the United States, and so soon as India should be again prosperous. But both these things have happened in greater or less degree, and we have even had an improved harvest year (after long waiting), which was to be another signal for the revival of trade; but trade revives not. Prices are and have been everywhere depressed—unless where temporary and local circumstances have at any time counteracted the general tendency.

What can be the cause of this declension? There are, no doubt, many causes; but there is one among them which our instructors in the Press steadily ignore, preferring rather to attribute the mischief to the spots in the Sun, or to any other recondite cause, than to one which lies at their very doors.

Prices of commodities are influenced, first, by the supply of and demand for those commodities, and by their cost of production ; and, secondly, by the quantity of material available for money, which is the measure of them, and which provides, in ordinary parlance, the very conception of *price*. If that material is rendered available in larger quantities, either (1) by increased production, (2) by diminished population, (3) by a falling off in the demand for use in the Arts, or (4) by the spread of banking expedients, which supply the place of coin and set the metal free, the prices of other commodities are, *cæteris paribus*, necessarily greater. Or, on the other hand, if (1) the production at the mines falls off, (2) population increases, (3) more money-metal is consumed in the Arts, or (4) metallic money takes, in any nation, the place of paper,—these causes, or any one of them, provided it be not counterbalanced by the existence of either of the points in the first category, must, so far as it goes, depress the prices of commodities.

The shrinking or increase of the worth of the sovereign, the measure of value, is precisely analogous to the shrinking or expansion of the inch, the measure of length. If the standard inch were enlarged, so that the foot of 12 inches were equal to 13 of our present inches, the buyer who bought a foot-length would get more stuff; or, if it were diminished, so that the foot of 12 inches were to be equal to only 11 of our present inches, the buyer would get less. The diminution of the quantity of sovereigns (that is to say, of gold, used as money) is an increase in the value of each particular sovereign; the buyer gets more stuff for it. The multiplication of sovereigns is a shrinking of the value of each particular sovereign; the buyer gets less stuff for it. The difference in actual fact is that the inch cannot increase or diminish without its being everywhere known:

the increase or diminution of the quantity of the money-metals is uncertain and insidious.

What is true of money-metals as a whole is, *à fortiori*, true of either one of them; either one being exposed to an additional strain, if it is taken into use as money in lieu of the other.

I have, then, to inquire—first—whether there *is* such a general fall in prices as is supposed; secondly—whether, if there is, it can be asserted with any degree of certainty that no other universal and persistent cause can be alleged for the fall; and, thirdly—whether either of those four things, to which I have above referred, has happened, which could disturb the proportion which existed some years back between gold and the commodities which it measures in English commerce, and cause such a fall.

Now, as to the second question, I must frankly say that there can be no *certainty* in the answer. Each article in the following table (*pp.* 358-9) may have had its own especial increase of production or diminution of demand, or both together, which may account for its steady fall in price; but if we find that the general result over all of them is the same, though differing in degree, we must search for some general cause which has overridden and either counteracted or increased the effects of the especial circumstances of each case.

That there has been such a fall the succeeding table, containing the prices of some of the principal articles of trade, clearly shows. It is mainly taken from Mr. Giffen's paper above referred to (*p.* 349), with additions and continuation to the present date (1883).

The results are admitted by the writer in the *Statist.* Prices, he says, have declined, to the present prejudice of trade and agriculture; and "if gold had not been appre-
" ciating in value, prices all round would have been higher
" than they are now."

Mr. H. H. Gibbs.

But, in treating the decline of prices which springs from this source as unimportant, he commits, I think, as grave an error as I should commit were I to attribute the decline to the appreciation of gold alone, and to no other cause; and I think I shall be able to show from his own words that he has not fully apprehended the cause of the complaint, nor the motives and reasoning of the complainers. He writes :—

"The appreciation, after all, cannot have been the main "factor, either in the agricultural distress or in the distress of "industry generally . . . . . . What causes distress "and suffering in business, moreover, is not a gradual fall in "prices extending over many years, such as would be due to "an appreciation of the standard, but a quick and violent fall, "which comes heavily upon the holders of large stocks, or upon "those who are carrying on considerable transactions with "borrowed money. To such people, the ups and downs of prices "in business from other causes are infinitely more important "than the insensible changes which are due to an appreciation "in the standard. The cases where the latter most cause "suffering are those of businesses which have large fixed "payments, and large payments in wages, that are difficult to "adjust to the new circumstances; but gradually, we may be "sure, the adjustment, even in those cases, will be made. We "are inclined to doubt, then, whether the appreciation of gold "which has been going on during the last ten years will have "more than temporary effects. When prices and wages and "many of the fixed payments have got adjusted to the new "conditions, business will go on as before."

No one can deny what he has here advanced, viz.:— that sudden and heavy falls of price cause distress, and greater distress than any which would result from the gradual appreciation of the metal forming the standard of value; or that legislative interference would be powerless to prevent, though it might lessen, this latter phenomenon.

Comparative List of Prices of sundry Articles of Pr

		1874.	1875.	1876.
COCHINEAL, fair silver ...	per lb.	2s. 1d.	1s. 11d.	1s. 9d
COCOA, Guayaquil	per cwt.	50s. @ 52s.	42s. @ 44s.	50s. @ 5
COFFEE, Middling Plantation Ceylon	"	133s.	98s.	105s.
COTTON—				
Middling Upland... ...	per lb.	8⅛d.	7¼d.	7d.
Fair Surat	"	5$\frac{5}{16}$d.	5d.	4½d.
HIDES—				
River Plate, heavy salted...	"	7⅛d.	9¼d.	8½d.
light " ...	"	7⅛d.	9⅛d.	7½d.
Australian heavy " ...	"	6d.	7⅛d.	5½d.
light " ...	"	5¾d.	7¼d.	5¼d.
INDIGO—				
Middling shipping Bengal	"	7s. 2d. @ 7s. 4d.	7s. 4d. @ 7s. 6d.	6s. 10d. @
JUTE, medium quality ...	per ton	15l. 10s. @ 16l. 15s.	14l. 15s. @ 15l. 10s.	15l. @ 1
RICE, Rangoon	per cwt.	11s. @ 12s. 3d.	8s. 9d. @ 9s.	7s. 10d. @ 8s
SALTPETRE	"	22s. @ 24s. 6d.	19s. 6d. @ 21s. 9d.	17s. @ 19s.
SUGAR—				
Brown Manilla	"	18s. 6d.	17s.	14s. 6d.
Good & fine West Indian...	"	25s. @ 26s.	23s.	20s.
TEA, sound common Congou	per lb.	1s. 0½d.	11d.	10d.
TOBACCO—				
Virginia leaf	"	3d. @ 1s.	7d. @ 1s. 2d.	5½d. @ 1s.
strips	"	7½d. @ 11d.	9½d. @ 1s. 4d.	9d. @ 1s. 2
Kentucky leaf	"	4d. @ 11d.	6d. @ 1s. 1d	3½d. @ 1
strips	"	7½d. @ 10d.	9d. @ 1s. 1d.	8d. @ 1s. 1
WOOL—				
English sheep's, ½ hog, ½ wether...	"	1s. 11d.	1s. 8½d.	1s. 6½d.
Australian: average Victoria washed	"	2s. @ 2s. 1d.	2s. 1d.	1s. 11d.
greasy	"	1s. 2d.	1s. 2d. @ 1s. 3d.	1s. 1d.
Mohair	"	2s. 9½d.	3s. 5d.	3s. 7½d.
Alpaca	"	2s. 8½d.	2s. 8d.	2s. 5d.

At commencement of January in respective years.		1873.	1874.	1875.	1876
COPPER, Chili bar	per ton	91l.	84l.	83l. 10s.	82l.
IRON, Scotch pig	"	127s.	107s. 6d.	80s.	64s. 3
LEAD, English	"	21l. 10s.	24l. 5s.	23l. 10s.	22l. 12s.
TIN, foreign	"	142l.	120l.	94l.	82l.
WHEAT, English Imperial average throughout the United Kingdom ...	per qr.	55s. 11d.	62s. 1d.	44s. 8d.	45s. 9

LONDON, 31*st January*, 1883.

…nuary of each of the undermentioned years:—

…877.	1878.	1879.	1880.	1881.	1882.
…. 9*d*.	2*s*. 1*d*.	2*s*.	3*s*.	1*s*. 9*d*.	1*s*. 6*d*.
… @ 69*s*.	71*s*. @ 74*s*.	108*s*. @ 110*s*.	78*s*. @ 80*s*.	59*s*. @ 60*s*.	61*s*. @ 63*s*.
…20*s*.	102*s*.	97*s*.	103*s*.	80*s*.	74*s*.
…⅞*d*.	6½*d*.	5⅜*d*.	6$\frac{15}{16}$*d*.	6$\frac{15}{16}$*d*.	6⅝*d*.
…$\frac{3}{16}$*d*.	4$\frac{13}{16}$*d*.	5*d*.	5¼*d*.	4⅜*d*.	4$\frac{5}{16}$*d*.
…¼*d*.	8*d*.	7¼*d*.	8⅛*d*.	7¼*d*.	7¼*d*.
…⅜*d*.	7*d*.	6¼*d*.	7½*d*.	7*d*.	6⅞*d*.
…½*d*.	5⅜*d*.	5*d*.	6*d*.	5¼*d*.	5½*d*.
…⅞*d*.	4½*d*.	4⅛*d*.	5⅞*d*.	5⅛*d*.	5¼*d*.
… @ 7*s*. 6*d*.	6*s*. 2*d*. @ 6*s*. 4*d*.	6*s*. @ 6*s*. 2*d*.	7*s*. 9*d*. @ 8*s*.	6*s*. 6*d*.@6*s*.10*d*.	6*s*. 10*d*. @ 7*s*.
….6*d*.@16*l*.	14*l*. 15*s*. @ 15*l*. 10*s*.	11*l*. @ 12*l*.	18*l*. 5*s*. @ 18*l*. 15*s*.	16*l*. 5*s*. @ 17*l*.	15*l*. 10*s*. @ 16*l*
…. 9*d*.	9*s*. 1½*d*.	8*s*. 7½*d*.	9*s*. @ 9*s*. 3*d*.	8*s*. 7½*d*.@8*s*. 9*d*.	8*s*. @ 7*s*. 10½*d*.
…*d*. @ 21*s*.	20*s*. @ 22*s*.	18*s*. @ 19*s*. 6*d*.	21*s*. @ 23*s*. 3*d*.	24*s*. 6*d*. @ 25*s*.	23*s*. 3*d*.
22*s*.	15*s*. 6*d*.	15*s*.	18*s*.	14*s*. 3*d*.	15*s*.
…*s*. 6*d*.	21*s*.	21*s*.	25*s*. 6*d*.	22*s*.	23*s*.
8½*d*.	9*d*.	8*d*.	11*d*. @ 1*s*.	6*d*. @ 6½*d*.	5*d*.
…. @ 1*s*.	4*d*. @ 11*d*.	3*d*. @ 10*d*.	4*d*. @ 1*s*.	4*d*. @ 11*d*.	4*d*. @ 1*s*. 3*d*.
…*d*. @ 1*s*.	5½*d*. @ 10*d*.	4½*d*. @ 10*d*.	5*d*. @ 10½*d*.	5*d*. @ 10½*d*.	6½*d*. @ 1*s*. 1*d*.
… @ 10½*d*.	2½*d*. @ 9½*d*.	2½*d*. @ 8½*d*.	3*d*. @ 10*d*.	3*d*. @ 10*d*.	4*d*. @ 10*d*.
…*d*. @ 1*s*.	5*d*. @ 9½*d*.	4*d*. @ 8*d*.	4½*d*. @ 9½*d*.	4½*d*. @ 9*d*.	5½*d*. @ 10*d*.
…1*s*. 6*d*.	1*s*. 4*d*.	1*s*. 1*d*.	1*s*. 2¾*d*.	1*s*. 1*d*.	1*s*. 0¼*d*.
…*d*.@1*s*.11*d*.	1*s*. 10*d*. @ 1*s*. 11*d*.	1*s*. 9*d*.	1*s*. 11*d*. @ 2*s*.	1*s*. 9*d*.@1*s*. 10*d*.	1*s*. 10*d*.
1*s*. 1*d*.	1*s*. 1*d*.	1*s*.	1*s*. 2*d*.	1*s*.	1*s*. 1*d*.
3*s*. 1*d*.	3*s*. 0½*d*.	1*s*. 10½*d*.	2*s*. 2½*d*.	1*s*. 10*d*.	1*s*. 9*d*.
2*s*. 1*d*.	1*s*. 8*d*.	1*s*. 5*d*.	1*s*. 5*d*.	1*s*. 3*d*.	1*s*. 5*d*.

…877.	1878.	1879.	1880.	1881.	1882.	1883.
…*l*. 10*s*.	66*l*.	57*l*.	65*l*. 10*s*.	62*l*. 10*s*.	70*l*. 5*s*.	65*l*. 5*s*.
…*s*. 6*d*.	51*s*. 6*d*.	43*s*.	67*s*.	53*s*. 4*d*.	51*s*. 9*d*.	48*s*. 9½*d*.
…*l*. 10*s*.	19*l*. 2*s*. 6*d*.	14*l*. 12*s*. 6*d*.	19*l*. 7*s*. 6*d*.	15*l*. 5*s*.	15*l*.	13*l*. 15*s*.
…*l*. 10*s*.	66*l*.	61*l*.	91*l*. 10*s*.	91*l*. 10*s*.	107*l*. 10*s*.	92*l*. 12*s*. 6*d*.
…1*s*. 6*d*.	51*s*. 9*d*.	39*s*. 7*d*.	46*s*. 11*d*.	41*s*. 11*d*.	44*s*. 9*d*.	40*s*. 7*d*.

But no sane man has ever hoped to prevent the "ups "and downs in prices which result from other causes" by legislative action, nor by any such action to forbid that gradual appreciation of the metal forming the standard which may spring from natural causes. Such an appreciation will take place under a bimetallic system of money, from the same cause as under a monometallic system, if the production of gold and silver both diminish at the same time, but, in contending that probability and history are both against such a thing happening and continuing to happen, I only follow some of the most able and most learned on the monometallic side of the question. What I do advocate is, not a futile attempt to interfere with the action of natural and slowly-acting causes, but the application of a remedy which will surely counteract those evils which hasty legislative action has caused and may cause again; and that remedy is a return by England to the bimetallic standard, or, at least, some practical encouragement on her part to induce other nations to return to the full use of it. Either policy would bring us back to the state of things as they existed before the violent action of Germany brought about the present difficulties.

The remarks of the *Statist* are mainly directed to show how much less dangerous appreciation of the standard metal is than depreciation; and he assumes that the aim of Mr. Goschen in his speech, and of all those who find danger in an abnormal contraction of the currency, is "to "substitute new conditions which would give the stimulus "to industry formerly given by the continually increasing "abundance of money."

But I may express my belief that Mr. Goschen desires no such thing, and my own assurance that I have no such wish.

I suppose that the ideal perfection of a monetary system is, that there should be just so much of circulating medium as will suffice for the commercial and domestic wants of the

Mr. H. H. Gibbs.

community—not so much as unduly to foster speculation—not so little as unduly to fetter legitimate trade; and, above all things, that there should be the greatest attainable steadiness in the volume of the currency. Some regularity in this respect is possible, but immobility is neither possible nor desirable; and the hope of the *Statist* that we shall in no wise alter "our determination to maintain an unchanging "standard for money in this country" is sufficiently proved to be utopian, by his own argument that by the operation of natural causes (and, I may add, by the operation of law) its value is continually liable to change.

To return to the question of the decline of prices; there is one notable exception. In wages there is no such fall. On the contrary, it would seem that there has been a marked improvement in the condition of the labourer, both in increase of wages and in diminished cost of some of the necessaries of life.

This is not the place for a disquisition on the causes which place the price of that fundamental commodity, labour, in a different category from the prices of commodities produced by labour; but, I may remark (1) that it seems obvious that, in the long run, the price of labour must be regulated by the ability of the labourer to live upon his wages, and by the ability of the occupier of the soil to pay him; (2) that the general increase of his wages seems consequent upon a conviction to which both he and his employers awoke some time since that he had been underpaid,—a conviction which bore substantial fruit, partly by reason of the flow of the wealth of the great towns into the country districts, and partly by the increased power of organization amongst the labourers themselves, both causes being helped by the greater facilities of communication and locomotion enjoyed in the present day; and (3) that, whereas the increase of his weekly pay must have tended to produce an increase in the prices of the commodities he consumes, the reverse seems to be the case.

But if the reverse *is* the case, and if those consumable articles have persistently fallen in price, it is one proof the more that there must be some general and abnormal cause for their fall.

To say that the real cause is the badness of trade is merely to argue in a circle, for we are at once driven to ask, "What, then, is the general and abnormal cause of the "badness of trade?"

Nor does it appear that over-production of commodities is an adequate cause for this continuous decline in prices; such a decline should naturally have checked production, and the facilities of telegraphic communication should rather tend to adjust production to demand; but the establishment of railways in producing countries has opened up new fields of production, and the increase of the means of rapid transit between those countries and England, has brought their produce nearer to its greatest market; and the result has been that many articles have been produced in abundance greater than the increase of population has demanded, and that over-supply has brought down their price. But the improvement of the means of transit, and the increased production which it has helped to cause, have been neither continuous nor universal, and a persistent decline of price would seem to suppose a persistent and universal cause.

One cause alone has been persistent; and that is the appreciation of gold. That commodity is produced less and is used more, and, like all other commodities in like case, it is consequently dearer. In buying it with other commodities we must give more of them than we should do if those two circumstances did not exist.

So much, then, for the second question—whether the alleged fall in prices is mainly or greatly due to the appreciation of gold.

The first question (whether there is such a fall) is abundantly answered by the foregoing table of prices.

Mr. H. H. Gibbs.

The third question—whether the proportion between the mass of gold money and the commodities it measures has been disturbed—is to be answered as follows:—

1.—The output of gold from the mines appears to have declined in the last 10 years, as will be seen by the following table (*p.* 364), the figures in which are taken from those compiled by Sir Hector Hay, and printed in the *Journal of the Institute of Bankers* of last month (March, 1883).

The production of gold in the year ending June 30, 1882, is, it will be seen, £2,070,000 less than that of the year 1870, and £4,200,000 less than that of the year of the greatest yield, 1878.

The estimates made in the United States give larger figures, but with few exceptions they show the same upward and downward tendency as Sir Hector Hay's. They show a falling off of £4,374,000 between 1882 and 1870, in the total production of the world; and £2,832,000 in that of their own country.

It appears, therefore, that the chief difference is in the estimated yield of other countries; and it must be admitted that there is great difficulty in arriving at a correct account of their production.

M. Alexander Del Mar, formerly a Director of the United States Bureau of Statistics, writes as follows in a letter to the *Mining World,* dated 4th January last (1883), as to the probable decline in production; and if we may take his opinions to be correct, we cannot consider the figures in the second column of the following table as likely to be maintained.

M. Del Mar says:—

"During the past ten years I have personally inspected "the principal goldfields and mines of Russia, Spain, Brazil, "California, Nevada, Arizona, North Carolina, Mexico, &c., "and, with the exception of Brazil and Spain, where little or

Year.	SILVER.			GOLD.				Total of Silver and Gold.
	United States.	Other Countries.	Total.	Australia.	United States.	Other Countries.	Total.	
	£	£	£	£	£	£	£	£
1870	3,200,000	8,150,000	11,350,000	5,830,000	10,000,000	5,540,000	21,370,000	32,720,000
1871	4,600,000	8,600,000	13,200,000	6,650,000	8,700,000	6,050,000	21,400,000	34,600,000
1872	5,750,000	8,200,000	13,950,000	6,810,000	7,200,000	5,900,000	19,910,000	33,860,000
1873	7,150,000	7,800,000	14,950,000	6,290,000	7,200,000	5,750,000	19,240,000	34,190,000
1874	7,200,000	8,000,000	15,200,000	6,000,000	6,400,000	5,750,000	18,150,000	33,350,000
1875	9,000,000	8,000,000	17,000,000	5,750,000	8,000,000	5,750,000	19,500,000	36,500,000
1876	7,700,000	9,000,000	16,700,000	5,500,000	8,500,000	6,600,000	20,600,000	37,300,000
1877	9,100,000	9,500,000	18,600,000	5,500,000	8,900,000	6,600,000	21,000,000	39,600,000
1878	9,000,000	10,700,000	19,700,000	5,800,000	10,000,000	7,700,000	23,500,000	43,200,000
1879	8,200,000	10,400,000	18,600,000	5,800,000	7,700,000	7,800,000	21,300,000	39,900,000
1880	7,800,000	10,400,000	18,200,000	5,200,000	6,000,000	7,800,000	19,000,000	37,200,000
1881	7,800,000	11,000,000	18,800,000	5,800,000	6,000,000	7,800,000	19,600,000	38,400,000
1882	9,500,000	11,000,000	20,500,000	5,500,000	6,000,000	7,800,000	19,300,000	39,800,000

"no gold is being now produced, I have derived a very firm "conviction that at least for five or ten years to come none "of these countries will be enabled to increase their present "output, but, on the contrary, that it will diminish. In all "of these countries there are certain mines which will doubtless "increase their product, and there are many new and probably "very rich mines yet to be opened in them; but speaking of the "countries generally, I cannot believe that their output of gold "will not diminish. The same must be said of Australia. There "is a future for gold in Africa; but this future, so far as any "product of importance to the world is concerned, is a long "way off. Mining depends on climate, water, the organisation "of labour, and the general condition of the mechanical arts. "Labourers who cannot handle a spade, a drill, a pick, a plane, "or a saw, will not make good miners; and countries where "these tools are not used or cannot be obtained, and where there "are no roads, foundries, mills, nor workshops, are poor places for "successful mining. India has all these disadvantages, together "with the further one of being, so far as gold is concerned, a "very old and thoroughly searched country. On the whole, "therefore, I am compelled to believe the future production of "gold must diminish."

2.—Population has largely increased, and with population must have increased also the quantity of gold money in the personal possession of the people; so that if £100,000,000 was a correct estimate of the amount of gold in the United Kingdom, exclusive of the Reserve in the Issue Department of the Bank of England, a quarter of a century ago, we may now well add, at least, £20,000,000 to the sum.

3.—Luxury also has greatly increased, and that fact, together with the increase of population, has doubtless increased largely the use of gold for ornaments, and otherwise in the Arts. M. Chevalier, writing in 1857, estimated the annual consumption of the metal for articles of luxury at 1,236,655 ounces, or about £5,000,000 sterling; and it may not be unreasonable to compute that, at the present time, the amount may have increased to £7,000,000 sterling, a quantity about equal to the whole yearly American output.

4.—Up to this time, paper—resting on no metallic basis—has largely taken the place of metallic money. Austria, Russia, Portugal, Brazil, the Argentine Republic, Turkey, Italy, Spain, Peru, Chili, and Japan, have all, at various times, suspended specie payments. Spain, I believe, has resumed them on a quasi-bimetallic basis; and Italy has made provision for resumption of specie payments on the 12th of this month (April, 1883). Should any or all of these follow her example, and in resuming specie payments adopt gold as the metal for their coinage, the effect cannot but be very great on the gold prices of the world.

The action of Germany in its adoption of a gold currency in place of silver, the action of the Scandinavian nations in following her example, and the possible action of the United States and of Holland in the same direction, cannot but make the strain more intense.

We see, then, that all the four things spoken of above have happened; that the production of gold has declined, is declining, and in the opinion of those well qualified to judge will continue to decline, and that the demand for it, both in the Arts and for money purposes, has increased, is increasing, and with the increase of population will continue to increase; and it seems to me that when this becomes evident to the gold-using nations, they will be inclined to adopt, or further the adoption of, the only measure which can lighten the strain upon them, and that is the associating silver with gold in the monetary work of the world.

Mr. H. H. Gibbs.

Should it be asked what harm can come of a diminished price, if it be caused by the increased value of that which the merchant receives for his goods,—if, that is to say, the diminution in quantity be compensated by an improvement in quality of the money received,—the answer is that, if and when the decline in price from this cause is a settled and concluded matter, and the price is once adjusted to the altered measure of value, then, as the *Statist* rightly says, in the passage above quoted, trade can go on without interruption, and without future injury from this source to any one. But while the four causes above-mentioned are in action, when one of them, the demand for gold for money purposes is likely to increase, and when, consequently, it is not only the case that prices have declined, but that they *are declining*, the condition is a very different one. A season of declining prices is almost necessarily a season of unprofitable trade. A merchant who has advanced his money on the market value of a commodity suffers loss when the goods arrive and he finds that the market value has diminished beyond his calculation; and not he only suffers, but the consumer suffers also in the long run; for though he is for the moment benefited by the cheapness of the commodities he uses, yet the decline in their price tries to the utmost the endurance of the producer; and no one will care to continue importing goods which may most probably fall in price by the time they arrive. So, then, the tendency of the continued decline must be to injure both producer and consumer, and to paralyse trade.

If it be asked, "Is it not a positive good to England "that gold should be appreciated?" "England," it may be said, "is a creditor nation, and her debts are due to her "in gold. The scarcity of gold has made that metal more "valuable, and she must needs be the gainer by this, and "must continue to be still more the gainer if gold becomes "scarcer still. Is it to be expected that she should throw "away this advantage, and by admitting silver to a "partnership with gold, exalt the value of the first, and "lower the value of the second?"

I must reply by another question: What *is* a creditor country? Are we all creditors, and creditors only? The meaning of the phrase is, no doubt, that, on balance, the nation has more to receive than to pay, and the inference is that the balance must come in the appreciated and appreciating metal. But who are they who are to receive it? Not so much the producers, the makers of the wealth of the land (though they, also, to the extent of their profits are recipients), as the holders of fixed incomes, the *fruges consumere nati.* But if we look to the advantage of England at large, we must admit that it is not these for whom we should be most solicitous; especially as every increase in the value of the three sovereigns which they duly and punctually receive on each hundred pounds of their Consols, is an addition to the burden of the National Debt, payable alike by the working bees as by the drones; alike by the debtor who loses by the appreciation of gold, as by the creditor who gains. My conclusion is, that the bringing back of gold to its old relation to commodities would be no real injury to England.

I have said above that it has been demonstrated that there is no analogy between fixing by law the ratio that gold money shall bear to silver money and fixing the money-prices of commodities; but if I am met with the answer that gold and silver are commodities like all others, and that their price must be governed, accordingly, by the cost of their production, I must reply that those two metals are no doubt commodities, but that neither gold nor silver, both being full money in the same country, can possibly be priced each in terms of the other; and though undoubtedly like all others in their essence as commodities, yet they differ from all others in their accidents. Every one, bimetallist or monometallist, must admit that both or either of them are differently conditioned from all other commodities; namely, in these four ways following:—

First.—They are the measures of all commodities, and are measured by them. Of no other commodities can this be affirmed.

Second.—It is of little importance to the world (though of great importance to the producer) whether the production of these measuring metals is greater or less. It is of the greatest importance to the world, as well as to the producer, whether other commodities (or almost all of them) are produced or not.

If no more wheat is produced, it is a world-wide calamity, immediate in its effect.

If no more gold and silver is produced the world is not visibly or immediately the worse. Circulation will be gradually contracted as wear and tear of the existing stock goes on, and prices will gradually and imperceptibly fall; but the hindrance to trade, though certain, is necessarily slow.

Third.—Ninety per cent. of the demand for the precious metals being for one purpose only, that of serving as money, the demand for either of them in any country, and consequently in all countries, is subject to be almost entirely and quite suddenly extinguished by the action of law. This can be said of no other commodity; nor, if it could, would the extinction of the demand for it affect all other commodities, as the extinction of the demand for gold or silver as money must do.

Fourth.—All other commodities—speaking generally—are consumable and produced to be consumed; their reason of existence is that they may be worked up and used, and perish in the using. Roughly speaking, there is no *stock* of any of them beyond a very few years' production:—where is the wheat of 1880?—but the stock of gold and silver is the production of a thousand years!

The production of gold and silver from 1493 to 1875 was estimated by Seyd to be £1,230,000,000 of gold and £1,469,000,000 of silver, £2,699,000,000 in all; and adding £101,000,000 for the production of 1876-8, we have a total of £2,800,000,000. He computes, further, that taking into account the production before 1493, there existed now, in the shape of coined money or bullion serving as money, a sum of £1,580,000,000.*

How small is the proportion which an annual increment of £25,000,000 or £30,000,000 in coin or bullion bears to this vast stock; and how little influence can the cost of production of that small addition have on the relative value of the stock of money-metals and the stocks of other commodities! But in the case of consumable commodities, the annual production of which bears a very large proportion to the existing stocks, the cost of that production must necessarily and immediately influence the price of the commodity.

The precious metals, we are told, experience, as all other commodities do, great changes of value from the action of Supply and Demand. That they will do so from the arbitrary cessation of Demand is incontestable; but Supply depends mainly on existing stocks, which may almost be considered a constant quantity, while if by Supply is meant annual supply, we have seen that it is relatively insignificant; but of the mass of commodities

* Allowing 1/20th for waste by abrasion, and a sufficient sum for loss and forgotten hoards, the £2,800,000,000 may perhaps be reduced by about £400,000,000 during the years from 1493–1878; and deducting the £1,580,000,000 supposed to exist in current coin and bullion, it would follow that no less than £800,000,000 must be stored in the form of articles of luxury, or hidden away in hoards.

Mr. H. H. Gibbs.

it may be said, that their existence depends on their annual supply.

So then, in arguing for the possibility of fixing and maintaining a definite ratio between gold and silver, serving as money, there is no need to show that they have any especial *quality*, as compared with the commodities they measure. It is enough that they are so differently conditioned from all others, and so like-conditioned with one another, that it is both possible and easy to yoke them together as one combined medium of exchange and measure of value.

The ground of controversy is narrowing. We are all practically agreed on the main features of the position. Gold has grown and is growing scarcer, prices have declined and are declining, trade has suffered and is suffering. Mr. Goschen, the late Mr. Stanley Jevons, Mr. Giffen, the writer in the *Statist*, and the writer in the *Daily News*, and a host of other writers, testify to these facts. But the monometallist writers, while they admit the evil, all tell us that time will cure it. No, not all. Mr. Jevons proposed as a remedy the issue of one-pound notes, and many writers and speakers are now putting forth this plan—some as a remedy, some as being itself a good. So, then, those of our opponents who look with horror on the association of silver as money with gold because forsooth it is an inferior metal, and because notes issued on silver would not have a solid basis of value, are not at all afraid to advocate the issue of millions of fiduciary notes having no basis at all,—promises to pay issued on the security of—promises to pay.

The more I consider the matter, the closer I look into it, the more sure I am that the system which I advocate, though it seem to contradict in words the dicta of Lord Liverpool, is yet the only real carrying out of his system. He urged unity and uniformity of metallic money of full weight and fineness as a necessity for the nation. Unity of money is impossible for that great nation which all commercial peoples form. No one desires it, or dreams of it. But a uniform metallic money is possible, and for the very reasons which Lord Liverpool gives, desirable, and that is what I advocate.

Some objectors are satisfied to accept, without inquiry, their own or other men's statement, that what I advocate is impossible. My answer is that it is not only not impossible, but has been practically done for 70 years in this century, and will be done again.

HENRY H. GIBBS.

LONDON, *April*, 1883.

P.S.—Since the foregoing paper was written, Mr. Goschen has delivered a very interesting address to the Institute of Bankers, strongly supporting my view that the scarcity of gold has lowered prices and injured trade. He expresses, indeed, the belief that the period of change in values, during which time alone is any hurt done to trade, will probably be short, and that all will soon subside into a normal condition; but Mr. Giffen, speaking on the same occasion, thought that there was greater probability that the production of gold would go on diminishing, and the demand for it go on increasing for an indefinite time, so that it was impossible to foresee the day when the desired steadiness in the relation of gold to commodities should be reached.

Mr. Henry Sidgwick, Professor of Moral Philosophy in the University of Cambridge, also, has made of late a very important contribution to the study of this subject in his book on the *Principles of Political Economy*, where he maintains the view advocated in these pages.

Referring to what I have written on p. 351 as to further demands for gold, I would observe that the resumption of specie payments by Italy there spoken of as imminent, has since taken place, and the predictions of those who believed that she would be unable to retain the gold have not as yet been verified. Gold will leave her shores, of course, just as it will leave ours, when its export is needed; and to retain it, or to recall it, she will have to do as we do in like case—raise her rate of discount.

Holland, also, has lost her silver to the amount of one million sterling, and has supplied its place with gold drawn from this country.

I must correct what I wrote on p. 361 as to wages. Agricultural wages have risen, and so have the wages of many handicrafts; but this has not been the case everywhere, nor in all trades. In some there has been a notable fall.

LONDON, *June*, 1883.

THE PRICE OF SILVER.

To the Editor of the *Economist*, September 19, 1885.

SIR,—I propose in this letter to make answer to three questions which were put to me in the Money Article of *The Times* of the 24th and 29th ultimo.

I am asked whether I should consider a violent rise in the price of silver to be bad for trade, and it is intimated that I say nothing on this point, "for reasons which those "who are familiar with the bimetallic controversy will not "fail to comprehend."

In everything that I have written or said on the subject I have advocated the bimetallic standard as productive of steadiness in the price of silver, and I have deprecated all violent fluctuations, whether in one direction or the other, as harmful to sound trade. The reasons which it has been thought might induce me to hold a contrary opinion are, I presume, a desire for high prices and "cheap money"; but as I have never expressed, and do not entertain that desire, I need say no more about them. Those slight oscillations in the price of silver which occurred before 1872, and which were for the most part due to the variations of exchange between London and Paris, cannot be considered as any injury to trade. I believe them to be inevitable and practically harmless.

2. I am asked whether I have abandoned the views expressed by me three years ago, and am prepared to advocate a bimetallic union on the basis of 18½ to 1.

I have abandoned nothing. The essence of bimetallism is free coinage of both metals to an unlimited extent, and at a fixed ratio. The question whether this or that shall be the ratio has nothing to do with the principle. I say now, as I have always said, that the ratio of 15½ to 1 is the most suitable; first, because I believe it would be found to be the proportion nearest to the truth, supposing the demand for silver for coinage purposes were again at the point at which it stood before the "demonetisation" of that metal by Germany; and secondly, because that is the actual legal ratio between gold and silver in France and Germany, and the change to 18½, or any other higher rate than the present, would be attended with very grave difficulties. I say now, as I have always said, that what I seek is a near approach to stability of price, and that if I cannot get it by the adoption of a more suitable ratio, I am content to take it by the adoption of 18½ to 1, or whatever be apparently indicated by the market price.

3. I am asked if I am not beginning to be afraid of so "dangerous" an arrangement as "an international "agreement for keeping up the price of silver."

I have never advocated any arrangement having that for its ultimate object, but I do not think the worse of the 15½ to 1 ratio, that it would deliver the Indian Government and officials from some embarrassment, and restore the value of silver remittances made to this country. I see no danger at all in an international agreement for fixing that or some other ratio between silver and gold, and for mints being freely open to the coinage of both metals. On the extreme improbability of the infraction of such a treaty, I wrote fully in an article in the *Bullionist* of the 15th April, 1882, entitled, "Concerning Faith in "Treaties." Self-interest would prevent any such infraction—even as self-interest now threatens the existence of the Latin Union, a combination which has very little in common with such a convention as I advocate, and which contains in itself those seeds of disruption which would be wholly absent from a Bimetallic Union constituted on the basis of the French Law. The Latin Union, on the contrary, in its present restricted form, involves the suspension of the French Law, and the Union will fall, if it does fall, not because it is a Union, but because it lacks the essential condition necessary to success. It maintains a fixed ratio between the two money metals, but fails to preserve the rule of a mint open to both to an unlimited extent, with perfect freedom of action to the Gresham Law.

I have long sought in vain from the hands of any writer on the subject a fair consideration of the one thing which is the base of my contention, viz., the statement that during the whole period of the unrestricted action of the French Law, when the mint was freely open for coinage at a ratio of 15½ to 1; there neither was nor could be any other price in the London market than that which was as near 60*d.* as the slight oscillations caused by the variations of the exchange, by sudden demand, or by political crises, would permit.

At last this assertion of mine is fairly met and boldly traversed by the counter opinion that the French bimetallic law was not, and could not be, the cause of the comparative steadiness of the price of silver; and that it is a delusion and an error into which I, in company with eminent economists, monometallist as well as bimetallist, have fallen, to suppose that it was; and the assertion has even been made that our advocacy of a fixed ratio between the metals is one of the causes why the price of silver is not steady. No attempt, indeed, has been made to prove the impossibility of the effect supposed by me to have been produced by the bimetallic law, nor to show how it could come to pass that, when the seller of silver could get the equivalent of 60*d.*, or thereabout, in Paris, he would be content to take a less price in London; but another cause for the steadiness of price has been suggested, viz., that in the first seventy years of the century, "the relation between the "masses of the two metals in existence was approxi- "mately unchanged," and this notwithstanding that the discoveries of gold, which had their first effect in 1852 (the production in that year increasing from 16 to 36 millions), poured in no less between the years 1852 and 1859, both inclusive, than £226,220,000, against £74,020,000 of silver, of which the production was then, and for two years more remained stationary at about £9,000,000 a year.

That influx had, it is said, as much influence as could be expected, inasmuch as it forced up the price of silver to over 62*d.*, and had the further effect that, notwithstanding the glut of gold in France, the Bank of France had to borrow from the Bank of England (in 1860) £2,000,000 of that metal to prevent having to pay out all its silver.

I will add a few words on the above three points. 1. The transactions between the Banks of France and England; 2. The price of 62*d.* per ounce to which silver was forced; and 3. The supposed parity of relations between the precious metals until 1849.

1. You, Sir, will be at no loss for the reason why there was any such persistent export of precious metals from France in 1860, for the *Economist* of the day, in a very able article, thoroughly explained it. The debtor no doubt had the choice which metal he would pay his creditor with; gold was then the cheapest and silver the dearest, relatively, of the two metals, and, given the necessity of export, silver would obey the Gresham Law, and be the one to leave the country. But why was there that necessity? Why was the Bank of France in any difficulty at all? Not because of the bimetallic law, but because the French Government would not permit it to adopt the only true remedy in such a case, the only one by which bullion

Mr. H. H. Gibbs.

can be retained at home or attracted from abroad—a rise in the rate of discount.

2. Why was silver the dearer metal? Not because of the bimetallic law, but for the very simple reason that large quantities of the metal were needed for export from England to India for railway purposes, and that there was no supply in England. It, therefore, became necessary to purchase it where it could be had in the shape of bars, and even of 5-franc pieces, the latter especially, by reason of loss of weight by wear, involving greater cost.

But to what did the agio amount? Silver rose to 62*d.* an ounce in 1853, and varied between 60*d.* and 62*d.* and a fraction during the succeeding 13 years; and this rise of about 3 per cent. can scarcely be as much as could have been expected, seeing that the total production of gold from 1849 to 1866 inclusive had been £430,000,000 (to add to a stock in the world at the end of 1848 estimated at £600,000,000, an increase of about 70 per cent.), and though the excess of gold production over silver production in the same period was no less than £253,000,000. It would seem, then, that if the price was governed solely by the relative production of the two metals, a much greater rise than 3 per cent. might have been expected, and a greater still when a further excess of gold of upwards of £56,000,000 was produced from 1867 to 1872 inclusive. But, on the contrary, the price of silver, in the face of that excess of gold, gradually declined to the normal 60*d.*

3. I have seen no attempt to prove the approximate parity of relation between the metals which is imagined as having existed from 1803 to 1872; but I think the foregoing figures conclusively disprove it. For had that parity existed up to 1849, and had it been, as is alleged, the cause of the maintenance of the price of 60*d.*, then it is clear that when the parity disappeared, and gold

streamed in in such abundance, silver must have been forced not to 62*d.* only, but to a price commensurate with the disparity. It is impossible, therefore, to avoid the conclusion that there was some other cause of the steady price.

Now the total production of silver from 1849 to 1872 inclusive was £249,000,000, and of gold £559,000,000; the annual production of silver from 1849 to 1860 inclusive was only about £9,000,000, increasing gradually to £14,000,000 in 1872; but the average annual production of gold from 1852 (when the increase began) to 1872 was £24,500,000, or an excess of gold over silver of about £15,000,000 a year; in the face of which excess silver had fallen again by 1872 to about 60*d.*

The supposed parity serves to elucidate another point above referred to. If that parity existed at the ratio of 15½ to 1, or if, in other words, that ratio exhibited anything like the real proportion of the masses of the two precious metals at the beginning of 1849, it follows that the yield of gold having been since then enormously in excess of that of silver, the true relation cannot now be as high as 15½ to 1, still less can it be 18½ to 1; and I repeat my contention that the former ratio would be found to be nearer the true relation than that which is indicated by the present price of silver.

My conclusion is,—1, that it cannot be the supposed parity of relation which maintained a certain steadiness of price from 1803 to 1872; 2, that, however great the disparity of production and stock between the two metals may have been, the bimetallic law did suffice to maintain the steadiness of price.

I am,

Yours faithfully,

HENRY H. GIBBS.

Aldenham House, near Elstree, Herts,
Sept. 17, 1885.

Passages from the concluding pages of Mr. H. R. Grenfell's *Speech at the Memorial Hall at Manchester, February 6th,* 1886:—

You are all aware that for some years past Mr. Gibbs and I have been the President and Vice-President of an association in London for the spread of the doctrine which I have endeavoured to lay before you, and which association Mr. Barclay and others are now desirous of enlarging upon a more popular basis. A great deal of the correspondence in which we have been engaged, I may say with leading economists in various parts of the world, has been to a limited extent confidential—that is to say, persons have been good enough to impart to us the state of political forces in these countries, so far as they were impediments in the way of action on this question. Legislative confusion is not limited to the English House of Commons. It exists everywhere; but this correspondence in which we have been engaged, enables me to set before you very briefly the actual condition of affairs in other countries.

The United States followed the example which we set in 1816, by enacting a gold standard at the close of their great war. They seemed to think it would be a feather in their cap. They paid off their debt with a rapidity which has astonished the world; but when they discovered the evils arising from the contraction of their currency, they passed the Bland Bill, which was a sort of compromise between the gold party in New York and the silver party of the West. And here I must be permitted to say, that the silver party does not mean those interested in silver mines alone, but the whole body of producers of agricultural wealth in the Western States. This limited coinage of silver makes what is called a "lame standard." Silver is legal tender to any amount for debts and taxes, but only when coined. On the whole, I am of opinion that the Government at Washington, though anxious to suspend the compulsory coinage of silver, are in favour of international bimetallism. Our latest information from Washington justifies the opinion we have long held, that the Bland Bill will not be suspended during the present Session of Congress.

France, and the Latin Union also, have had a lame standard since 1873; all debts can be paid in coined silver, as well as gold, but the coinage of silver is limited by treaty between the States of the Union. Last autumn, fears were entertained that the renewal of the treaty would not be carried out; but it was signed and ratified not long ago, and the French Government has very recently instituted a permanent commission to study the question.

The state of affairs in Germany is extremely difficult to portray accurately. Notwithstanding that we are in daily communication with the bimetallists of that country, we have failed to procure reliable statements as to the definite opinions of the Great Chancellor. Nobody understands the question better, for to him is attributed the most epigrammatic summing-up of the whole gold position, when he said, "The counterpane is too small for "three to sleep in the bed." One thing is quite certain, the matter has not been pooh-poohed in Germany, but is now the subject of the most warm and eager debate.

With regard to our Indian Administration, the present phase of the question seems to be one of helplessness. Two proposals have been made, to each of which there are insuperable objections. One is to limit the coinage of silver till the coined dollar be artificially enhanced in value. The other is to change the standard to a gold one. This latter course would intensify the evil we are met to

Mr. H. R. Grenfell.

consider. The Indian Administration will either find itself with an ever-increasing deficit, or else it must augment its taxation. I have reason to believe that it is now putting a very strong pressure on the Imperial Government in the direction of negotiating for a double standard with the nations.

I have now, gentlemen, shown you why we appealed to a Platform agitation. Next, I entered into, I am afraid very inadequately, the salient features of the question, and I hope I was able to prove the truth of the doctrines we are preaching; and, finally, I have explained to you the existing state of the question in America, Germany, the Latin Union, and Indian Empire.

Now, what do we want you to do? It is to give us your support in endeavouring to press on the Government the advisability of doing that which all other Governments have done, namely, of studying it as the Germans have, of coming to a conclusion on it as the Americans have, or of appointing a permanent special commission to watch it as the French have, and to negotiate with these Governments, if they are willing, through our diplomatic agents.

We believe that the other nations *are* perfectly willing to enter into treaties, not only if we will bind ourselves, but even if we are ready to take minor measures short of an immediate and absolute adhesion.

INDEX.

A

PAGE

AFRICA, Future production of gold in 365
AGRICULTURE, Effect of fall in prices on 349, 356-7
AMERICA. See *United States.*
ARENDT (Dr.) on bimetallism 269, 350
ARGENTINE REPUBLIC. Suspension of specie payments . 366
ARISTOTLE on the function and duty of money . . . 144, 191, 192, 200, 201, 216, 217
ARTS, Use of gold and silver in the 355
  Increased use of gold for ornaments 365-6
ASHBURTON (Lord). Opinion regarding a legal-tender silver currency 122-3, 127
AUSTRALIA. Gold. Cost of production 33
  —— Decrease in the supply of 4, 7, 367
  —— Discoveries, and the relative price of the precious metals 85, 205, 208, 246, 282
  —— Effect of the discoveries on prices and wages 157
  —— Mint price in England and market price in Australia 288, 291
AUSTRIA, Attitude of, as to bimetallism 42, 95
  Suspension of specie payments 366

B

BAGEHOT (Walter). Examination before the Silver Committee 74
  His objection to discuss bimetallism 95, 97
  on the influence of the price of silver on Indian exports 137

PAGE

BAMBERGER (Dr.) 316

BANK CHARTER ACT, 1844, aimed at the extinction of the country and Scotch bank issues 276
Effect of a repeal of the Act 278
Power given to the Bank to hold gold and silver . 51
Professor Jevons on the expediency of carrying out the third clause 108-9
Sir Robert Peel on the principle of the metallic standard 111
Steps taken in 1881 towards authorising the Bank to carry out the provisions of the Act as to silver . 167, 351

BANK FAILURES. 279

BANK MONEY as described by Lord Liverpool 120, 121, 127, 221

BANK NOTES. See *Notes.*

BANK OF ENGLAND. Disposal of a shipment of silver under a bimetallic law 50-52
If authorised to use silver at the market price of the day 180, 181, 213
Its action in raising the discount rate to six per cent. 231
Monopoly of note issue a part of the Government business 277
See *Notes,—Bank of England. Bank Charter Act.*

BANK OF FRANCE. Borrower of gold from Bank of England in 1860 378
Depletion of the gold reserve in 1848 83
Effect of the adoption of bimetallism on . . . 136-7
Italian currency lying in the 168
Large stock of five-franc pieces in hand . . . 162
See *Notes,—Bank of France.*

BARTER among the ancients 193
The use of silver with us approaches to 22-3

"BIMETALLIC ENGLAND." H. H. Gibbs. Reprinted from the *Bullionist* 267-74

BIMETALLIC circulation in England before 1819 . . . . 113, 116, 220
Effect of a bimetallic law 25, 26, 253, 264
law in France 16, 223, 377
—— existing in a single country 29
—— affecting the intrinsic ratio of value between gold and silver 251
standard, Stability of the 88, 100, 375
———— in France defended by Sismondi 215
———— as affecting the value of money . . . 245-8
treaties. Fear of breach in time of war 124, 240

"BIMETALLISM." Professor Jevons. Reprinted from the *Contemporary Review* 99-110

"BIMETALLISM AGAIN." Professor Bonamy Price . . . 293-333

BIMETALLISM, Advantages of 17, 207, 267-9
as affecting contracts 107, 159, 166, 278

BIMETALLISM—*continued.* PAGE

Disadvantages of 29, 93, 102, 195
Effect of, on trade 77, 135, 226
——— on the price of silver 26, 136, 156
——— on stability of prices 10, 146, 202, 380
Fundamental propositions 117
Object of 291
Objections to 34-6, 124, 165, 212

BLAND ACT, Dollars coined under provisions of 353

BOMBAY, Traders of 262

BRAMWELL (Lord). Letter to the *Times.* "Is the Value of Gold and Silver Money artificial?" 131-8
Letters to Mr. H. H. Gibbs 337-9, 340-41, 343, 344
Answer to Col. Smith 66

BRAZIL. Suspension of specie payments 366

BULLION COMMITTEE (Report of). The foundation of the English system of metallic currency 113
Use of the expressions "standard," and "chief coin in use" 200

BULLION PRICES. Adoption of the prices of the day of legislation 316, 317

BULLIONIST (The) adopted as the organ of bimetallism, 184, 186
Reprinted from :—
"Bimetallic England." . . . . (H. H. Gibbs) 267-74
"Concerning Faith in Treaties." . . (H. H. Gibbs) 237-43
"Paper, or Metallic Inflation." . (H. R. Grenfell) 275-80
"The Ratio of Value between Gold and Silver." (Clarmont Daniell) 251-8
"The Scramble for Gold." . . (H. H. Gibbs) 231-6
"The Value of Money." . . . (H. H. Gibbs) 245-9
"Whither would the Dearer Metal Go?" (H. R. Grenfell) 259-65

BULLIONISTS believe that coining is an attribute of the State 277

C

CALCUTTA, Uncertain value of silver a disadvantage to the trade of 21
Bank of, note circulation 263

CALIFORNIA, Cost of gold discovered in 33
Effect of gold discoveries on value of the precious metals 205, 208, 246, 283
Refusal to receive greenbacks at the time of the civil war 91, 96

PAGE

CAMPBELL (Sir George) on the stability of a double standard. 227

CANTILLON. Influence of fluctuations in the precious metals on the price of commodities 100

The market price decides the proportionate value of gold and silver 105

CAPITAL. Distinction between the "value of money" and the interest paid on a loan of capital 247-9

CAZALET (E.) 184

CERNUSCHI (H.) Contention that France gained by paying away her gold 16-17, 165

Letters to the *Times* 142-3, 149-50

on the ratio of gold to silver to be adopted 134, 252

Professor Jevons on M. Cernuschi's project. . . . 102, 104

Sir T. H. Farrer's replies to 147, 150-51

CHAPMAN (Mr.) Memo. on an international bimetallic standard of value 203

CHEQUES, Economy of coin due to use of 14, 60, 123, 150, 272, 343

Under a bimetallic law payments would continue to be made in 49

CHEVALIER (M.) Estimate of the value of gold used in the Arts 365

CHILI. Suspension of specie payments 366

CHINA, Effect of a gold or silver standard in 41

——— the demonetization of silver in 42, 120

COBBETT'S PARLIAMENTARY HISTORY. Sir Isaac Newton on the value of the guinea 143

COCHINEAL. Comparative prices, 1874-1882. (Table) . . 358-9

COCOA. " " " " . . 358-9

COFFEE. " " " " . . 358-9

COMMONS (HOUSE OF), Party feeling in the 198

COMSTOCK MINE 144

"CONCERNING FAITH IN TREATIES." Article reprinted from the *Bullionist*. (Mr. H. H. Gibbs) 237-43

CONTEMPORARY REVIEW, Reprinted from :—

"Bimetallism" . . . . . (Professor Jevons) 99-110

References to "How Money does its work." (Professor B. Price) 298, 304, 308

COTTON. Comparative prices, 1874-1882. (Table) 358-9

COPPER. ——————— 1873-1883. " 358-9

CRUMP (Arthur). Views on bimetallism examined . . . 270, 272

D

DAILY NEWS. Article on Trade and Finance 353, 371

DANIELL (Clarmont) :—

"Gold in the East," Correspondence reprinted from the *Economist* on 65-9, 70-74

DANIELL (Clarmont)—*continued.* PAGE
on gold monometallism for the world 213-14
"On the Rates of Value between Gold and Silver." Reprinted from the *Bullionist* 251-8
As to where the dearer metal would go 259-65
Scheme of occasional adjustments of the ratio . . 304-10, 313, 315, 317, 319, 320, 321, 328, 332, 333
DARU (Count). Argument for the French law of 1803 . . 77
DEL MAR (Alex.) on the probable decline in the production of gold 363
DEPRESSION OF TRADE accounted for by the appreciation of gold 78, 81
As to trade being permanently contracted 82
Effect of a revival of trade in India and the United States 354
Mr. Goschen's paper read before the Institute of Bankers 372
Over-production of commodities 362
DOUBLE STANDARD (The). . . . . . (H. H. Gibbs) 1-63, 225-9
Correspondence between Earl Grey and Mr. H. R. Grenfell 153-81
DRUMMOND (Henry). Elementary propositions on the currency 63

E

ECONOMIST, Letters to the :—
On "Gold in the East" . . (H. R. Grenfell) 65-8, 70-72
——————— . . . (Clarmont Daniell) 68-9, 72-4
On the ratio between gold and silver. (H. H. Gibbs) 282-4, 284-6, 288-92
Editorial, in reply to Mr. H. H. Gibbs 287-8
Effect on money and prices of the adoption of bimetallism 245, 249
On the existence of the double standard in England up to the suspension of cash payments 199
On the breach of a bimetallic treaty 240
ENGLAND. Centre of international payments 51, 95, 119-20
Debts payable in gold or silver, 1717-1778, up to £25 . 116
Gold stock 149
has the largest stock of gold 104
Hindrance to monetary concord 40, 42
Inconvenience of a single standard 24
Silver standard abolished inadvertently . . . 127
Stocks of debased silver coin. 149
EUROPE. Limitation of silver coinage 7
Lord Sherbrooke's proposal to alter the standard of value 209-10

F

PAGE

FARRER (Sir T. H.) Letters to the *Times* 138-42, 147, 150-51
——— Mr. H. H. Gibbs . . . 335-6
FAUCHER (Leon). Depreciation of silver in 1842 83-5
FAWCETT (Right Hon. Henry) :—
Question to Mr. Bagehot before the Silver Commission 74
FORTNIGHTLY REVIEW, Reprinted from :—
"The Case against Bimetallism." . (R. Giffen) 75-98
FOWLER (Wm.) on the issue of one-pound notes 277, 280
FRANCE, a clearing house between England and India . . 24, 29
Cessation of the coinage of silver 1, 174
Cernuschi's opinion that the loss of gold has been a gain to 16, 17
Dearer metal disappearing from common use in . 16
Double standard in 24, 44, 45, 104, 200
Exports of the precious metals 378
Franco-German war 222
Free mintage in 25, 350, 351
Glut of gold in 1860 378
Interest to become bimetallic if England led the way 173-4
Intermediary between gold and silver-using countries 78
Legal tender in 200
Power to obtain as much gold as she requires . . 232
Premium on gold 170
Profit to, by return to old ratio with gold . . . 124
Silver, if made legal tender up to 50 francs . . 163
Single standard in 25, 91, 174
See *Notes,—Bank of France. Mint,—Paris.*
FREE TRADE. Want of reciprocity an argument against bimetallism 198

G

GARBETT. Variation in the price of silver bullion . . . 84
GAUDIN (M. M. C.) on the ratio of $15\frac{1}{2}$ to 1 105
GAZETTE (The), Market price of silver to be published in . 160
GERMANY. Gold. Consequences of absorption of . . . 19, 62
—— Coinage of 114, 128, 224
—— Demand for 2, 67
—— Ratio between gold and silver . . . 283, 376
Silver. Effect of remonetisation 225, 291
—— Loss by sale of 18

PAGE

GIBBS (Henry Hucks), Papers by:—
- "Bimetallic England." Reprinted from the *Bullionist* 267-74
- "Concerning Faith in Treaties." Do. . . . 237-43
- "The Double Standard" 1-63
- "The Gold Question and the Fall of Prices." Reprinted from the *National Review* 345-73
- "The Price of Silver." Reprinted from the *Economist* 375-80
- "The Value of Money." " " *Bullionist* 245-9
- "The Scramble for Gold." " " " 231-6
- Speech at meeting of International Monetary Standard Association, March, 1882 225-30
- Letters to Lord Bramwell 338-9, 341-2
- ——— the *Economist* 282-4, 284-6, 288-92
- ——— Sir T. H. Farrer 336-7
- ——— the *Times* 142-6
- Criticisms on "the Double Standard" in correspondence between Earl Grey and Mr. H. R. Grenfell . 153-76

GIFFEN (Robert). Decline of prices 114, 275, 371
- Decrease in the production of gold 372
- Paper read before the Statistical Society . . . 349, 356
- Single standard in France 25
- Statistical information of bimetallists derived from . 202
- "The Case against Bimetallism." Reprinted from the *Fortnightly Review* 75-98

GOLD, Absorption of 352, 353
- Between reigns of James I. and Charles II. rose in value against silver 32 per cent. 252
- coined by Germany 114, 128, 224
- Consumption of, for articles of luxury. 365
- Convenience of 92
- Cost of transmission 49
- Demand for 2, 7, 212, 213
- ——— as influencing value 322, 369
- ——— effect on the markets of the world . . . 67
- ——— in the East 281
- Estimate of amount in the United Kingdom . . . 365
- International struggle for 19, 231
- is always to be had at a price 188, 232, 233, 351
- legal tender in England 148, 150
- Mint price in England regulated market price in Australia 288
- Not legal tender till 1816 . . . . 139, 252
- Preference for 91, 92
- Price of, before 1717 148
- —— Mint 206
- Production, Average annual 380
- ——— in the United States, 1877-1880 . . . 4
- ——— of the world 370
- ——— Mr. Giffen on the probability of diminished 372
- ——— Mr. A. Del Mar's contention that, must diminish 363-5

GOLD—*continued.* PAGE

Scarcity of, an advantage to England 157
——— affecting trade 81, 82
——— diminishing cost of production . . . 157
——— Efficiency of a high Bank rate to counteract 231-2
Stocks of the world 370
——— unused in India. 66, 68, 73
Source of prosperity to England 352
"Gold in the East." Correspondence between Mr. H. R. Grenfell and Mr. C. Daniell. Reprinted from the *Economist* 65-74
"Gold in the East." (H. R. Grenfell.) Reprinted from the *Bullionist* 259-65
"The Gold Question and the Fall of Prices." (H. H. Gibbs.) Reprinted from the *National Review* 345-73

GOSCHEN (Right Hon. G. J.) Appreciation of Gold . . . 348, 349, 360, 371
Business in countries where fluctuations in exchange are great 23
Paper read before the Institute of Bankers . . 372

GOVERNMENT, Action of, on value of metals as money . . 138, 139, 140-41

GREAT BRITAIN. Gold the only standard 1, 50, 148

GRENFELL (H. R.), Papers by :—
"Paper or Metallic Inflation." Reprinted from the *Bullionist* 275-80
"What is a Pound?" Reprinted from the *Nineteenth Century* 111-29
"What is a Standard?" Do. 197-217
"Whither would the Dearer Metal go?" Reprinted from the *Bullionist* 259-65
Speech at meeting of International Monetary Standard Association, March, 1882 219-24
Correspondence with Earl Grey on the double standard 153-81
——— Professor Bonamy Price . . 294-333
Letters to the *Economist* 65-8, 70-72
——— *Times* 294-5, 299-300

GREENBACKS (United States) equal in value to gold . . 163
Refusal of California to receive 91, 96

GRESHAM'S LAW, Operation of 148, 241, 271, 328, 377, 378

GREY (Earl, K.G.) Letters to Mr. H. R. Grenfell . . . 153-64, 169-75, 179-80
The general law of the cost of production in relation to the precious metals 204-5
Conclusions arrived at as to bimetallism . . . 212-14, 275

GROESBECK (W. S.) Statement as to the demonetisation of silver in the United States in 1873 127

GUINEA. Preference for the coin, determined the Government of George I. to fix the value by law 140-42
Value fixed in 1717 . . . . 105, 148, 149
——— at the time of the Revolution 139
Weight of 206

H

PAGE

HALIFAX (Lord). Objections to bimetallism 179
HARRIS (Mr.) on gold monometallism 57, 82, 199
HAUPT (Ottomar). Criticism on his pamphlet, "Bimetallic England" 267-9
HAY (Sir Hector). Estimate of the world's production of precious metals 363
HIDES. Comparative prices, 1874-1882. (Table) . . . 358-9
HOLLAND, Bimetallism in 346
Demonetisation of silver 2
Gold standard 366
Sale of silver 352, 373
HORTON (Dana). Partial list of modern publications on the subject of money 110, 350
"HOW MONEY DOES ITS WORK," Extract from. (Professor Bonamy Price) 298
HUME. Influence of fluctuations in the precious metals on the price of commodities 100
HUSKISSON on the abolition of small notes after the panic of 1825 175

I

INDÉPENDANCE BELGE, M. de Laveleye's article in . . . 102
INDIA. "A simple way out of the Indian difficulty" . . 212
Council Bills 2, 3
Damage to, by fall in exchange, imaginary . . . 87, 124, 137
——— by German demonetisation, exaggerated 211
Effect of the depreciation of silver on the finances of 19, 30, 211, 353
Exchanges, State of the 71, 137
——— Bimetallism would steady 87
——— How rate checks exports 124
Gold coinage, Scheme of 259
—— Increased imports of 7, 8
—— legal tender 71, 73
—— production small and uncertain 4, 365
—— Secret stock of 66, 69, 73, 257
Improvement of trade 354
Mr. Clarmont Daniell's proposals, Correspondence on . 65-72
Paper currency founded on gold 211, 212, 263
Proposals of Indian Government at Conference, 1881. 128
Protection from a general fall in prices 72, 74
Result of a bimetallic law in 87
Rupee coinage, Col. Smith's proposal to restore . . 65, 71, 75
Silver absorption 8
—— Cessation of coinage of 67, 69, 71, 212

INDIA—*continued.* PAGE

Silver, Free mintage of 351
—— Imports of 7, 379
—— Largest employer of 255
—— shipments to Europe under a bimetallic law . 265
—— Stock of 137, 260

INDIGO. Comparative prices, 1874-1882. (Table) 358-9

INTEREST ON NATIONAL DEBT, Effect of a bimetallic law on payments of 159
Rate of, the weapon with which the battle of bullion will be fought 19
—— depends on the demand for and supply of capital 248-9
—— if a gold currency were adopted in India . 257

INSTITUTE OF BANKERS. Mr. Goschen's paper 372
Journal of the, Extracts from 187, 363

INTERNATIONAL MONETARY STANDARD ASSOCIATION :—
Object 187
Report of meeting 219-30

"IS THE VALUE OF GOLD AND SILVER MONEY ARTIFICIAL?"
Letters to the *Times* 131-51

ITALY, Failure of the Latin Convention as regards 95
Change from a paper to a metallic currency easy but costly 239
Demand for gold 233
Loan to meet the cost of redeeming the forced currency 6, 163, 215
not prepared for a gold currency 232, 235, 241
Stock of gold 234, 285, 351
Suspension of specie payments 366
Resumption of " 18, 168, 241

IRELAND, Preference for one-pound notes in 91, 110, 207
Issue of small notes to supply the place of silver coin . 126

IRON. Comparative prices, 1873-1883. (Table) 358-9

J

JAPAN. Suspension of specie payments 366

JEVONS (Professor Stanley) :—
Article on "Bimetallism." Reprinted from the *Contemporary Review* 99-110
"Money and the Mechanism of Exchange" . . 11, 118, 146, 202, 249, 305, 312
on the fall of prices 275
Steadiness in value of money 214, 330
Variations in the precious metals measured in commodities 121, 246

JUTE. Comparative prices, 1874-1882. (Table) 358-9

K

PAGE

KISCH (B.) on the ratio of value between gold and silver . 259

KURRACHEE, Influence of the silver question on the traders of 262

L

LARDNER (Dr. Dionysius). The "paradox" of proposing to send steam-vessels across the Atlantic . . . 273

LATIN UNION. Bimetallism 1, 17, 95, 253, 351, 376, 377
- Demonetisation of silver 31, 62, 120, 224, 283
- Gold standard 118
- Ratio of gold to silver 2, 7, 177, 269, 301, 306, 328, 330

LAVELEYE (E. DE) on the fall of prices occasioned by the demand for gold 102-3. 298, 350
- Reference to, in M. Ottomar Haupt's Pamphlet . . 269

LEAD. Comparative prices, 1873-1883. (Table) 358-9

LEGAL TENDER. Bank notes in England and Scotland . . 200
- Contention that gold was not, for payment of debts in the reign of William III. 139, 148, 150
- Difference between legal tender coin and bullion . 70
- Duty of Government in regard to 75, 76
- Earl Grey on the effect of making silver unlimited legal tender 155, 170-71
- Effect of making gold legal tender in India . . 71, 73
- in France 163, 174
- Lord Liverpool on 120
- of silver dollars in the United States 5, 9, 301
- Possible refusal to accept silver as unlimited legal tender 95, 106
- Preference for non-legal tender gold in England in 1696 . . . . 91-2, 140-41
- The privilege of legal tender increases the value of the metals 299, 327
- Two standards of different values both legal tender . 190, 194, 205, 206, 235, 240, 252, 293, 310
- under Mr. Clarmont Daniell's scheme 321

LENEUIL (COURCELLE) on the French currency law . . 119

PAGE

LIVERPOOL (Lord). Application of his argument to other nations 14
Basis of his proposal for a gold currency 111, 177, 221, 276
Changed aspect of the monetary system since the days of 58, 59, 119, 121, 220, 222, 279
Conversion of silver coins into a token currency in 1816 252
Discussion on Ricardo's proposal of a paper currency convertible into bullion 167
His system and bimetallism 371, 372
History of our coinage 139-41, 150-51
On paper currency 126-7
On the depreciated currency of the 17th Century . 80
Reasons which decided him against a double standard 89-90
Recognition of his principles by Germany 104
Treatise on the coins of the realm 56
———— the foundation of our present system of money 56, 113
Variations in the price of silver bullion 84
Want of commercial education 122

LOCKE. On fluctuations in the precious metals 82
On the double standard 10, 57, 153, 165
Recall of old silver coins under William III. . . . 139, 140
Sense in which he used the word "money" . . . 13
State of England when he was writing 120
Violation of contracts by an alteration of the standard 94, 115

LUZZATTI (M.) Purchase of gold by the Italian Government 103

M

MACLEOD (Henry D.) Letter to the *Times* 148-9

MADRAS, Bank of. Note issue 263
Influence of silver question on Traders of 262

MALLET (Sir Louis). Propositions made at the Paris Conference 128

MARKS. (German.) Recall of five-mark pieces 128
Ratio of thalers to marks 134

MCCULLOCH. Cost of production determining the value of money 204, 294
Effect of the cost of production on perishable or non-perishable articles 326

MEXICO, Gold as merchandise in 41

MILL (John Stuart) on a double standard 10, 205
The rate of interest and the quantity of money in circulation 248
The expressions "labour" and "cost of production" . 307, 311

PAGE

MINT, Royal. No seignorage on standard coin 91
—— Coinage of guineas 148, 206
—— Price of gold fixed in 1717 148
—— Profit on coinage of silver 108
Paris. Coinage of gold, but not of silver 200
India. Coinage of silver 69, 71, 351

MONEY, Abundance of, not so much required as stability . 226-7
Coined, existing at the present time 370
Consent and law, establishing the use of gold and silver as 12, 144
International, the idea premature 98
Is not a commodity, but a measure of commodities . 13
Paper. See *Notes.*
The action of Government gives it value 138, 143
"What is Money?" (Lord Sherbrooke.) Reprinted from the *Nineteenth Century* 183-96

MONTAGU. Defective silver coinage in the reign of William III. 139

MORTGAGES. Effect of a bimetallic law on payments of interest 159

N

NATIONAL DEBT. Effect of a bimetallic law on payments of interest 136, 159, 368

NATIONAL REVIEW (The), Reprinted from :—
"The Gold Question and the Fall of Prices." . . . 345-72

NEWMARCH (William). Price of gold bullion in Australia in 1851 238-91

NEWTON (Sir Isaac). Adoption of 21*s.* as the value of the guinea in 1717 . . . . 105, 140, 142, 143, 148, 149
Limitation of the functions of silver as legal tender 151, 220

NEW YORK BANKS. Decision not to accept silver coined under Bland Act 96

NINETEENTH CENTURY (The), Reprinted from :—
"What is a Pound?" . . . . (H. R. Grenfell) 111-29
"What is Money?" . . . (Lord Sherbrooke) 183-96
"What is a Standard?" . . (H. R. Grenfell) 197-217

NOTES, Bank of England. Effect of increasing the fiduciary issue 278
—— Limit of silver bullion against which notes may be issued 109, 160
—— Temporarily legal tender during the suspension of cash payments 60
Bank of France, inconvertible, circulated at par with coin in 1874 149
—— Proposed issue against silver 160, 161, 167, 174, 177, 180, 181

NOTES—*continued.* PAGE

One-pound, Proposal of an issue of 110, 175, 207, 273, 277, 280, 341, 371

—— Economy of issuing paper in lieu of gold . . 178

—— Lord Liverpool's letter 167

—— Preference for, in Scotland and Ireland . . 91, 126

Scotch 200

O

ONE-POUND NOTES. See *Notes, One-Pound.*

OVERSTONE (Lord) 207

ORNAMENTS, Demand for gold for. See *Arts.*

P

"PAPER OR METALLIC INFLATION." (H. R. Grenfell.) Reprinted from the *Bullionist* 275-80

Tokens 317

PARIEU (M. De) on the standard in Russia 112

PARIS CONFERENCES. Year 1867 . . . . 121, 221

—— 1878 . . . . 110, 113, 222, 229

—— 1881 127-8

PEEL (Sir Robert), Changed aspect of currency since the time of 221, 276-9

on the principle of the metallic standard 111, 127, 321

on the resumption of cash payments in 1819 . . 113, 129, 220, 343

Reason assigned for permitting one-fifth of the bullion to be silver 167

PETTY (Sir William) 57

PERU, Suspension of specie payments in 366

PLATINUM, Cost of, relative to gold 223, 295, 297, 320-22

Early sales of Australian gold speculative, as the metal was believed to contain platinum 291

POPULATION. Influence of increased or decreased population on prices 355, 362

increases the quantity of gold in the personal possession of the people 365

increases the demand for gold 366

PORTUGAL. Suspension of specie payments 366

PAGE

PRICE OF SILVER (The). Letter to the *Economist*. (H. H. Gibbs) 375-80

PRICES, Comparative statement of, 1873-1883. (Table) . . 358-9
Fall of, partly due to collapse of credit speculation . 103
—— Mr. Giffen on 114
—— cannot be attributed to ordinary trade oscillations 275
—— produced by demands for gold for coinage . 118
of commodities affected by the scarcity of gold . . 81
of silver, 1827-1880. (Table) 27
Regulation of, by currency however appreciated . 195
Steadiness of, under a double standard . . . 10
Two, of either metal, under a bimetallic union . . 285-6
"The Gold Question and the Fall of Prices." Reprinted from the *National Review* 345-73

PRICE (Professor Bonamy). Letter to the *Times* . . . 297-9
Correspondence with Mr. H. R. Grenfell . . . 300-32

R

RATE OF INTEREST. See *Interest, Rate of.*

RATIO, Alterations in the 47
as affected by cost of production 133, 223, 225
between gold and silver in the time of Adam Smith . 206
between other metals or commodities 134
Exactness of, a matter of less importance than the principle 287, 289, 332, 376
Occasional adjustments of the. (Mr. C. Daniell's scheme) 304, 307, 321, 332
Whatever ratio the law lays down will regulate the prices of gold and silver 315
of 15½ to 1, Continuity of 305, 308, 309
—— Expanding or contracting circulation . 287, 289
—— Fallacy of 330
—— has existed for a longer period than any other 43, 101, 105, 117
—— M'Culloch on the 294-5
—— Objection to, on the ground that it would stimulate production of silver, examined 54
—— practically the ratio of the world . . 34, 134
—— No special virtue in, except that it has been in actual practice 225
—— Steadiness in price of silver during period of French bimetallism 377
—— the best ratio, as having been maintained for nearly the whole of the present century 117
of 18 to 1 would prohibit a return to the volume of circulation as existing in 1873 . . . 289
—— Professor Price on the adoption of the bullion ratio of 316, 319

RATIO—*continued*. PAGE

of $18\frac{1}{2}$ to 1, Change to, would be attended with difficulty 376
"The Ratio of Value between Gold and Silver." Letter to the *Bullionist*, by Mr. Clarmont Daniell . . . 251-8
"The Ratio of Value between Gold and Silver." Letters to the *Economist*, by Mr. H. H. Gibbs 281-92

RECOINAGE, Expense of 91

REVOLUTION OF 1688, Position of silver at the time of the . 139

RICARDO. Proposal of a paper currency convertible only in gold bullion 111, 160-61, 209
Adoption of the scheme for India 211
Advantage of his practical education 207
Benefit of a paper currency and test of its security . 276, 278
His proposal discussed in Lord Liverpool's letter . 167

RUPEE. Col. Smith's proposal to restore the rupee coinage of India 65, 66, 75
Loss to the Indian Government on the 88

RUSSIA, Bimetallism in 95
The standard in 112
Suspension of specie payments 366

S

SALARIES, Effect of depreciation on Indian 87

SALTPETRE. Comparative prices, 1874-1882. (Table) . . 358-9

SARATOGA, Bankers' Convention at 6

SATURDAY REVIEW (The) on the results of the six per cent. rate 231-3
on bimetallism 273

SEIGNORAGE. Exemption of standard coin from seignorage at English mint 91
under a bimetallic law 93

SEYD (Ernest). Prices of silver, 1827-1853. (Table) . . 27
Estimate of the production of silver, 1493-1875 . . 370
The demonetisation of silver in Germany and the silver discoveries in America 306, 308
Scheme of a four-shilling piece 108

SHERBROOKE (Lord). "What is Money?" Reprinted from the *Nineteenth Century* 183-96
M. Ottomar Haupt on Lord Sherbrooke's denunciation of bimetallism 267-70
on the scarcity of gold 67, 92

SHILLINGS. Distinction between silver standard money and token coinage 54-5
Four-shilling pieces 108, 268
Value of the British shilling a century ago . . 171-2
Weight and definition 206, 327

SIDEBOTHAM (Mr.) 211

SEDGWICK (Professor). "Principles of Political Economy" . 372

SISMONDI on the bimetallic standard in France . . . 215-16

PAGE

SILVER, Appreciation of, involving a depreciation of gold . 44
as a commodity 22, 178
Bank of England notes, Partial payment in . . 160, 167, 173, 177, 180, 213
Cost of transmission of, relatively to gold 49
Demonetisation of, as affecting trade 78
Depreciation of. Chief causes 2
——— in 1842 83-4
Discoveries of, Effect of new 31, 312
——— in America, influencing German demonetisation 304, 306, 308
Effect on trade of fluctuations in price of 21-2
Exports to India for railway purposes. 379
Fall in price due to German demonetisation . . 296, 304, 306
France, Legal tender in 163
—— Stock of 137
—— Token coinage, Relation of five-franc piece to. (Table) 55
Germany, Demonetisation of 2, 114, 128, 309
——— Sales of. 30, 224
Holland, Demonetisation of. 2, 352
India, Absorption of 255
—— Mint, coinage of, has kept up price 198
—— Loss to, by depreciation of 23, 87, 211
Legal tender in England in 1696. 91
——— Legislation commencing in 1774 depriving silver of its character as. . 141, 151
——— limited to £25 in 1774 . . . . . 148, 200
——— Proposal to permit increase of the limit to £5 . . . . 108, 125
Market value of 282
More subject to depreciation than gold 101
Payments of, in bulk under a bimetallic law . . 116, 209, 272
Preference for, by half the world 48
Price of, years 1774-1797 84
——— 1827-1880. (Table) 27
——— at the time of Adam Smith 206
Production of, from 1493 to 1875. 370
Remonetisation. Effect on prices 144
Scandinavian States. Demonetisation of 2
Stock of coin in England 149
Token coinage. Necessity of recoinage 35, 54
United States. Demonetisation of 4, 112, 353
——— Failure to force dollars into use. . 123
——— Production of 7-8
Value of, determined by cost of production . . 144, 293, 325
"Is the Value of Gold and Silver Money Artificial?" Letters to the *Times* 131-51
"The Ratio between Gold and Silver." Letters to the *Economist*, by Mr. H. H. Gibbs 281-92

SILVER—*continued.* PAGE

"The Price of Silver."
Letter to the *Economist*, by Mr. H. H. Gibbs . 375-80

SMITH (Adam). The question of a single or double standard . 206, 207, 208

His use of the word "labour" as equivalent to "cost of production" 307, 310

SMITH (Col.) Proposal to restore the rupee coinage of India to a level in value with gold 65, 71, 75

SPAIN. Suspension of specie payments 366
Resumption of " " 368

SPECTATOR (The). Comments on Mr. Goschen's speech on the appreciation of gold 348

STATIST (The). Comments on Mr. Goschen's speech on the appreciation of gold 349, 353, 356, 360, 371

STATISTICAL SOCIETY. Professor Jevons' paper, 1865 . . 103
Mr. Giffen's paper, 1879 349

SUGAR. Comparative prices, 1874-1882. (Table) . . . 358-9

T

TEA. Comparative prices, 1874-1882. (Table) 358-9

THIELMAN (Baron de). Propositions on behalf of Germany . 128

TIMES (The), Letters to, by:—
Lord Bramwell 131-8, 341
M. Henri Cernuschi 142-3, 149-50
Sir T. H. Farrer 138-142, 147, 150-51
Mr. H. H. Gibbs 143-6
Mr. H. R. Grenfell 294-5, 299-300
Mr. H. D. Macleod 148-9
Professor Bonamy Price 297-9, 322

TIN. Comparative prices, 1874-1882. (Table) 358-9

TOBACCO " " " 358-9

TOOKE'S HISTORY OF PRICES 103

TRADE, Balance of, in favour of this country notwithstanding debased currency during the 17th century . 80
——— Gold only leaves this country to redress the 232, 236, 248
Expansion of, between 1833 and 1839 103
Foreign, only a fraction of the business of great countries 86
General revival of trade would stimulate demand for gold 8
Hindrance to trade by scarcity of gold 369
Predicted revival of 354
Stimulated by discovery of new mines 135
See *Depression of Trade.*

TREATIES (Bimetallic), Risk of breach of 46, 238, 240, 243

TURKEY. Suspension of specie payments 366

U

PAGE

UNIFICATION OF COINAGE. Advantages to be derived from . 112

UNITED STATES. Bland Act, Purport of the 112
—— Causes of agitation for repeal of 352
—— Dollars coined under provision of 353
—— Repeal would further contract gold supply 168, 301, 330
Coinage law and its results 4-8
Desire for foremost place in national and commercial credit 112, 124
Dollars, Weight of, under the law of 1878 4-5
—— coined under provision of Bland Act . . 353
—— Failure of attempt to force into use . . 105, 123
Double standard, Not likely alone to introduce . . 9, 352, 366
Gold, Absorption of, has been large and continuous . 7, 352
—— Demand for, since 1872 2
—— Production of 3, 4
Decrease in 363
—— standard, Large party in favour of . . . 19
Greenbacks, Refusal of California to receive . . 91, 96
—— now equal in value to gold . . . 163
Ratio between gold and silver 34, 253, 283
Silver. Certificates in circulation 353
—— Coinage of 352
—— Disinclination to use 17, 123
—— Production of 3-8
—— Standard abolished accidentally . . . 127
—— Stock of 352
Trade revival predicted, not fulfilled 354

V

VALUE, Artificial or actual, defined 299-301, 322, 325
Artificial greater than real 131
Change in, period during which trade suffers . . 372
Comparative, of gold and silver changed by German demonetisation 294
Determined by cost of production 39, 100, 144, 169, 176, 322
—— supply and demand 138, 149, 335, 370
Fixity of, the advantage of a standard . . . 216, 227, 303
In exchange, Gist of the question involved in . . 296, 298
Market, of silver 282

VALUE—*continued*. PAGE

Measure of, Gold as a 11
———— Adam Smith on money as a 207
———— Essentials of a 33
of a commodity limits its quantity 193
of coined money 141
of gold, Variations in, affecting the gold price of commodities 157
—— being governed by cost of production is a question of degree 205
—— influenced by demand 322
—— Intrinsic, affected by the demand for it for ornaments 172
of metals increased by privilege of being legal tender when coined 299, 301, 322, 325
of precious metals as measured in each other shown by market price 289
under a bimetallic law 264
"The Value of Money." (H. H. Gibbs.) Reprinted from the *Bullionist* 245-9
"Is the Value of Gold and Silver Money Artificial?" Letters to the *Times* 131-51

W

WAGES. Economic meaning of the word. 311
Effect of the appreciation of gold on large employers of labour 357
Increase or decrease in rate of 361, 373
Influence of, on the cost of production . . . 157-8
Position of the Indian producer in regard to . . 67-8, 262

WEALTH, Distinction between money and 191

"WHAT IS MONEY?" (Lord Sherbrooke.) Reprinted from the *Nineteenth Century* 183-96

"WHAT IS A POUND?" (H. R. Grenfell.) Do. 111-29

"WHAT IS A STANDARD?" (H. R. Grenfell.) Do. 197-217

WHEAT. Comparative prices, 1873-1883. (Table) . . . 358-9
Value determined by cost of production . . . 67

"WHITHER WOULD THE DEARER METAL GO?" (H. R. Grenfell.) Reprinted from the *Bullionist* 259-65

WOOL. Comparative prices, 1874-1882. (Table) . . . 358-9

WOLOWSKI'S "L'or et l'Argent" 77, 78, 89, 91, 118, 350